Contents 3

4   **Contents**

English Result

Intermediate Student's Book

Mark Hancock & Annie McDonald

The people in my life

acquaintance /əˈkweɪntəns/ aunt /ɑːnt/ best friend boss (brother)-in-law colleague /ˈkɒliːg/
cousin /ˈkʌzn/ ex-(boyfriend) flatmate neighbour /ˈneɪbə/ nephew /ˈnefjuː/ niece /niːs/
parents step-(father) uncle widow widower

Wanda's World

I'm Wanda Jones. I'm 24, single, and I live with another girl in a small flat in Notting Hill. These are the people in my life …

Family

I've got four parents! My mum and dad are divorced and both of them have remarried. My mum, Tina, lives with my step-father, Costas, in Wimbledon. My dad, Harry, lives in Marbella with his new wife, Roxette. She's the same age as me, and we get on really well!

I've got a younger sister called Sandra. She's married to a guy called Ray. They have a young baby called Grace. That means I'm an aunt!

Friends

Well, there's my flatmate, Fatima. She's from Lebanon. I haven't got a boyfriend. My ex-boyfriend, Warren, still phones me every week, but I'm not interested. It's a bit complicated because Warren is my brother-in-law's brother.

My best friend is Stan. He's a 54-year-old barber and his shop is just below my flat. He's a widower and he's got a teenage son, Danny. Danny's learning to play the trumpet.

Acquaintances

Let's see, there's our neighbour, Mrs Mirren. I know her because she calls every day to complain about something. Her cats fight on our balcony.

Work

I'm a secretary in an insurance company. My boss is called Tom and I think he's secretly in love with me. My colleague is called Tracey and she's secretly in love with Tom. What a mess!

How to talk about the people in your life

G subject questions and object questions   V the people in my life

A Vocabulary the people in my life

1 Work with a partner. Write a list of family words.
Example mother, son, grandfather ...

2 Look at **The people in my life** opposite. Say if they are *male*, *female*, or *either*.
Example aunt = female

3 Look at the photos in **Wanda's World** opposite, but don't read the text. Work with a partner and guess the relationships between the people.

4 Read the text and name the people in the photos.
Example a = Fatima

5 Look at the mind map of Wanda's World. How are the people related to Wanda? Tell a partner.

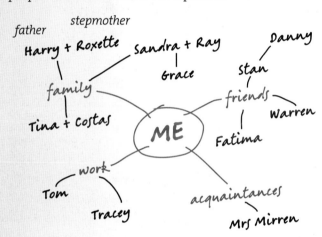

B Listen for specific information

6 1A.1▶ Wanda and Fatima got eight messages on their telephone today. Listen and decide who they are from.

7 Read the audio script on ▶ p.150 and answer the questions. Compare with a partner.
1 Who visited Wanda?   *Warren*
2 What does Mr Robbins ask Wanda to do?
3 Who did Warren visit?
4 Who wants Wanda to go to their house?
5 Who left a message for Fatima?
6 Who does Harry want Wanda to meet?
7 Who wants Wanda to stay home tomorrow?
8 Who left an umbrella at Wanda's house?
9 Who wants to see Wanda tomorrow evening? (more than one person!)

8 Make a list of things that people want Wanda to do tomorrow. What do you think she should do? Why? Decide in groups.

C Grammar subject questions and object questions

9 Complete the grammar box.

	subject	verb	object
1	Tom	loves	Wanda.
2	Sandra	married	
3	Warren	visited	
4	Warren	loves	
5		forgot	her key.
6		divorced	Harry.

10 Complete the questions about the sentences in the grammar box and underline the correct word in the rule.
Object questions (when you don't know the object)
1 Who does Tom love?
2 Who did Sandra _____?
3 Who did _____?

Subject questions (when you don't know the subject)
4 Who loves Wanda?
5 Who forgot _____?
6 Who _____?

Rule Use *do*, *does*, or *did* in subject/object questions.

11 Look at the questions in exercise 7. Are they subject or object questions?

12 Look at the mind map in exercise 5 and ask your partner questions about **Wanda's World**.
Example A Who loves Tom?
           B Tracey!

More practice? **Grammar Bank** ▶▶ p.136.

ABC Put it all together

13 Draw a similar mind map of people in your life.

14 Look at your partner's mind map and guess who the people are.
Example A Is Adam your uncle?
           B No, he's my brother-in-law.

15 Think of questions to ask about the people in your partner's map. Ask and answer with your partner.
Examples Does your sister live near you?
           Who do you speak to most on the phone?
           Who lives with you?

bow   hug each other   kiss each other on the cheeks   kiss each other on the lips
put your hand on the other person's shoulder   shake hands with each other   wave to each other

How do you **meet** and **greet**?

What do you do or say in your country? Choose the best answer.

1 What do people do when they meet in your country?

a shake hands with each other
b put their hand on the other person's shoulder
c bow
d hug each other
e kiss each other on the cheeks
f kiss each other on the lips
g wave to each other
h *something else*

2 How do you greet these people? Is your greeting different if the person is of the same sex or of the opposite sex?

a a good friend
b an acquaintance – a friend of a friend, for example
c an older neighbour
d somebody important – your boss, for example
e one of your parents when you haven't seen them for a long time
f a six-year-old child – your nephew or niece, for example

3 How do you address the people in question 2?

a Sir or Madam
b Mr / Ms / Mrs / Miss and their surname
c their first name
d a nickname
e *other*

4 You're by yourself and you walk into a café. You see a friend sitting with a group of people you don't know. What usually happens?

a Your friend introduces you to the people.
b You say 'hi' to your friend and introduce yourself to the people.
c The people stand up and introduce themselves to you.
d *something else*

5 A new colleague at work introduces himself or herself to you. Do you ever say any of these things? Say *never, it's possible, sometimes*, or *often*.

a Enchanted.
b Pleased to meet you.
c How old are you?
d Hi, I'm Mr / Ms … (surname)
e Hi, I'm … (first name)
f Peace be with you.
g Greetings.

6 You meet a teacher from your school in the street. What do you say?

a Hello, teacher!
b Hello, Mr / Ms … (surname)
c Hello, … (first name)
d Hello, Sir / Miss.
e *something else*

7 You want to get someone's attention. What do you normally say? Are any of these rude?

a Excuse me!
b Hey, Mister / Miss!
c Listen!
d You there!
e *something else*

How to talk about greeting customs

A Vocabulary ways of greeting

1 Look at **Greetings** opposite and match them with photos a–g.

2 Which greetings do you use? When? Tell a partner.
   Examples I never hug my boss.
   I kiss a friend on the cheeks when we meet after a few days.

B Read and respond

3 Read **How do you meet and greet?** opposite and choose the best title for each question.
   a ☐ Introducing friends
   b ☐ Getting attention
   c ☐ Addressing people
   d ☐ Meeting new colleagues
   e ☐ Men and women
   f ☐ Body language
   g ☐ Meeting your teacher

4 Do the questionnaire. Compare your answers in small groups.

5 You will listen to Greg Brown, a 20-year-old student from Britain. Guess his answers to the questionnaire.

6 **1B.1▶** Listen to Greg and check your guesses. How are his answers different from yours? Compare with a partner.

7 **Pronunciation** Match the titles and the pronunciation.
   Mr Ms ~~Miss~~ Mrs

   /mɪs/ *Miss*   /mɪz/ _____
   /ˈmɪsɪz/ _____   /ˈmɪstə(r)/ _____

8 **1B.2▶** Listen and say if you hear *Mr*, *Ms*, *Miss*, or *Mrs*.
   Example **Audio** This is Mrs Mirren.
            You   Mrs!

C Grammar reflexive pronouns

9 Match the sentences with the photos.
   1 ☐ They're hugging each other.   ←——→
   2 ☐ She's hugging herself.   ⬸
   3 ☐ She's hugging someone else.   ——→

10 Complete the grammar box. Then match the rules and examples.

pronouns			
subject	possessive	object	reflexive
She introduced me.	*He introduced his wife.*	*I introduced them.*	*We introduced ourselves.*
	my	me	myself
you		you	yourself
	his		himself
she	her		
we		us	ourselves
they	their	them	themselves

Rules
Use a reflexive pronoun:
1 when the subject is the same person as the object.
2 to make it clear you did it and not someone else.
3 in the phrase *by* + reflexive pronoun, meaning *alone*.

Examples
a ☐ We didn't get a painter – we painted the house ourselves.
b ☐ Come and join us – don't just sit there by yourself!
c ☐ He's an adult now and he can look after himself.

11 Underline examples of reflexive pronouns in **How do you meet and greet?** and compare with a partner.

12 Complete the sentences with a reflexive pronoun or *each other*.
   1 In France, people kiss *each other* when they meet.
   2 Nobody introduced me so I introduced _____.
   3 If you're hungry, get something for _____.
   4 How long have you and Jo known _____?
   5 In Britain, relatives give _____ presents at Christmas.
   6 Danny didn't have trumpet classes – he taught _____.
   7 I hate eating in restaurants by _____.

   More practice? **Grammar Bank** >> p.136.

ABC Put it all together

13 Work with a partner. Make notes to answer questions about two countries.
   Student A Read **Two countries** on >> p.126.
   Student B Read **Two countries** on >> p.133.

14 Ask your partner the questions from exercise 13 about his/her countries. Did you learn anything new?

I can talk about greeting customs.

Las Meninas

In 1656, Diego Velázquez painted *Las Meninas*, one of the most famous works in the history of Western art. Today, the painting is on display in the Prado Museum in Madrid. Thousands of people visit the museum every day, and most of them want to see this masterpiece by Velázquez before they leave.

When you look at the picture, the first thing you see is five-year-old Princess Margarita ⬚6. She's standing in the middle of a group of girls and she's looking directly at you. The girls are wearing expensive dresses with very wide skirts. Margarita's dress is white and shines brightly in the light from a window on the right. The two girls on either side of the princess are her maids of honour, Maria and Isabel. Maria ⬚ is kneeling and offering Margarita a drink. Isabel ⬚ is standing to the right of Margarita and she's looking in our direction.

Apart from her maids of honour, little Margarita also has two dwarfs to keep her company. Their names are Nicolas ⬚ and Maribarbola ⬚. You can them at the front on the right. A dog is lying in front of them and Nicolas is trying to wake it up with his foot.

Behind Isabel, the maid of honour, we can see Marcela ⬚, the woman who looks after the princess. She's saying something to the princess's bodyguard ⬚. At the back of the room, through the doorway, we can see José Nieto ⬚. He looks after the palace buildings. He's going up the stairs, or perhaps he's coming down, it isn't clear. He's looking towards us.

Finally, on the left of the scene is the painter himself, Diego Velázquez ⬚. He's working on an enormous painting, but we can't see what it is. Is he painting the whole scene in a mirror, or is he painting something else? We will never know.

Position

at the back (of the room)
in the middle (of ...)
at the front (of ...)
on the left (of ...)
on the right (of ...)

in front (of the girl)
to the left (of ...)
to the right (of ...)
behind (the girl)

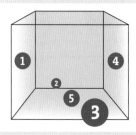

How to explain who people are

1C

A Read an art catalogue description

1 Look at the painting opposite with a partner. Do you know anything about this painting? Do you like it?

2 Read **Las Meninas** opposite and answer the questions.
1 Who's the little girl in the white dress?
2 Who's the painter and what is he painting?

3 Write the numbers of the people in **Las Meninas** in the text. Which people in the picture are *not* mentioned?

B Vocabulary position

4 Look at the phrases in **Position** opposite. Match them with the numbers in the diagrams.

5 <u>Underline</u> the correct words.
1 The driver sits <u>at the front</u>/in front of a bus and the passengers sit at the back of/behind the driver.
2 In Britain, cars drive on the left/to the left of the road. If you want to pass a slow lorry, you have to pass on the right/to the right of it.

6 Test a partner about the people in the painting.
Example **A** Where's Marcela?
B She's to the left of the bodyguard.

C Grammar present simple and continuous

7 Read this text. Which man in the painting is it about?
I'm studying[1] art history so I spend a lot of time in the Prado. Sometimes I watch[2] the visitors. When they see Las Meninas, they usually look[3] at the princess first. But later, they usually notice this man. He works[4] in the palace – he checks[5] that all the palace rooms are clean and in order. At this moment, he's standing[6] on the stairs and he's looking[7] into the room. Perhaps he wants[8] to look at the painting. Some historians believe[9] he was a relative of the artist.

8 Match the verbs in red in exercise 7 with the rules in the grammar box.

Use present simple for …	Use present continuous for …
a verbs which describe states.* *I like art.*	d actions happening at this moment. *She's looking at the princess.*
b an action which happens often. *Tourists always visit the Prado.*	e actions happing these days, but perhaps not at this moment. *I'm learning to paint.*
c permanent or long-term facts. *He lives in Madrid.*	

* State verbs include: *believe, know, like, see, understand, want,* etc.

9 Work with a partner. Put the verbs in the present simple or the present continuous.
1 Nicolas _wants_ to wake the dog – he _____ it with his foot. want/touch
2 José Nieto _____ something in his hand – I _____ it's a book. hold/think
3 Diego _____ a picture. He _____ a lot of pictures of the royal family. paint/paint
4 Maria and Isabel _____ a lot of time with the princess. They _____ her now. spend/help
5 Marcela and the bodyguard _____ about something. They _____ for the king. talk/work
6 I _____ Las Meninas – I _____ an essay about it for my class. like/write

10 Write a sentence about you for each of the rules a–e in exercise 8. Then tell a partner.
Example rule a – I like European films.

11 Change partners. Talk about your first partner.
Example Magda wants something to eat.
More practice? **Grammar Bank** >> p.136.

D Listen for detail

12 **1C.1▶** You will hear a tourist, Barbara, and a guide talking about **Las Meninas**. What two parts of the painting do they talk about?

13 Listen again and answer the questions.
1 Where are King Phillip and Queen Mariana?
2 Who is looking at them?
3 Where is the red cross?
4 Who gave it to the painter?
5 Who painted it?

14 Read the audio script on >> p.150. <u>Underline</u> the words in red below and match them with their meanings.
1 [b] oh   a to show you're going to answer a
2 [ ] uh huh?   question.
3 [ ] well   b to show surprise, or that the information is new to you.
           c to show that you're following what the person is saying.

ABCD Put it all together

15 Work with a partner. Look at a photo and ask and say who the people are. Then compare your information.
Student A Look at **Family photo** on >> p.126.
Student B Look at **Family photo** on >> p.133.

I can explain who people are.
Tick ✓ the line.   with a lot of help   with some help   on my own   very easily

Misunderstandings

I don't understand.   No, I meant (pair).   I thought you said (pear).   Oh, I see!   Pardon?   Sorry, I misunderstood.

MEDICAL EXAMINATION

Age?

Eighteen.

Height?

One metre seventy.

Weight?

Weight?

Why aren't you saying anything?

I thought you asked me to wait ...

Puzzle time

We use language to communicate and understand each other. But quite often we *misunderstand* what the other person is saying. Can you explain the misunderstandings in these situations?

1 An English teacher was doing some vocabulary work with his class. He was asking questions and inviting students to give the answers. 'What is the opposite of right?' he asked. A student called Jenny put her hand up. 'Go ahead, Jenny', said the teacher.

'The opposite of write is read!' she shouted. The other students all laughed and Jenny didn't understand why.

2

A young man was talking to his colleague at work. 'How's Anita?' his colleague asked. Anita was the man's girlfriend.

'Oh, she's not very well, actually', said the man. 'She arrived back from Ireland yesterday and she's been in bed with a temperature since then.'

'Flu?' asked the man's colleague.

'Yes, she flew', replied the man, 'I went to the airport to meet her.'

His colleague looked at him very strangely.

3 I was doing a crossword and I needed help. My mum was in the room, and I said to her, 'Can you think of a word meaning boat with five letters?'

'Do you know what the first letter is?' she asked.

'Y', I said.

'Because it's much easier if you know the first letter, isn't it?' she replied.

4

Maria Teresa was in a greengrocer's in England buying fruit. She asked for some bananas and the greengrocer asked which ones she wanted. There were lots of bunches of five or six bananas, but she didn't want that many. Then she noticed there was a bunch with just two bananas, and said, 'I'll take that pair, please'.

The greengrocer was confused. 'Pardon? Don't you want any bananas, then?' he asked.

How to correct a misunderstanding

v cognates and false friends; misunderstandings **p** the alphabet

A Vocabulary cognates and false friends

1 Match the definitions and examples.
  1 ☐ Cognate (There is a similar word in my language and it has a similar meaning.)
  2 ☐ False friend (There is a word in my language which looks similar but has a different meaning.)
  3 ☐ The word is completely different in my language.

  a The Italian word *calcio* means *football*.
  b The Polish word *paszport* means *passport*.
  c The Spanish word *carpeta* doesn't mean *carpet*. It means *file*.

2 Are these words cognates, false friends, or completely different in your language? Write 1, 2, or 3. Check in a mono-lingual dictionary if you aren't sure.

  ☐ actually ☐ apple ☐ camera ☐ exit
  ☐ large ☐ novel ☐ parent ☐ police
  ☐ smoking ☐ taxi ☐ tennis

3 Can you think of more cognates and false friends in English and your language? Do you think they could cause misunderstandings? Discuss in groups.

B Read and identify misunderstandings

4 Read **Medical Examination** opposite. What is the misunderstanding? Complete the explanation with a partner.
  Weight sounds the same as _____.
  The doctor meant _____.
  The young man understood _____.

5 Read **Puzzle time** opposite. Match stories 1–4 with these titles.
  ☐ Buying Fruit   ☐ Crossword
  ☐ Chatting at Work   ☐ English Class

6 Work with a partner. Read the puzzles again and explain the misunderstandings. These words are clues.
  right   flu   why   pair

C Pronunciation the alphabet

7 Which letters rhyme with these words? Match them.
  S F ~~B~~ A Z X Q O N L I R M
  1 ☐B tree   6 ☐ spell   10 ☐ necks
  2 ☐ day   7 ☐ them   11 ☐ know
  3 ☐ new   8 ☐ pen   12 ☐ car
  4 ☐ fly   9 ☐ dress   13 ☐ bed
  5 ☐ Jeff

8 Work with a partner. Answer these questions about the full alphabet.

abcdefghijklmn opqrstuvwxyz

  1 Which seven other letters rhyme with *tree*?
  2 Which two other letters rhyme with *day*?
  3 Which two other letters rhyme with *new*?
  4 Which other letter rhymes with *fly*?
  5 Which letter doesn't rhyme with any of the words in exercise 7?

9 **1D.1▶** Listen and complete the sentences. Here are the words you need.
  bored   guessed   knows   meat
  new   peace   rode   through

  Example **Audio** Nose, N-O-S-E, is pronounced the same as …
  You   … knows; K-N-O-W-S

D Listen and follow a conversation

10 Read puzzle 4 in **Puzzle time** again and put this conversation in order.
  A ☐ I'm sorry, I don't understand …
  A ☐1 Can I have some bananas, please?
  A ☐ Oh, I see! No, I meant pair, P-A-I-R! I'd like those two bananas, please.
  A ☐ Oh, ehm … I'll take that pair.
  B ☐ Pardon? Don't you want any bananas then?
  B ☐ Oh, ha ha. OK. Sorry, I misunderstood. I thought you said pear, P-E-A-R!
  B ☐ Yes, of course. Which ones do you want?
  B ☐ You want a pear?

11 **1D.2▶** Listen and check.

12 **1D.3▶** Look at **Misunderstandings** opposite. Listen and repeat the phrases.

13 Practise the conversation in exercise 10 with a partner.

ABCD Put it all together

14 Work with a partner. Look at **Misunderstandings** on **» p.126**. Choose two of the misunderstandings and write a conversation similar to the one in exercise 10. Practise saying your conversations.

15 Do your role play for another pair. What is the misunderstanding?

I can correct a misunderstanding.
Tick ✓ the line.   with a lot of help   with some help   on my own   very easily

Writing A self-introduction

A Get ideas to write about

1 Read email A. Work with a partner and <u>underline</u> the best option.

1 Wanda's writing to people she doesn't know / a friend / her boss.

2 Wanda wants to learn new things / meet new people.

3 Wanda's sending a photo in the post / attaching a photo with the email.

2 How is Wanda's email organized? Put these headings in order 1–6.

☐ my general background and interests

☐ my hopes for the future

1 greeting

☐ goodbye

☐ my interest in the topic of the discussion group

☐ my name and how I heard about the discussion group

3 Organize these notes into the six sections from exercise 2.

24 Notting Hill   secretary   Japan   yoga
Best wishes   ~~Dear~~   photos of people, capture personality
sending photo   Wanda J, invited by Tony G
want learn more, contribute

Wanda
1	*Dear*
2	
3	

4 Imagine you want to join a discussion group. Decide what the group is about. Write some notes, not full sentences, for the six sections.

5 Talk about your ideas in small groups. Do you want to change or add anything to your notes?

B Drafting and editing

6 Read email B. Warren wants to join the discussion group and wrote this first draft. What changes should he make before he sends his email?

7 Work with a different partner or in a small group and compare your ideas.

AB Put it all together

8 Use your notes in exercise 4 to write a first draft of your self-introduction email.

9 Work with a partner and edit your writing together. Look for mistakes like Warren's.

10 Write your final draft. Are you happy to send it now?

A

✉ Self-introduction ＿□✕

Dear list members,

I'm Wanda Jones and I was invited to join this photography discussion group by Tony Garcia.

I'm 24 and single and I live in Notting Hill with my flatmate Fatima. I'm a secretary at Safeguard Home Insurance. I'm studying Japanese at evening classes because I want to go and work in Japan. I enjoy Tai Chi and Yoga.

My biggest passion is photography and I love taking photographs of people. I believe that if you take the picture at the right moment, you can capture their personality. I'm sending a photo of myself with my first camera as an attachment. It's a Leica. It was my grandfather's, and he gave it to me when I was ten.

I'm looking forward to learning more about photography from you all and I hope I can contribute something too.

Best wishes,

Wanda

B

✉ Self-introduction ＿□✕

Dear Mr Tony,

I'm Mr Warren and I was invited to join the discussion group by Wanda.

I'm look forward to learning more from you all and I hope I can contribute something too.

I work for a Japanese company which makes cameras for people who work in the film industry. I'm studying Japanese at evening classes so I can communicate myself better with people in the company.

My biggest passion is photography and film and I love going to the cinema. I'd like to learn more about film and photography. I believe that a good film can be made better if the people who do the filming know a lot about photography too. I'm 22 and single and I live in notting Hill.

Warren

I can write a self-introduction.

Tick ✓ the line.   with a lot of help   with some help   on my own   very easily

Unit 1 Review

A Grammar

1 Subject questions and object questions Write questions about the missing information.

1 Tom loves __?__ . *Who does Tom love?*
2 __?__ loves Wanda.
3 __?__ left a message for Fatima.
4 Roxette kissed __?__ on the cheeks.
5 Tracey thinks __?__ is nice.
6 __?__ wants to see Wanda tomorrow.
7 __?__ called Wanda to invite her to dinner.
8 Warren visited __?__ yesterday.
9 __?__ saw Warren outside Wanda's flat.
10 Mrs Mirren lives with __?__ .

2 Reflexive pronouns Complete the sentences with a reflexive pronoun or *each other*.

1 I never introduce *myself* using my full name.
2 It's normal for people to live by _____ when they go to university.
3 Come and join us – don't just sit there by _____!
4 In Turkey, friends greet _____ with one or two kisses on the cheek.
5 He's old enough to look after _____ now.
6 In many countries, people give _____ Christmas presents on 6th January.
7 We made this wedding cake _____. I hope it tastes OK!

3 Present simple and continuous Put the verbs in the correct tense.

The Musée d'Orsay in Paris ¹*has* have a large collection of French Art. I really ²_____ like the paintings by Edouard Manet. One picture ³_____ show a young soldier boy. He ⁴_____ wear red trousers and a hat, and he ⁵_____ play a small flute. The boy ⁶_____ seem happy enough, but I ⁷_____ feel sad when I look at him – will he live to be an adult? I ⁸_____ know this picture well because I ⁹_____ see it every week – I ¹⁰_____ learn to play the flute and my teacher ¹¹_____ have a poster of it on his wall.

B Vocabulary

4 The people in my life Match these words with the correct definition.

acquaintance aunt brother-in-law colleague cousin neighbour ~~niece~~ widow

1 The daughter of my sister. _____*niece*_____
2 A women whose husband has died. _____
3 The sister of my mother or father. _____
4 Somebody I work with. _____
5 The brother of my husband. _____
6 My uncle's daughter. _____
7 A person who lives near me. _____
8 A person who I know. _____

5 Ways of greeting Complete the sentences with these words.

~~bow~~ cheeks hug kiss put shake shoulder wave

1 Musicians sometimes *bow* to the audience at the end of a concert.
2 When people meet for the first time, they often _____ hands.
3 Brothers often _____ when they greet each other.
4 Women friends often _____ each other on the _____ when they meet.
5 Men sometimes _____ their hand on the other person's _____.
6 People often _____ when they say goodbye.

6 Position Where's the smiley ☺? Write sentences for the pictures.

1
He's behind the box.

2

3

4

5

6

7 Misunderstandings Put the conversation in order.

☐ A Oh, I see! No, I meant a pot of tea.
☐ A Pardon? I don't understand.
☐[1] A Can I have a pot of tea, please?
☐ B Ah, I misunderstood. I thought you said 'pot of cheese'! Sorry about that.
☐[2] B I'm sorry, we don't sell food.
☐ B We don't sell cheese.

People and places

This is a young man called Tariq from Morocco in North Africa. He and his family are Muslims and they live in the Atlas mountain region. In this picture, we see him in front of the white walls of the village mosque. He's wearing the traditional blue cloth of his people.

age and gender	*young man*
nationality	*Moroccan*
religion	
ethnic background	*Berber*
(part of) continent	
country	
region	
environment	*mountains, desert*

1 a Huli man

2 an Aymara woman

3 a young Berber man

4 a young Wodaabe man

5 a Maasai woman

6 a Maori man

7 a Mayan girl

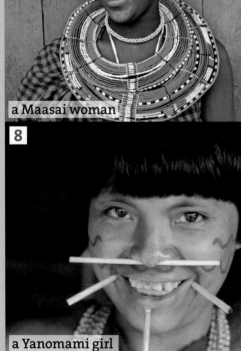

8 a Yanomami girl

9 an Inuit man

10 a Bedouin boy

How to talk about your background

G *the* before geographical names   V people and places   P spelling and pronunciation *c* and *g*

A Vocabulary people and places

1 Work with a partner and match these names with the three categories.
~~Bolivia~~ Christian Guatemala Muslim
Central America   the Middle East   the South Pacific
Jewish Tanzania East Africa

religious groups	regions / parts of continents	countries
		Bolivia

2 Add more names to the three categories.

3 Look at the information in People and places opposite. Which photo is it about? Complete the information.

4 Work with a partner. Guess at least two pieces of People and places information for the other people.
Example Well, in photo 1 there's a young man, maybe 17 years old …

B Listen for key words

5 **2A.1▶** Listen and read this text. Which photo is it about? Underline the words which helped you.
This picture shows a woman standing beside Lake Titicaca in Bolivia. She's wearing a traditional black hat and carrying a brightly coloured cloth bag. The Aymara people have their own language, called Aymara.

6 **2A.2▶** Listen to these descriptions and match them with the photos. Were your guesses correct in exercise 4?

7 Listen again. Find one extra piece of information for each photo. Compare with a partner.

C Grammar *the* before geographical names

8 Write these names in the grammar box.
Asia   the Alps   the Arabian Desert   India   the Atlantic
North Island   the Canary Islands   London   the Nile
~~Polynesia~~   the United States   the Far East   Lake Victoria
Mount Everest

use *the* before …	don't use *the* before …
mountain ranges –	regions – *Polynesia*
rivers –	single mountains –
oceans and seas –	countries –
island groups –	continents –
deserts –	single islands –
some countries* –	cities –
some regions* –	lakes –

*Examples the United Kingdom, the Czech Republic; the Middle East

9 Write *the* or nothing in the gaps.
1 _____ Lake Titicaca is in   *the*   Andes mountains.
2 _____ Atlas Mountains are north of _____ Sahara Desert.
3 _____ Baffin Island is in _____ Canada.
4 _____ Lake Victoria is in _____ Africa.
5 _____ Jordan is in _____ Middle East.
6 _____ Polynesia is in _____ Pacific Ocean.
7 _____ Britain is also called _____ United Kingdom.
More practice? **Grammar Bank >>** p.137.

D Spelling and pronunciation *c* and *g*

10 Add these words to the rule box.
Africa   background   city   country
gender   group   place   religion

spelling rule	the letter *c* =	the letter *g* usually =
Before *e, i, y*	/s/	/dʒ/ *
	the Pacific /pəˈsɪfɪk/	age /eɪdʒ/
Before any other letter or at the end of a word	/k/	/g/
	the Arctic /ˈɑːktɪk/	Mongolia /mɒŋˈgəʊliə/

*Except *give, get, begin, together*

11 Read this text. How are the letters in green pronounced? Say them with a partner.
My name's Gerry. I'm 19 and I work in a garage. I'm from a village near Galway in the west of Ireland. I speak English and Gaelic. I'm not religious but my parents are Catholic. I come from a working class family. I've got cousins in America because my aunt Celia married an American man and moved to the USA. They live in Georgia. I enjoy motor racing and I write articles for a car magazine.

12 **2A.3▶** Listen and check.

13 Work with a partner. Close your book. What do you remember about Gerry?

ABCD Put it all together

14 Write notes about yourself and your background. Choose at least five of the topics below.
name age home region country job religion
family background   ethnic background   interests

15 Work in groups. Tell the others in your group about your background. Use your notes to help you.

I can talk about my background.

Tick ✓ the line.   with a lot of help   with some help   on my own   very easily

17

Chinese tourists hurry to Britain to find shoes, fog, and the 'big stupid clock'

Britain receives crowds of Chinese tourists after Beijing changes visa rules.

A bus with a large group of Chinese tourists stopped outside the Clarks shoe shop in the Bicester Village Shopping Park near Oxford. 'I've never seen anything like it', said one of the shop assistants, 'They were queuing right out of the door.' The tourists wanted to buy shoes for their family back home and some of them bought six pairs. Many of them came with paper cut-outs of their relatives' feet – a clever idea, as you can never be sure that shoes sizes are accurate.

In the past, only business people and students could get visas to visit the UK, and people hardly ever visited as tourists. But the visa rules have changed. Now, Chinese tourists are allowed to travel to Britain in groups. Also, the Chinese economy is strong and airlines are introducing more direct flights from China to Britain. This is all good news for British tourism.

But what do the Chinese expect to find when they come here? According to Calum MacLeod of the Great Britain-China Centre, they sometimes have old-fashioned ideas of Britain. They think of Charles Dickens's book Oliver Twist and the famous London fog. 'When I tell people I live in London, they often ask me how bad the fog is,' says MacLeod.

'They are interested in the UK's history and traditions,' says MacLeod. Lai Gaik Ung Polain, a tour guide, agrees. 'We usually take them to see the famous tourist attractions in London and the south east of the country such as Buckingham Palace and the Houses of Parliament, and they always want to see Big Ben.' In Chinese, they call it Da Ben Zhong, meaning 'Big stupid clock'. But they are quite often interested in less well-known sights too, such as Winston Churchill's home or Karl Marx's grave.

But they don't only want to go sightseeing while they are in Britain. 'We always take our groups to Soho to eat Chinese food', says Polain. Most tourists enjoy food from home when they are abroad. Shopping is important, too. Chinese tourists rarely stay in Britain for more than a few days before continuing to another European country. They often buy presents for family and friends. Apart from Clarks, well-known British goods such as Burberry raincoats are also popular. You can buy many of these goods in China, but people usually prefer to buy them in the country of origin if they can.

People in the British tourism business are very pleased. They are comparing it to twenty years ago, when tourists suddenly started coming from Japan.

In Chinese, Big Ben is called 'Big Stupid Clock'

Karl Marx's grave is also popular

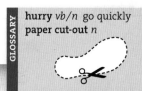

GLOSSARY

hurry vb/n go quickly
paper cut-out n

expect vb to think or believe that something will happen
tradition n a custom; a habit which has continued for a long time
attraction n an interesting thing for tourists to see

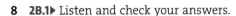

How to talk about tourism

G adverbs of frequency **P** adverbs of frequency

A Read a newspaper article

1 Think of at least one example of each of these things which are famous or typical of your country. Compare your list with a partner.

books   clothes   famous people   food   geography
places that tourists visit   souvenirs   weather

2 What things do you think are typical of Britain? Make a list with your partner. Compare with another pair.

3 Read **Chinese tourists ...** opposite. Find examples of the things in exercise 1.

4 Change one or two words in each sentence to make it correct. Compare with a partner.
   1 They ~~always~~ have old-fashioned ideas about Britain. *sometimes*
   2 The tour guides sometimes take them to see the usual sights.
   3 They hardly ever want to see Big Ben.
   4 They are never interested in less well-known sights.
   5 The tour guides sometimes take them to Soho to eat Chinese food.
   6 They usually stay in Britain for more than a few days.

5 Answer the questions with a partner.
   1 Why do you think the tourists have paper cut-outs of their relatives' feet?
   2 Why are more tourists coming from China now? Find three reasons in the text.
   3 Why do the tourists think that London is foggy?
   4 How do we know that these tourists are more interested in history than typical visitors to London?
   5 Why is shopping important to these Chinese tourists while they're in Britain?

6 Would you do the same things these Chinese tourists do? Tell a partner.

B Grammar adverbs of frequency

7 Put these adverbs of frequency in order to complete the rhyme.

sometimes   usually   never   often

They	always	like the city lights
They	_____	go to see the sights
They	_____	go to see Big Ben
They	quite often	visit 'Number Ten'
They	_____	take a photo there
They	{ rarely	miss Trafalgar Square
The action	{ hardly ever	stops
They	_____	want to miss the shops

8 **2B.1▶** Listen and check your answers.

9 **Pronunciation** Say the rhyme. Try to keep to the rhythm.

10 Read the sentences in exercises 4 and 7 and answer the questions.
   Do the adverbs of frequency come before or after ...
   1 a main verb?
   2 the auxiliary verb *be*?
   3 the subject of the verb?

11 Add adverbs of frequency to these sentences to make them true. Compare your ideas with a partner.
   1 Tourists visit my home town. *Tourists hardly ever visit my home town. They usually prefer to go to the coast.*
   2 I go abroad on my holidays.
   3 I eat Chinese food.
   4 Tourists are interested in the history of my country.
   5 Foreigners have old-fashioned ideas of my country.
   6 I visit the usual tourist sights in my own country.

More practice? **Grammar Bank** >> p.137.

C Listen for detail

12 **2B.2▶** You will hear a quiz about typical images of four countries. For each country there are three clues. After each clue, work with a partner and discuss which countries you think it could be.
   Audio First clue – When people think of this country, they usually think of mountains ...
   Example A I think this is in Europe – maybe Austria?
             B Yeah, it could be, or Switzerland. But I don't think it's in South America.

13 Listen again. What type of information do you hear about each country? Choose from the topics in exercise 1.
   Example Country 1: geography ...

14 Work with a partner. Think of three countries and make a list of typical images of them. Use the topics in exercise 1 to help you.
   Example Eiffel Tower, The Louvre ...

15 Work with another pair of students. Give them clues about your three countries. Use the clues in exercise 12 as an example. Try to guess the other pair's countries.

ABC Put it all together

16 Think about *your* country or region (or a country you know). Make notes about some of the topics in exercise 1.

17 Tell your partner about your country. Listen and say which topics from exercise 1 they tell you about.

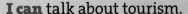

I can talk about tourism.
Tick ✓ the line.   with a lot of help   with some help   on my own   very easily

19

Pieces in a Museum

1 _____ ~ Zambia

This item is made of wood and it looks like the letter T. It has a round leg and a curved piece across the top. The leg is wider at the bottom than at the top. It is used as a pillow. It is also used for sitting on, like a stool. There is a piece of rope tied around the top part of the leg. This is used for carrying the headrest around with you on your belt. These headrests are still used today.

3 _____ ~ Ireland

This item has a wooden handle. At each end of the handle, there are metal plates. There are a lot of curved wires connected to the metal plates. The whole thing looks like a capital D. It was used in the kitchen for mashing vegetables, especially potatoes. Modern potato mashers usually have a different shape.

2 _____ ~ USA

This item is a kind of glove made of leather. It has tubes for the four fingers and thumb, but they are tied together. There is a wide piece of leather connecting the thumb and first finger. Baseball players use this glove for catching the ball, because the ball is hard and moves fast.

4 _____ ~ England

This item is a ball made of green glass in a net connected to a piece of rope. Fishermen used these balls for keeping fishing nets near the surface of the water. The glass balls contain air so they don't go under the water. Modern fishing floats are usually made of plastic instead of glass.

5 _____ ~ Brazil

This is a round container made of dried gourd. The top part is covered with silver, and there is a metal tube inside the container. The container is a cup for drinking 'maté', a kind of tea. The metal tube is used as a straw for drinking the tea from under the tea leaves.

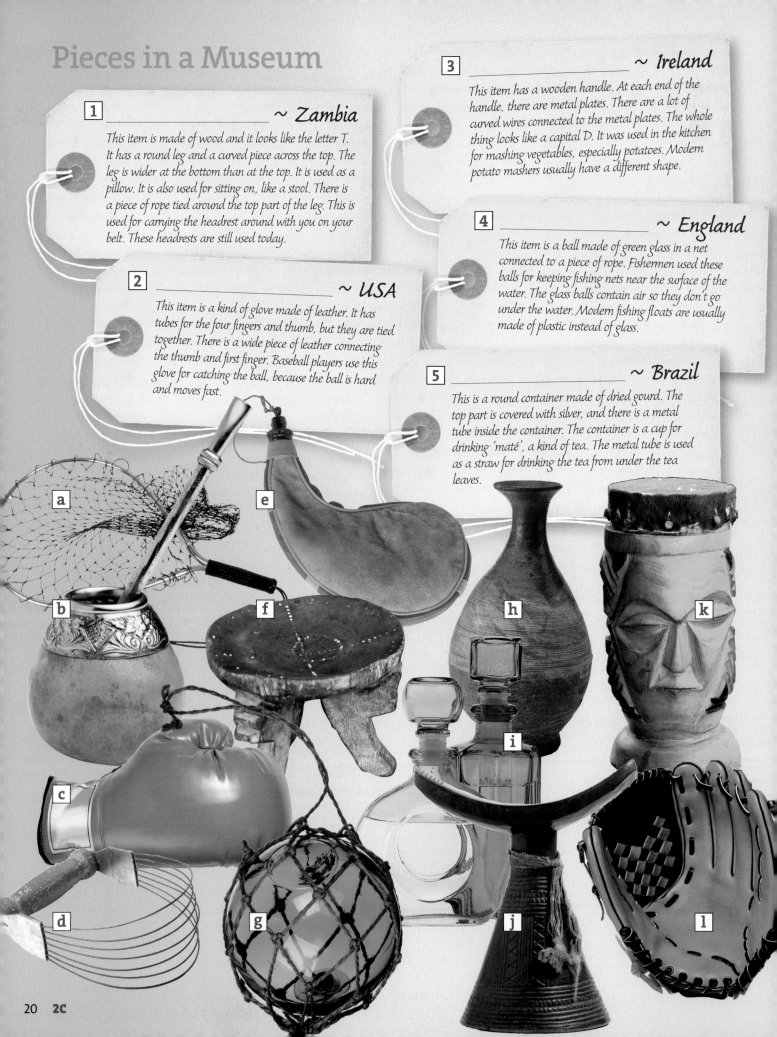

a

b

c

d

e

f

g

h

i

j

k

l

How to describe objects

v words and phrases for describing objects   P stress of prepositions

A Read for detail

1 Work with a partner. Think of as many words as you can to continue these lists.
material *wood, leather, metal* ...
shape and size *wide, flat, long* ...
parts of an object *top, side, handle* ...

2 Look at the photos opposite. Say or guess what the things are with a partner. Try to use some of your words from exercise 1 to describe them.

3 Read **Pieces in a Museum** opposite and match texts 1–5 with these titles.
- [ ] Fishing Floats
- [ ] Baseball Glove
- [ ] Maté Cup and Straw
- [ ] Potato Masher
- [ ] Wooden Headrest

4 Match texts 1–5 with five things in photos a–l.

5 Choose one new word from each text. Guess the general meaning, then check in your dictionary.

B Vocabulary phrases for describing objects

6 What is *it*? Match the sentences with photos a–l.
1 It's made of wood.   *f, j, k*
2 It's used for drinking wine from.
3 It could be used as a water container.
4 The top of it is covered with animal skin.
5 It's a kind of glove.
6 The top part of it looks like a dish.

7 Underline examples of the phrases in green in exercise 6 in **Pieces in a Museum**.

8 What is the difference in meaning? Decide with a partner.
1 a It's a pillow.
    b It's used as a pillow.
Example b = It isn't a pillow, but you can rest your head on it.

2 a It's a glove.
    b It looks like a glove.
3 a It's covered with leather.
    b It's made of leather.
4 a It's used for carrying water.
    b It's a water carrier.

2C

9 Pronunciation 2C.1▶ Listen and repeat. Notice how the preposition sounds different in A and B.

A end of sentence (stressed)	B middle of sentence (unstressed)
What's it used for? /fɔː/	It's used for cutting fruit. /fə/ It's used for opening tins.* /fər/
What's it made of? /ɒv/	It's made of metal. /əv/
Where's it from? /frɒm/	It's from Africa. /frəm/
What's it used as? /æz/	It's used as a stool. /əz/

*Pronounce the *r* in *for* if the next word starts with a vowel sound.

10 Work with a partner. Point and ask about the objects in the photos in **Pieces in a Museum**.
Example **A** What's this made of?
          B It's made of wood.

C Listen to a description of an object

11 You will hear a conversation between two friends, Elaine and Nilson. Nilson is from Brazil and he tells Elaine about photo b opposite. Work with a partner and write six words you think you will hear in the conversation.
Example cup ...

12 2C.2▶ Listen to the conversation and tick ✓ the words you wrote in exercise 11 if you hear them.

13 Answer the questions.
1 Where in Brazil do they use these maté cups?
2 What did Elaine first think the metal straw was for?
3 What happens if you drink maté directly from the cup?
4 What happens if you put the cup directly on a table?
5 What do people do when they've finished the drink?

14 Work in pairs. Write notes to answer the questions.
Student A Look at **Object A** on ≫ p.126.
Student B Look at **Object B** on ≫ p.133.

1 Where is it from?
2 What's it used for?
3 What's it made of?
4 What does it look like?

15 Ask about your partner's object. Use the questions from exercise 14. Do you know what the object is?

ABC Put it all together

16 Work in groups. Look at **Guess the objects** on ≫ p.127. Take turns to choose an object. The other students ask questions to guess which object it is.

Culture**Shock**

Part 1

A couple of years ago I worked in Japan for a while. During the first week, I didn't go out much because I had a terrible cold. In the second week, I was feeling a bit better, and when some work colleagues invited me out, I said 'yes'. We went to
05 a restaurant in the evening, and my new friends explained to me how to use chopsticks. It was difficult at first, but after some practice, I was using them really well and I didn't need to ask for a fork. It was my first time outside Britain, and I was eating Japanese-style like a native. I was feeling
10 quite pleased with myself. Then the problems started.

Part 2

My cold was not quite finished and my nose was still running a little. I took out a tissue, turned away from the table and quietly blew my nose. I noticed a person at the next table was looking at me strangely. When I turned to my friends again, they looked
15 away. Something was wrong. Anyway, the moment passed and the conversation started again. The person I knew best in the group was sitting next to me, and a bit later I quietly asked him if there was something wrong. He explained to me that in Japan, people don't blow their noses in public – especially at
20 the table. Oops! That was my first mistake of the evening.

The next time I needed to blow my nose, I decided to leave the table and go to the toilet. I didn't know where to put my chopsticks, so I stuck them in my bowl of rice. My friend said 'No, don't do that. Just leave them on the table.' Later, I discovered that leaving your
25 chopsticks in your rice means death in Japanese culture! That was my second mistake of the evening, and I wanted it to be the last.

When I returned from the toilet, it was nearly time to leave. I noticed there were some little bowls of tea with lemon next to everybody's place on the table. It was hot, and I started
30 drinking it before it got cold. Then I noticed some of my friends were covering their mouths and looking at each other. They were trying not to laugh. 'What's wrong?' I asked the friend next to me. 'That's not for drinking,' he explained, 'it's for washing your fingers.' That was it – mistake number three!
35 For a moment, I didn't know whether to laugh or cry. But in the end I started laughing, and little by little everybody else started laughing. Finally, we were all crying with laughter.

Simon Kerrigan *Leicester*

Time expressions

Time period

in the evening   during the first week
for a moment   for a while

Relating two times

before it got cold   after some practice
a couple of years ago   a bit later
when I returned

Putting events in order

my first time   at first
the second week   then
the next time   in the end   finally

How to tell an anecdote

G past simple and past continuous   V time expressions

A Read an anecdote

1 Compare the place you live and somewhere in another country or region you've visited. What differences did you notice? Tell a partner.

   Example   I visited Palermo last year. The buses were a different colour and the water tasted different.

2 Read **Culture Shock** part 1 opposite. Find one good and bad thing about Simon's first couple of weeks in Japan.

3 Look at the photos and cover part 2. Work with a partner and guess how the story will continue.

4 Read **Culture Shock** part 2. Were your guesses in exercise 3 correct? What events do the photos show?

5 Work with a partner and discuss these questions.
   1 Which of Simon's mistakes do you think was the worst? Put them in order.
   2 What do you think Simon learnt from this experience?

B Grammar past simple and past continuous

6 Read the grammar boxes. Underline the correct words in the rules below.

the context of the story	the events of the story
|- ↓ ↓ ↓	
I was feeling quite pleased with myself. Then the problems started.	

a shorter action *in the middle of...*	I noticed ... ↓
	|- -|
a longer action	some of my friends were covering their mouths.

Rules
1 Use the past continuous for the **context/events** of the story.
2 Use the past simple for the **context/events** of the story.
3 Use the past continuous for a **shorter/longer** action.
4 Use the past simple for a **shorter/longer** action.

7 Underline examples of the past simple and past continuous in **Culture Shock**.

8 Work with a partner. Decide which is the best tense for the verbs – past simple or past continuous.

   I sit[1] on a busy underground train one day, and I read[2] a newspaper when an old woman get[3] on. She wear[4] dark glasses and a hat. I stand[5] up to offer her my seat. When she sit[6] down, I notice[7] she have[8] big shoulders. Then I see[9] she had a beard. She say[10] 'Thank you' and she have[11] a man's voice! I get[12] off at the next stop, and while I go[13] up the stairs, the 'old woman' come[14] past me. A police officer run[15] after her. Or him!

   More practice? **Grammar Bank** >> p.137.

C Vocabulary time expressions

9 Look at the phrases in **Time expressions** opposite. Find and underline them in **Culture Shock**.

10 Work with a partner. Add one time expression to each sentence in the story below. Practise telling the story.
   I lived in Spain.
   I didn't go out because I had a cold.
   I was feeling better.
   Some friends invited me out to eat.
   We met at ten and went to a bar.
   My friends ate the 'tapas', or bar snacks, but I didn't eat because I wanted to be hungry for dinner.
   I asked, 'When are we going to have dinner?' My friends laughed and said, 'The tapas WERE the dinner!'
   I went to bed hungry.

D Listen to an anecdote

11 **2D.1▶** Listen to Linda telling a friend the story in exercise 10. What extra facts do you hear?
   Example   Linda was studying Spanish.

12 Do you remember (or can you guess) who says these words and noises – Linda or the listener? Put them in the correct box. Compare with a partner.
   well   oh   uh huh   ~~anyway~~   you know   mmm

story teller words	listener words and noises
anyway	

13 Look at the audio script on >> p.151 and check.

14 What do the listener words and noises mean?
   a I'm not listening.
   b I'm interested.
   c I've heard this story before.

ABCD Put it all together

15 Think of an anecdote of something that happened to you or someone you know. Make notes about it. Here are some ideas and questions to help you.

   an evening out   a bad journey   an interesting experience   a visit to another country

   Where did it happen?
   How did it start?
   Who were you with?
   How did you feel?

16 Tell your anecdote to a partner. Listen to your partner's story and make listening noises to show you're interested.

I can tell an anecdote.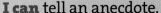

Tick ✓ the line.   with a lot of help   with some help   on my own   very easily

Writing An intercultural experience

A Vocabulary review

1 Are these words and phrases used to talk about people, places, or things?

bowl Christian colleagues container East Africa ethnic background fork gender glove handle leather Muslim region The Middle East tour guide tourist attraction weather

2 Can you remember any other words? Compare your ideas with a partner.

B Read and understand a narrative

3 Read the story and choose the best title.
1 Going on Holiday
2 A Different Way of Doing Things
3 The British Cup of Tea

Last year I went abroad for the first time – to Britain. In Brazil, when we think of Britain, we often think of pubs as typical places, so I decided to find one. It wasn't difficult! As I was walking along the street in Notting Hill, I found a traditional pub selling home-made food and traditional English beer.

I went inside and sat down at a table. I waited for a few minutes, but nobody came to serve me. While I was waiting, I noticed that there wasn't any table service and people went to the bar themselves. I went and asked for a cup of tea. The barman filled a small pot with hot water, put a tea bag in it, and then put the pot and a cup on a tray. I asked for some milk and sugar and he pointed to a small table in a corner of the room. I picked up the tray, took it to my table, and then went to get the milk and sugar.

Suddenly I heard the barman shouting 'Excuse me, excuse me!' I turned to look at him, and he said 'That's one pound fifty, please!' Then I understood that you have to pay when you get your drink. I felt really stupid, but I'll know what to do if I go there again.

Monica Ribeira Santos Brazil

4 Read the story again. Work with a partner and decide if the sentences are *true* or *false*. If there is no information in the text, write *doesn't say*.
1 It was raining. *Doesn't say*
2 Monica has travelled in foreign countries a lot.
3 She went to the pub at lunchtime.
4 The first thing she did was sit down at a table.
5 She watched other people.
6 The barman gave her some milk and sugar.
7 In English pubs, you don't pay for your drinks when you leave.

C Organize your writing: paragraphs

5 Look at Monica's story. Underline the correct option.
1 There are two/three/four paragraphs in her description.
2 Each paragraph has one sentence/more than one sentence.
3 Paragraph 1 tells the reader about the result of the main event/the context/the main event.
4 Paragraph 2 tells the reader about the result of the main event/the context/the main event.
5 Paragraph 3 tells the reader about the result of the main event/the context/the main event.

6 What does Monica include in her paragraphs? Tick ✓ the information.

Paragraph 1 (context)	when and where I went ✓
	the place
	the people
	what I knew about the place before I went
	what sights I saw
Paragraph 2 (event)	where I was when the event happened
	what I did/said
	what the weather was like
	what other people did/said
Paragraph 3 (result)	what happened in the end
	what things are for
	what I learned

D Get ideas to write about

7 Work in small groups. Talk about intercultural experiences similar to Monica's story. The story can be about you, somebody you know, or a character in a film. Choose the best story and write notes next to some of the headings in exercise 6.

8 Use your notes and tell your story to a partner from another group. Do you need to add more information?

ABCD Put it all together

9 Use your notes in exercise 7 to write a description of an intercultural experience. Remember to use paragraphs.

10 Check your writing.

11 Read your partner's description. Have they used paragraphs? Are the context, main event, and result clear? Is any information missing?

I can write a description of an intercultural experience.

Tick ✓ the line. with a lot of help with some help on my own very easily

Unit 2 Review

A Grammar

1 *the* before geographical names Write *the* or nothing in the gaps.

1 _The_ River Nile flows through many countries in _____ Africa.
2 _____ Brazil and _____ Argentina are two large countries in _____ South America.
3 _____ New York is on _____ Atlantic Ocean side of _____ United States.
4 _____ Mauritania is in _____ Sahara Desert.
5 _____ Lake Titicaca is in _____ Andes mountains, on the border between Peru and _____ Bolivia.
6 _____ Mount Everest is between _____ Nepal and _____ Tibet and is in _____ Himalayas.

2 Adverbs of frequency Put the words in order to make sentences. Then change the sentences to make them true for you.

1 late bed always I to go *I always go to bed late.*
2 cinema go My never parents the to
3 ever hardly my Tourists town visit
4 I Internet news on read the the usually
5 at go mountains sometimes the the to We weekend
6 father in My often quite shower sings the
7 Atacama Desert in It rains rarely the

3 Past simple and past continuous Write sentences about the pictures. Use the words given.

1
I/when the phone
I was having a shower when the phone rang.

2
Someone/while we

3
The light/while I

4
A fish/while I

5
We/when a thief

6
I/when a dog

7
I/when someone

B Vocabulary

4 People and places Find two examples of each of the things in the list.

nationalities religions ~~ethnic backgrounds~~ continents
countries   regions   types of environment

C	S	E	A	R	G	E	N	T	I	N	A	T
M	O	U	N	T	A	I	N	W	G	O	B	O
A	V	F	M	A	O	R	I	E	C	R	O	F
B	E	D	O	U	I	N	R	R	B	T	L	D
O	C	H	R	I	S	T	I	A	N	H	I	E
E	U	R	O	P	E	L	K	F	N	A	V	D
Q	U	I	C	H	D	L	I	I	P	F	I	E
H	W	I	C	O	Y	J	A	M	U	R	A	S
U	E	D	A	A	I	E	P	S	K	I	D	E
F	R	E	N	C	H	E	I	A	I	C	S	R
T	H	E	M	I	D	D	L	E	E	A	S	T

5 Words and phrases for describing objects Complete the sentences with these phrases.

~~made of~~ made of used for used as
covered with kind of looks like

1 Her belt was _made of_ leather.
2 The table top was _____ plastic to protect it.
3 This box was _____ keeping jewellery in.
4 At one time, these knives were _____ money.
5 It _____ a book, but in fact it's a box.
6 The brush handle is _____ wood.
7 A stool is a _____ chair with no backrest.

6 Time expressions Complete the text with these words.

after ~~ago~~ end evening finally
first later then when while

A few years ¹_ago_, I was camping in Scotland. I put up my tent next to the river and then sat outside for a ²_____. At ³_____, everything was fine, but ⁴_____ a while, lots of flies came out so I went inside the tent to escape. A bit ⁵_____ in the ⁶_____, I decided to make dinner on my small gas cooker. I put some powdered soup in a pan and ⁷_____ added some water. I heated it and ⁸_____ it was ready, I started to eat. However, I forgot to switch off the gas. It burnt a hole in the tent, and all the flies came in. I hid inside my sleeping bag but I couldn't breathe and ⁹_____ I had to put my head out. The flies started biting me again. In the ¹⁰_____, I had to pack up and leave that place.

Bernadette

20 years ago

The things I remember most about my first school are the smell of boiled vegetables in the canteen, the noise of games and fights in the playground, and Bernadette. Bernadette used to sit at the front of the class, and she was perfect. She was the teacher's pet, and she always got the correct answers. She was top of the class and got A grades in all her subjects. I used to love her, secretly.

Bernadette was good at everything. She used to sing well in assembly. She played the clarinet and never made mistakes. She was the captain of the hockey team. She ran around the playing field faster than anyone and she didn't use to get tired or sweat like the rest of us. She was too good to be true. I used to smile at her. I stood by doors and waited for her to pass. I wanted her to see me, but she never even looked. Was I invisible? Did she think she was too good for me? That's what I thought at the time.

But now I know I was completely wrong. I was looking on the Internet a couple of weeks ago and I typed in Bernadette's name, just out of interest. Eventually, I found her email address and I wrote a message to her. I didn't get a reply immediately and I thought that was the end of the story. However, a couple of days later, Bernadette made contact. After exchanging a couple of emails, we decided to meet for coffee. I was really curious to know what she was like now, this girl of my childhood dreams. But when we finally met, she looked completely different from how I remembered. I couldn't believe that I used to fancy her.

We talked a little about what we'd done since leaving school and our lives now. She's married with two kids and has a part-time job in a supermarket. Then we started talking about school, and we laughed together over our memories of those days. I was enjoying the conversation and I confessed that I used to love her. I thought she would laugh, but instead, she said something which completely changed the way I see my schooldays. She said, 'I used to love you too, but I didn't say anything because I was too shy.'

> **GLOSSARY**
> **canteen** *n* school dining room
> **playground** *n* play area outside school building
> **assembly** *n* meeting of students and teachers at start of school day
> **shy** *adj* nervous or embarrassed about meeting people

Now

How to talk about your schooldays

G *used to*   V school words   P rhythm

A Read a short story

1 Do you agree with these opinions? Compare with a partner.
1 Schooldays are the happiest days of your life.
2 I'd love to meet my old school friends again now.

2 Add more words to these lists with a partner.
School subjects   *History, Maths ...*
Things in the classroom   *blackboard ...*
Events in the school day and year   *break ...*
Places in school   *playground ...*

3 Read Bernadette opposite. Choose the best description.
a Our memories of school are better than the reality.
b One piece of information can change your memories.
c Our first love is the strongest.

4 Answer the questions with a partner.
1 What places in the school does the writer mention?
2 What was Bernadette good at?
3 How did Bernadette treat the writer?
4 Does the writer still love Bernadette?
5 How did Bernadette surprise the writer?

B Grammar *used to*

5 Underline examples of *used to* in Bernadette.

6 Read sentences 1 and 2. Are a and b *true* or *false*?
1 Bernadette used to sit at the front of the class.
 a She sat at the front once.
 b She probably sat at the front every day.
2 I used to love her.
 a I don't love her any more.
 b I still love her today.

7 What is the difference between *used to* and past simple? Tick ✓ the correct rules and ~~cross out~~ the wrong rules.
Rules We can choose *used to* instead of past simple to ...
1 talk about single actions in the past.
2 talk about repeated actions in the past.
3 talk about a state in the past which is still true now.
4 talk about a state in the past which isn't true now.

8 Complete the grammar box.

+		He used to love her.
−		He didn't use to love her.
?	Did she use to sing?	

9 Can you choose *used to* in these sentences? If you can, write the *used to* sentence.
1 I <u>took</u> the bus to school every day.
 I used to take the bus to school every day.
2 Bernadette <u>ate</u> an apple in the break one day.
 (*used to* not possible)
3 She <u>didn't speak</u> to me when we were at school.
4 I <u>met</u> Bernadette last Saturday.
5 Did you <u>fancy</u> anybody in your class?
6 How did you <u>find</u> Bernadette's email address?

10 Work with a partner. Look at the pictures of the classroom opposite. How was it different 20 years ago?
Example   The walls didn't use to be white. They used to be yellow.

More practice? **Grammar Bank** >> p.138.

C Pronunciation rhythm

11 **3A.1▶** Listen to a song about the Bernadette story. What information from the story is *not* mentioned in the song?

12 Write these phrases in the box.
front of the class   get it wrong   teacher's pet
last week   make mistakes

1 ● ●	2 ● ● ●	3 ● ● ● ●
first time	used to sit	sit at the front

13 **3A.2▶** Listen, check, and repeat.

14 Practise saying the song lyric on >> p.151. Keep the rhythm.

D Listen for general meaning

15 **3A.3▶** Listen to Antonia and Jeremy talking about their memories of school. Do you think they liked school?

16 Listen again. Tick ✓ the topics they talk about.
☐ subjects (best and worst)   ☐ teachers and pupils
☐ the building   ☐ clubs and extra activities
☐ special events   ☐ the classroom   ☐ clothes

17 Work with a partner. Try to remember what they said about each topic. Then listen again and check.

ABCD Put it all together

18 Choose three or more of the topics in exercise 16 and write notes about your memories of school.

19 Work in pairs or groups. Talk about your school memories. Which school sounds the best?

I can talk about my schooldays.

Tick ✓ the line.   with a lot of help   with some help   on my own   very easily

Dictionary entries

achieve /əˈtʃiːv/ *verb* [T] to complete sth by hard work and skill: *He has worked hard and achieved a lot this year.*

achievement /əˈtʃiːvmənt/ *noun* [C, U] sth good you have completed successfully through hard work and skill: *Winning the first prize was one of her greatest achievements.*

fail /feɪl/ *verb* [I, T] not to be successful in sth e.g. a test or exam: *I've failed my driving test three times.*

give up sth to stop trying to do sth, perhaps because it is too difficult: *He started flute lessons but it was too difficult so he gave up in the end.*

keep doing sth to continue doing sth or repeat an action many times: *If you keep trying, you will succeed in the end.*

manage /ˈmænɪdʒ/ *verb* [I, T] to do sth successfully or deal with sth difficult: *Did you manage to reach the top of the mountain?*

pass /pɑːs/ *verb* [I, T] to get the necessary result in an exam or test: *She passed her Maths exam with a grade A.*

succeed /səkˈsiːd/ *verb* [I] to achieve what you want to do: *He's finally succeeded in completing the puzzle.*

success /səkˈses/ *noun* [U] the fact that you have achieved what you wanted to do: *The project was a great success.*

successful /səkˈsesfl/ *adj* having achieved what you wanted to do: *The diet was successful and I lost five kilos.*

World's oldest primary pupil arrives in New York

Kimani Ng'ang'a from Kenya, aged 85, is the world's oldest primary school pupil. He has arrived in New York this week to speak at the United Nations about the importance of free primary education.

Kimani started at primary school last year, when the Kenyan government introduced free primary education. He didn't go to school as a child because his family couldn't pay the fees.

A successful student

Kimani is a successful student. He is only in the second year but he has achieved a lot since he started. He has managed to become head boy of the school this year. He gives help and advice to the teachers and other pupils in the school. The head teacher is very pleased with Kimani's achievements – 'When Kimani started school, he couldn't hold a pen. Now he has learnt to write a few words in Swahili.'

The Swahili and Kikuyu languages, and Maths are Kimani's

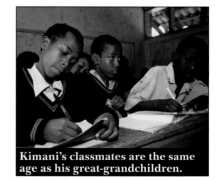

Kimani's classmates are the same age as his great-grandchildren.

favourite subjects, and he also enjoys Science. He says English is very difficult but he will keep trying. He says he has learnt a lot from the other pupils. 'They teach me games,' he says, 'and I tell them stories of the colonial days.'

It's never too late …

Kenya used to be a British colony, and in the 1950s, Kimani fought for independence with the Mau Mau rebels. He wants to learn Maths to count his compensation money, he says. He also wants to learn to read the bible. 'You are never too old to learn,' he told reporters.

It's a record!

Recently, Kimani has achieved a place in the Guinness Book of Records as the world's oldest primary school pupil. He has 30 great-grandchildren. Two of them are in the same school as him, but they are in higher years.

Kimani waited a long time for his first day at school, but he never gave up and finally he succeeded. He wants to tell world leaders that all children should be able to go to school. 'To me, freedom means going to school and learning,' he told reporters. But he has other plans for his visit to New York, too. 'I would also like to marry a rich American woman,' he said. We wish him every success.

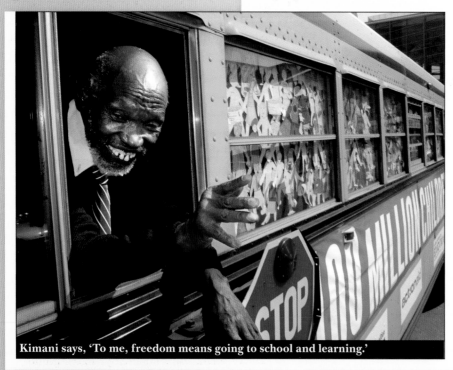

Kimani says, 'To me, freedom means going to school and learning.'

How to talk about your achievements

G present perfect and past simple   V achievement words; time phrases

A Vocabulary achievement words

1 Think of interesting things you've done in your life, or things you'd like to do. Tell a partner.
Examples I've learned to drive.
I'd like to climb Mount Everest.

2 Look at **Dictionary entries** opposite. Find these words.
1 the noun of *achieve*   *achievement*
2 the opposite of *fail*
3 the opposite of *keep trying*
4 the noun of *succeed*
5 the adjective of *succeed*
6 a verb meaning *to be able to do sth difficult*

3 Write a second sentence with the same meaning, using the word in blue. Use **Dictionary entries** to help.
1 He succeeded in getting a place. managed
  He managed to get a place.
2 He managed to pass his exams. succeeded
  He succeeded in ...
3 He kept trying. gave up
  He never ...
4 The teachers are pleased with what he's achieved.
  achievements
  His teachers ...
5 He has succeeded in learning to write. successful
  He has been ...

B Read a newspaper article

4 Look at the photos in **World's oldest primary pupil ...** opposite. Guess what the article is about. Compare with a partner.

5 Read the article. Were your guesses correct?

6 Read the article again. Write *true* or *false*.
1 Kimani's parents wanted him to go to school.   *True*
2 Kimani couldn't write before he started school.
3 Kimani teaches the children games.
4 He has learnt to read the bible.
5 There are no primary school students in the world older than Kimani.
6 He has married a rich woman.

7 Discuss these questions with a partner.
1 Why was Kimani invited to speak in New York?
2 Why is Kimani's teacher pleased with his achievements?
3 Why is free primary education important to Kimani?

C Grammar present perfect and past simple

8 Write the missing words in the grammar box.

past simple	present perfect
Kimani arrived in New York yesterday.	Kimani has arrived in New York today.
I _____ study much last week.	I haven't studied much this week.
Did you achieve much last year?	_____ you achieved much this year?
I _____ Kenya in 2002.	I've visited Kenya once in my life.
She phoned a few minutes ago.	_____ phoned three times in the last few minutes.
What _____ you learn when you started?	What _____ you learnt since you started?

9 Look at the time expressions in blue in exercise 8. Do they refer to a finished time or unfinished time? Underline the correct words in the rules.
Rules Use the past simple / present perfect for past actions which happened in a finished time.
Use the past simple / present perfect for past actions which happened in an unfinished time.

10 Put the verb in the past simple or present perfect.
1 They *'ve had* a very successful year this year.   have
2 They _____ a very successful year last year.   have
3 She _____ much when she was at university.
  not achieve
4 She _____ much since she started university.
  not achieve

11 Match the time phrases with the sentences. Then match the sentences with *a* and *b* in the grammar rule.
in the last few minutes   in my / your life
1 I've never been to Africa.   *in my life*
2 Your mum's just phoned.
3 Oh no, I've lost my passport!
4 Have you ever broken your leg?

Rule We often use the present perfect ...
a [1] to talk about experiences in life.
b [ ] to give news about recent events.

12 Use the rules in exercise 11 and make three true sentences about you. Tell a partner.
More practice? **Grammar Bank** >> p.138.

ABC Put it all together

13 Write notes about your achievements. Use some time phrases from exercise 8. Discuss with a partner.
Example A What have you done this year?
     B I've learnt some new songs on the guitar.
     A Oh really? What songs have you learnt?

I can talk about my achievements.

Tick ✓ the line.   with a lot of help   with some help   on my own   very easily

Teen **Dream**

1

Mum Daniel Peter Marston! Just look at the time! Where have you been? This isn't a hotel, you know!

2

Daniel I wish my mum understood me!

3

M You look tired, Danny. Don't get up. Shall I wake you up when the football starts?
D What? Eh ... yeah, thanks Mum.

4

Emma Mum – Danny's left the bathroom floor wet!
M I'm sure that's not true, Emma. Don't make up stories about your brother. Hurry up Danny, the football's about to start. Don't tidy up. I'll put away your clothes if you like.

5

M I'll turn on the telly for you. Just sit down, take your trainers off, and put your feet up. Help yourself to crisps.

6

M Lunch is on the table, Danny!
D Oh, Mum! I'm watching The Simpsons!
M Oh, sorry! Would you like me to bring your lunch on a tray?
D Yes, please.

7

M Don't worry about the dishes, Danny. I'll wash up today. Why don't you turn up your music – it's very nice! Is everything alright?
D No. I'm fed up!

8

M Why don't you try something new? Take up the electric guitar. Get a tattoo.
D Alright! I'll invite 30 friends for a party next Friday. We'll put on heavy metal music, turn it up really loud, and dance on the furniture. Is that OK?

9

M Oh, that sounds great! I'm looking forward to it already!
D Aargh! I can't stand it! You're too NICE! You're my mum – you're supposed to shout at me and tell me off! If you carry on like this, I'll grow up SPOILT!

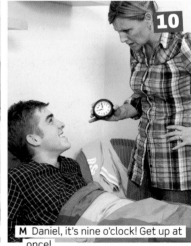

10

M Daniel, it's nine o'clock! Get up at once!
D Oh! Good morning, Mum! I love you!

Hospitality phrases

- [ ] Don't worry about the dog.
- [ ] Help yourself to some of these biscuits.
- [ ] I'll take your coat if you like.

- [ ] Do you need anything, or is everything alright?
- [ ] Just leave your bag on the sofa.
- [ ] Shall I change the channel for you?

- [ ] Why don't you watch TV for a bit?
- [ ] Would you like me to make you a cup of tea?

How to offer hospitality

G phrasal verbs   v phrasal verbs; hospitality phrases

A Read a photo story

1 Do you agree with these statements? Discuss with a partner.

Teenagers should ...
1 tidy their rooms.
2 pay for their clothes.
3 clean the bathroom.

Parents should ...
1 do everything for their teenage sons and daughters.
2 ask teenagers to help in the house.
3 pay teenagers to do housework.

2 Read Teen Dream opposite. Is Danny happy about the situation in his dream?

3 How do you think Danny feels in each picture? Why? Discuss with a partner. Use these words.

angry   fed up   happy
pleased   surprised   unhappy

4 3C.1▶ Listen to Teen Dream and find the differences in the six sentences.
1 Don't make up stories.   *Don't make stories up.*
2 I'll put away your clothes.
3 I'll turn on the telly.
4 Take your trainers off.
5 Why don't you turn up your music?
6 We'll put on heavy metal music.

B Grammar and vocabulary phrasal verbs

5 Match the phrasal verbs with their meanings.
~~make up~~   put away   put on   take off   turn on   turn up
1 invent a story   *make up*
2 start a machine
3 put things you aren't using in their correct place
4 remove something you're wearing
5 increase the volume, for example on a TV or radio
6 play a CD or DVD

6 Complete the examples and underline the correct words in the rules. Compare with a partner.

I made a story up. ✓   I made it up. ✓
I made up a story. ✓   I ~~made up it.~~ ✗

He took his shoes off. ✓   He took _____ off. ✓
He took off _____. ✓   ~~He took off them.~~ ✗

Rules
Nouns/Pronouns can go before OR after the particle.
Don't put nouns/pronouns after the particle.

7 Tick ✓ the correct sentences and correct the wrong ones.
1 I washed the dishes and put away them.
   ✗ *... and put them away.*
2 He had a shower and put his best clothes on.
3 After we got off the plane, we turned on our mobile phones.
4 I can't hear the TV – can you turn up it, please?
5 Don't go to bed in your socks – take off them!

8 Find phrasal verbs in Teen Dream with these meanings.
1 leave your bed   *get up*
2 stop sleeping
3 be quick
4 start a new hobby
5 speak angrily to somebody
6 continue
7 become an adult

9 Work with a partner. Complete the sentences with phrasal verbs from Teen Dream.
1 When I _____, I want to be a doctor.
2 Be quiet! You'll _____ the baby!
3 The story isn't true – you _____ it _____!
4 I didn't do my homework and the teacher _____ me _____.
5 If you're hot, _____ your jacket _____.
6 You should _____ until the job's finished.

More practice? **Grammar Bank** >> p.138.

C Listen for detail

10 3C.2▶ A visitor calls at Danny's house. Listen. What is her name and who does she want to see?

11 Listen again. Put the Hospitality phrases opposite in the order you hear them. Compare with a partner.

12 3C.3▶ Listen and repeat.

13 Look at audio script 3C.2▶ on >> p.152. Practise the conversation with a partner.

ABC Put it all together

14 Work with a partner. Read Hospitality role play on >> p.127 and decide what you are going to say.

15 Do the role plays. Take turns to be host and visitor.
   Example   **A** Hello, come in! I'll take your coat if you like.
             B Oh, thank you. It's a bit wet, I'm afraid ...

I can offer hospitality.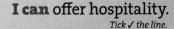
Tick ✓ the line.   with a lot of help   with some help   on my own   very easily

>START

A You are a 16-year-old in Britain and you have just finished your GCSE exams at a state secondary school. Your exam results weren't bad. What do you do?

1 You leave school. ➤ *Go to Q.*
2 You carry on at school for two more years to get your 'A' levels. ➤ *Go to B.*

B Your 'A' level results are quite good and you decide to go to university. Your parents want you to go into medicine but you prefer literature and languages. What do you do?

1 Apply for a place to study medicine. ➤ *Go to P.*
2 Follow your interests. Apply for a place to study modern languages. ➤ *Go to C.*

C In your third year of modern languages, you go to Berlin on an Erasmus programme. You love Germany and you start going out with a person you meet there. What do you do?

1 Quit university, stay in Germany, stay with your partner, and look for a job. ➤ *Go to F.*
2 Go back to Britain to finish your degree. ➤ *Go to O.*

D You hate the work and it isn't well-paid. You quit the job. ➤ *Go to Q.*

E After two years, you lose your job. ➤ *Go to Q.*

F You don't get on with your partner and you decide to leave. You return to Britain and look for a job. ➤ *Go to L.*

G You study to become an electrician. What do you do when you qualify?

1 You get a job in a local company. ➤ *Go to K.*
2 You go self-employed. ➤ *Go to J.*

H Finally, you are a 'doctor', but not a medical doctor as your parents wanted! You spend your days in tutorials and giving lectures.

Are you happy with this?

I You graduate and you become a doctor. You don't like the job at first, but after a while it isn't so bad, and you are well-paid. You've got a big house, a nice car, and a safe job.

Are you happy with this?

J Your electrical business grows. You have a lot of people working for you. You can earn a lot in a good year. You have a nice home and good holidays, but you never know if the business will do well next year.

Are you happy with this?

K Your job isn't well-paid, but it isn't bad. You get on well with your colleagues. You like the work. It's close to home and you can walk to work. You don't have to take work home with you, so your free time is really free.

Are you happy with this?

L You teach German in a private secondary school. You're never going to be rich, but it's a secure job. You get a bit of extra money by teaching evening classes in a further education college.

Are you happy with this?

M In the end, you get a job in an international advertising agency. The money's great, life is fast, and you travel a lot. The job's very competitive, but it isn't secure.

Are you happy with this?

N You get a place to study medicine. But after a few months, you hate it. You feel sick every time you watch an operation. What do you do?

1 Carry on with the course. ➤ *Go to I.*
2 Apply for a place to do modern languages instead. ➤ *Go to C.*
3 Leave university. ➤ *Go to Q.*

O You get a BA degree in German language and literature. What do you do next?

1 Get a job as a teacher. ➤ *Go to L.*
2 Go back to Germany to live with the person you met there. ➤ *Go to F.*
3 Stay at university to do a master's and then a doctorate. ➤ *Go to H.*

P Your 'A' levels aren't good enough to do medicine. What do you do?

1 Take your 'A' levels again. ➤ *Go to N.*
2 Apply for a place to study modern languages. ➤ *Go to C.*
3 Go to a further education college to get technical qualifications. ➤ *Go to G.*

Q What do you do next?

1 Sign on at the job centre. ➤ *Go to S.*
2 Go to a further education college to get technical qualifications. ➤ *Go to G.*
3 Go to an advertising agency and do in-service training in the photography department. ➤ *Go to R.*

R You do well in the job, but you can't go further without getting more qualifications. What do you do?

1 Do 'A' levels and apply for a place to study medicine at university. ➤ *Go to N.*
2 Carry on in the same job. ➤ *Go to K.*
3 Do a course in marketing and publicity at night school. ➤ *Go to M.*

S You sign on at the job centre and they offer you three jobs. Which one do you take?

1 Telephone sales operator for an Internet service provider. ➤ *Go to D.*
2 Assistant in an old-people's home. ➤ *Go to R.*
3 A secretary in an advertising agency. ➤ *Go to E.*

How to **talk about your education and career**

v education   **P** word endings which can affect stress

A Vocabulary education

1 What is the system of education in your country? Discuss with a partner.
Example We start primary school at the age of five.

2 Work with a partner. Guess the order of these British qualifications. What are the equivalents in your country?

- [ ] 'A' level [ ] Masters [1] GCSE
- [ ] doctorate [ ] degree (BA or BSc)

3 Complete the sentences with these words.

classes college ~~department~~ faculty
professor school (x2) teacher

1 She's a lecturer in the history *department*.
2 Is the economics department in the science or arts _____?
3 I left school at 16 and went to a further education _____.
4 He studied economics in evening _____.
5 At what age do children start secondary _____ in your country?
6 Her father was a university _____.
7 She used to be a school _____.
8 People study foreign languages at night _____.

B Read and make decisions

4 Read text A in **Leaving School** opposite. Work with a partner and discuss all the advantages and disadvantages of the two options.

5 Work alone. Choose option 1 or 2 in text A and follow the instructions. Make a note of your route. Don't worry if there are a few words you don't understand.

6 What happens in the end? Compare with a partner.

C Pronunciation word endings which can affect stress

7 Complete the boxes.

-tion		-ogy, -aphy, -ity	
verb	noun	noun or adjective	subject of study
●●● educate	●●●●● education	●●● technical	●●●● technology
●●● qualify	●●●●●● qualification	●●● photograph	●●●●
●●● graduate	●●●●●	●● public	●●●●
●● apply	●●●●●		

8 **3D.1▶** Listen and repeat. Copy the stress pattern.

9 Notice that the word endings in the box can affect the stress. Complete the rules.

1 In words ending with -_____, the stress is always one syllable from the end.
2 In words ending with -_____, -_____, or -_____, the stress is always two syllables from the end.

10 Work with a partner. Can you think of any more words with these endings?

D Listen and make notes

11 **3D.2▶** Listen to Karim talking about his education and career and answer the questions.
1 Did he go straight to university after leaving school?
2 What's his job now?

12 Listen again. Make notes about these topics for Karim.
leaving school   *left at 16*
first job
further education
current job

13 Follow Karim's route in **Leaving School** opposite. Work with a partner and use your notes from exercise 12.

14 Tell your partner about your own route through the reading maze in exercise 5. Listen to your partner's description and follow their route through the reading maze.

ABCD Put it all together

15 Write notes about your real education and career using the topics in exercise 12. If your career is still very short, imagine what might happen in the future.

16 Talk to other students. Use your notes to describe your education and career. Whose education and career is most similar to yours?

I can talk about my education and career.

Tick ✓ the line.   with a lot of help   with some help   on my own   very easily   33

Writing A CV

A Vocabulary review

1 Put these words in the correct column. Add two or more words about you in each column. You can use your dictionary. Be honest!

bad at maths   cycling   drawing   faculty   geography   ~~hard-working~~   lazy   manager   self-employed

education	work	personality	interests
		hard-working	

2 Underline any negative ideas in exercise 1. Would you include these in a job application? Discuss with a partner.

B Read a CV

3 Look at Patricia's CV. Find four pieces of information which you think she should cut from it.

4 Which of these careers would fit with Patricia's CV? Discuss with a partner.

accountant   computer technician   English teacher
French teacher   reporter   tour guide   web designer

5 Underline the best description of the CV from each pair. Why do you think it is like this?

1 brief/conversational   *the reader wants a quick idea if the applicant is suitable*
2 full sentences/phrases
3 opinions/facts
4 informative/entertaining
5 quick notes/carefully written and checked

C Text building

6 Find the section in the CV where Patricia puts all this information in one brief bullet point. With a partner, write the information in 1–3 in brief bullet points.

I'm ambitious. I'm hard-working. I'm a school leaver. I've got good computer skills. I've got good language skills.

1 I'm reliable. I'm punctual. I'm a graduate. I've got a driving licence. I've got a car.
2 I'm qualified. I'm experienced. I'm a flight attendant. I've got good first-aid skills.
3 I'm trained. I'm highly skilled. I'm a computer technician. I've got good qualifications. I've got good references.

7 Write two Personal Profile bullet points for you. Use your information in exercise 1.

Curriculum Vitae

Personal Details

Name	Patricia Leahy
Address	28 Coldhall Lane, Accrington, Lancs
Telephone	829 882 8887
Email	pleahy@telcom.net
Date of Birth	14/09/89

Personal Profile

- An ambitious, hard-working school leaver with good computer and language skills
- Good attitude and creative ideas
- Not very communicative in the mornings

Education

2006 to 2008	Nelson 6th Form College 16 Ribblesdale Road, Nelson, Lancs
A-levels	• IT A • French B • Economics C
2001 to 2006	Accrington Comprehensive 190 Kelvin Street, Accrington, Lancs
GCSEs	• Maths A • History C • Science A • English Literature C • French B • English Language C • IT B • Geography *Fail*

Work Experience

2008 to present	Unemployed
Summer 2007	Technical assistant *Computers R Us*
Summer 2006	Shop assistant *Carlin's Books*

Interests

- Website design   • Singing   • Basketball
- Graffiti painting • Clarinet

Referees

ABC Put it all together

8 Think of a job you would like to have. Write a list of qualifications, skills, and experience you would need. Compare your ideas with a partner.

9 Write a CV to go with your application for the job.

10 Check your spelling and punctuation.

11 Read your partner's CV. Do you think he/she will get the job?

I can write my CV.
Tick ✓ the line.   with a lot of help   with some help   on my own   very easily

Unit 3 Review

A Grammar

1 *used to* Change the verbs in blue to the *used to* form if possible. If not, put — in the gap.

As a child, I lived [1] *used to live* in a small village and the nearest school was ten miles away. On my first day of school, when my mum put [2]_____ — me on the bus, I cried [3]_____ for the whole journey. However, after a couple of weeks I started [4]_____ to enjoy it. Every Monday morning, I got [5]_____ on the bus happy to return to school after the weekend. There weren't [6]_____ many kids of my age in the village, so I was lonely, but at school I had [7]_____ lots of friends. Nowadays, I always look [8]_____ forward to the holidays, but at that time, I didn't want [9]_____ the school terms to end.

2 *Present perfect and past simple* Put the verbs in the present perfect or past simple.

1 I *'ve seen* some good films this week. see
2 I _____ to North Africa in 2004. go
3 I _____ to hospital since I was a child. not go
4 My parents _____ a new car last year. buy
5 Your sister _____ a few minutes ago. phone
6 _____ anyone _____ in the last few minutes? phone
7 _____ you _____ any new clothes this month? buy
8 _____ you _____ to a good school when you were a child? go
9 I _____ a summer holiday last year. not have
10 The teacher _____ us any homework this week. not give

3 *Phrasal verbs* Put the words in order to make sentences. Then put the sentences into the conversations below.

a up I it made *I made it up.*
b heating up I'll turn the
c don't take you off Why them ?
d put away them I've
e coat on You put should your
f them I'll off turn

1 **A** Is that story true?
　B No, *I made it up* _____.
2 **A** Hey Mum, where are my toys?
　B _____.
3 **A** It's cold in here, isn't it?
　B Yes. _____.
4 **A** We don't need the lights on any more.
　B No. _____.
5 **A** Is it cold outside?
　B Yes. _____.
6 **A** My shoes are wet.
　B Oh. _____?

B Vocabulary

4 *Achievement words* Complete the text with the correct form of these words.

~~achieve~~ achievement fail give up keep manage pass succeed successful

Your daughter has [1] *achieved* a lot this year. She has [2]_____ nearly all her exams and she has [3]_____ to get an A in three of them. She has [4]_____ in improving her spelling and she has [5]_____ working hard on her maths. She has published an article in the school magazine – a great [6]_____! She has been a little less [7]_____ in music, and unfortunately she [8]_____ her violin exam. We think that perhaps she should [9]_____ playing the violin.

5 *Hospitality phrases* Write the best word in each gap.

A Hello Melinda, come in! [1] *Would* you like [2]_____ to take your coat?
B Oh yes, thanks.
A Just leave your umbrella here. [3]_____ don't you come into the kitchen?
B Thanks.
A [4]_____ yourself to some tea – I've just made a pot. Or I'll make you some coffee [5]_____ you like?
B Thanks. Tea is fine.
A Is everything [6]_____? Are you warm enough? [7]_____ I turn the heating on?
B No, I'm fine, thanks.
A OK, I'm going out now. [8]_____ worry about washing up. Just leave your cup in the sink.

6 *Education* Write the words for these definitions.

1 Studies after leaving school. *f u r t h e r* education
2 A history lecturer works in the history d_____m_____ of the university.
3 Where school children play in the break. p_____g_____
4 Night school. e_____ classes
5 After primary school. s_____d_____ school
6 A teacher at a university. l____t_____
7 A school subject with a lot of numbers. m_____
8 Is the economics department in the arts or science f_____?
9 Time between lessons in the school day. b_____
10 Not the science faculty. The a_____ faculty.
11 A university qualification. d_____
12 The head of a university department. p___f_____

What's your idea of fun?

BASE Jumping

As soon as I saw someone BASE jumping off a Swiss mountain, I knew I wanted to do it. This guy just jumped off a cliff and fell for a few seconds before opening his parachute and floating down to land in the valley. It looked amazing.

BASE jumping's great because you don't have to go up in a plane. The word BASE comes from Building, Antenna, Span (the middle part of a bridge), Earth (mountain or cliff) – the four kinds of places that BASE jumpers jump from. I've jumped from all of these except an antenna, so that's my next objective.

The most important thing in BASE jumping is to stay calm when you're falling. You have to make very fast and accurate moves and the smallest mistake will kill you. Most people think my hobby is terrifying, but I actually enjoy being terrified!

Chuck Calderon Tennessee, USA

Karaoke

A lot of my friends say they feel embarrassed when they sing in front of people, but I don't think it's embarrassing at all. People are so worried about what other people think that they can't have fun any more. I think it's crazy. When I get up on stage, I just forget what people think of me.

Last year I entered a karaoke competition in my home town, Wicklow, and I won a place in the national championship. I was so excited! I went up to Dublin with all my friends and family, it was fantastic. There were some brilliant singers there from all over the country and I didn't think I had a chance, but in the end I won second place. Was I embarrassed? No, I wasn't!!!!

Shania Brady Wicklow, Ireland

a

b

c

d

Bodybuilding

I started bodybuilding when I was a teenager. I was in a hockey team and I went to the gym a lot to train. I discovered that I really enjoyed lifting weights and feeling my muscles work. I was fascinated by the photos of bodybuilders I saw in magazines and I wanted amazing muscles like that too. After a while I stopped playing hockey and spent all my time in the gym instead.

As a bodybuilder, I have to eat a lot of protein-rich food like meat and eggs, and I don't go out much at night because you need lots of sleep when you're working out a lot. That's probably the only bad thing about the sport. Some people say that bodybuilding is disgusting, especially for women, because they think enormous muscles aren't natural. I think they're just embarrassed about their own weak little bodies and too lazy to work out. I've got a great body now, and I've had my photo printed in several magazines.

Petra Bruneau Winnepeg, Canada

Sudoku

For me, there's nothing more satisfying than doing a sudoku. I love the way the numbers all fall into place. People think a sudoku is a boring mathematical puzzle, but it hasn't got anything to do with maths. The pieces of the puzzle are numbers, but you don't do any calculations with them. I suppose most people try to solve the puzzle by logic, but I don't. I put a number in place by intuition – because it looks right. Then one thing leads to another, and suddenly it's finished. I can usually do a difficult sudoku in under ten minutes. I sometimes do 15 or 20 puzzles one after the other, and I never get bored.

I was in the National Championship last year, and that was really exciting. There were 160 competitors and I finished in the top ten. My friends used to get annoyed about my sudoku habit. You can't have an interesting conversation with someone who is doing a sudoku! But now I think they accept it.

Jake Daniels Portsmouth, UK

How to say how you feel about things

A Read for detail

1 Think of hobbies. Use these categories to help you. Tell your partner what you and people you know do in their spare time.

art and music   collections   games and puzzles
outdoor activities   sports

2 Look at the headings of **What's your idea of fun?** opposite and match them with photos a–d.

3 Work in pairs. Look at **What's your idea of fun?**
Student A read about Chuck and Shania's hobbies.
Student B read about Petra and Jake's hobbies.

Make notes about these topics for each person.

1 Person's name   *Chuck Calderon*
2 Name of hobby   *BASE jumping*
3 What this person does in their hobby   *jumps off* ...
4 Why he/she likes the hobby
5 What other people think of the hobby
6 One problem connected with the hobby
7 Something he/she has achieved

4 Describe the two hobbies you read about to your partner. Use your notes from exercise 3. Which of the hobbies would you like to try?

B Grammar and vocabulary -ed and -ing adjectives

5 Work with a partner. Find -ed or -ing adjectives in **What's your idea of fun?** to describe the following.

BASE Jumping
1 something fantastic   *amazing*
2 feeling very afraid

Karaoke
3 feeling stupid and ashamed
4 feeling concerned and afraid
5 feeling happy and enthusiastic

Bodybuilding
6 feeling very interested
7 something horrible and unpleasant

Sudoku
8 something pleasing that makes you feel good
9 something uninteresting
10 feeling a little angry

6 Check your answers in a dictionary.

7 Match these words with pictures 1–4. Then complete the rules.

☐ disgusted   ☐ terrifying   ☐ terrified   ☐ disgusting

| 1 He's ... | | 2 She's ... |
| 3 It's ... | | 4 It's ... |

Rules
Use adjectives ending with -_____ to talk about how a person feels.
Use adjectives ending with -_____ to talk about the cause of that feeling.

8 Finish the words in these sentences.
1 Chuck's hobby is terrif*ying*____, but he enjoys being terrif____.
2 Shania thinks Karaoke is excit____, and she never feels embarrass____.
3 Some people feel disgust____ by bodybuilding, but Petra thinks it's fascinat____.
4 Jake feels satisf____ when he finishes a puzzle – he never feels bor____.

More practice? **Grammar Bank** >> p.139.

C Pronunciation -ed endings

9 Write these adjectives in the box in normal spelling according to how -ed is pronounced.
/əˈmeɪzd/   /ɪkˈsaɪtɪd/   /ˈfæsɪneɪtɪd/   /bɔːd/
/ɪmˈbærəst/   /dɪsˈɡʌstɪd/   /ˈɪntrəstɪd/

/d/	/t/	/ɪd/
amazed		

10 **4A.1▶** Listen and repeat.

ABC Put it all together

11 Work in pairs. Follow the instructions and write the answers in the shapes. Then ask about the words in your partner's shapes.

Student A Look at **Feelings** on >> p.127.
Student B Look at **Feelings** on >> p.134.

I can say how I feel about things.
Tick ✓ the line.   with a lot of help   with some help   on my own   very easily

Are you into music?

Some people live for music while for others, it is just noise. But most of us lie somewhere between these two extremes. **What about you – how into music are you? Do this test and find out!**

1 Every few years, a new way of listening to music is invented. Put these in order from the oldest to the newest and tick the ones you've got at home.

a ☐ MP3 player
b ☐ 1 Radio
c ☐ Tapes
d ☐ CDs
e ☐ Records

2 People listen in different ways. Can you guess what the people below are listening to? Match the photos and descriptions. Which photo is missing?

a A Carlos Santana guitar solo.
b A news podcast.
c A Mozart symphony.
d A Spice Girls track.

3 Does music make you move? Tick the things you do when you're listening.

a Tap your feet.
b Sing along.
c Dance.
d 'Conduct' the orchestra like the old man in the photo in 2.
e Play the 'air guitar' like the young man in the photo in 2.

4 Some of these are more difficult to name than others. Which can you name? Write a name on the line – if you can!

a A singer _____
b A composer _____
c A guitarist _____
d A drummer _____
e A female drummer _____

5 What are the differences between these instruments?

a Which is bigger – a keyboard or a grand piano?
b Which is usually louder – a Spanish guitar or an electric guitar?
c Which is heavier – a saxophone or a recorder?
d Which are the biggest and smallest of these – a violin, a double bass, and a cello?

6 A lot of music fans are great collectors. How many of these have you got? Tick them.

a Books or magazines about music.
b A collection of CDs by one artist.
c A T-shirt with the name of a singer or group.
d An autograph of a famous musician.

7 Look at the six singers above. What styles of music are they singing? Which style is the oldest?

country   jazz   opera
rap   reggae   rock

8 Some fans prefer bigger venues, others prefer smaller, more intimate venues, and some people aren't interested in live music at all. How many of these have you been to? Tick them.

a A massive concert in a stadium or other outdoor venue.
b A big concert in a concert hall or other indoor venue.
c A small concert in a club or other small venue.

9 You're going on a long, boring car journey. What do you do? Tick your answer.

a Have a conversation.
b Listen to the radio.
c Take the first few CDs you find.
d Carefully choose some good 'driving music'.

How to talk about music

G comparatives and superlatives   V music   P comparative -er

A Read and respond

1 What music do you listen to? Tell a partner.

2 Read **Are you into music?** opposite and choose or write your own answers.

3 Exchange books with your partner. Look at the **Answer Key** on >> p.127 and calculate your partner's score. Read out the result to your partner. Do you agree with the result?

B Vocabulary music

4 Find words in the quiz with these meanings.
   1 a part of a song where a single instrument is most important   *solo*
   2 a piece of classical music for an orchestra
   3 a single song or piece of music
   4 lead an orchestra with your hands
   5 the signature of a famous person as a souvenir
   6 any place where you see a concert or other live entertainment

5 Find words in **Are you into music?** to add to these lists. With a partner, add more words of your own.
   1 instruments and musicians   *saxophone, drummer* ...
   2 styles of music   *rock* ...
   3 music products   *CD* ...
   4 events and venues   *stadium* ...

C Grammar comparatives and superlatives

6 Complete the text with the comparative or superlative forms of the adjectives and adverbs in brackets.

Guitar or piano?

A guitar is ¹*cheaper* (cheap) than a piano to buy and it's a lot ²_____ (small), so it's ³_____ (convenient) if you live in a small flat. Also, you can carry it much ⁴_____ (easily) so it's ⁵_____ (good) if you move around a lot. You can also buy special guitars for kids – these are slightly ⁶_____ (small) than normal guitars.

On the other hand, a piano is probably the ⁷_____ (good) instrument of all for learning about music. You can see all of the notes a bit ⁸_____ (clearly) than on a guitar. If a piano is too big and expensive, you could buy a keyboard. These are far ⁹_____ (cheap) and ¹⁰_____ (convenient). A toy keyboard is probably the ¹¹_____ (popular) instrument of all for small children.

7 Which adjectives in exercise 6 are comparatives? Which are superlatives?

8 Underline these words in the text in exercise 6 and complete the rules.

slightly   much   far   a bit   a lot

Rules
Use _____, _____, and _____ to compare two things that are very different.
Use _____ and _____ to compare two things that are NOT very different.

9 **4B.1▶** Pronunciation Can you hear the difference? Listen and say *A* or *B*. Test a partner.

A	B
a nice venue	a nicer venue
an old song	an older song
a deep sound	a deeper sound
a big stage	a bigger stage
a small studio	a smaller studio

10 Which would you choose, a guitar or a piano? Tell a partner and say why.

More practice? **Grammar Bank** >> p.139.

D Predict and listen for key words

11 Which is better, listening to music on CD or MP3? List some good and bad points of both with a partner.

12 **4B.2▶** You will hear Andrea and Jan talking about how they listen to music. Do you hear any of your good and bad points from exercise 11?

13 Listen again. Underline what they prefer and write notes about the reasons.

	prefers ...	because ...
Andrea	CDs / MP3	*better quality, clearer sound*
	iPod / stereo system	
	speakers / headphones	
Jan	CDs / MP3	
	iPod / stereo system	
	speakers / headphones	

ABCD Put it all together

14 Work in pairs or small groups. Look at **Music** on >> p.128 and make notes about the music, venues, and entertainment you prefer. Discuss your ideas.

I can talk about music.

Tick ✓ the line.   with a lot of help   with some help   on my own   very easily

Restaurant Reviews

Thinking of going out for a meal? Why not try somewhere different?
Here are our top eight recommendations for the weekend …

Café Paradiso

You won't find pizzas as good as these anywhere in town. The pasta dishes are excellent too, and there's a salad bar where you can take all you can eat. This bright, cheerful restaurant is popular with families and it offers good value for money. If you prefer a quieter atmosphere, try it later in the evening when it isn't as busy as early evening.

$**$$$ **SEATS 96
OPEN 5.00 till midnight

The Chestnut

I've never had vegetarian food as tasty as this. Save space for something from the excellent dessert trolley, too. This tiny restaurant is often fully booked, so book as early as you can. Highly recommended, even for non-vegetarians!

$$**$$$ **SEATS 16
OPEN 7.00 till 10.30

The Red Lion

This pub restaurant offers traditional home cooking in a warm, cosy atmosphere. The servings are very generous and the prices are reasonable. The staff are very friendly and the waitress likes to stop and chat – which means that the service isn't as quick as some people would like.

$**$$$$ **SEATS 24
OPEN 5.30 till 10.00
FREE PARKING

El Paso

Nowhere serves steaks as big as the ones at the El Paso. And it doesn't stop – when you empty your plate, a waiter arrives with a skewer of meat and serves you more. But save your appetite – they bring the best meat last. This restaurant seats over 100 people, making it ideal for large groups. There's live music on Friday and Saturday evenings.

$$$**$$ **SEATS 110
OPEN 6.30 till 1.00
FREE PARKING

Chez Dominique

The modern art on the walls gives this place an elegant, stylish atmosphere. Everything on the menu is cooked to perfection, and the wine list is impressive. Yes, it's expensive, but you get what you pay for. But be warned – the main course servings aren't as big as you'd expect, so don't skip the starters!

$$$$ **SEATS** 30
OPEN 7.00 till 11.30

Old Peking

The Old Peking is under new ownership, but it's just as good as ever. There are all the usual Chinese dishes and plenty of options I haven't seen elsewhere. The staff are friendly and do everything to make your meal as pleasant as possible. It's great value for money and you won't get a good meal as cheap as this anywhere else in town.

$**$$$$ **SEATS 50
OPEN 6.00 till midnight

Bombay Palace

I've never had a curry as hot as the vindaloo at the Bombay Palace! But if you'd rather have something milder, there are plenty of other options on the menu. They don't serve wine, but you may take your own. There's a small charge for opening the bottle, but it isn't as expensive as a restaurant wine price.

$$**$$$ **SEATS 50
OPEN eight till late

Home Sweet Home

This is home cooking at its best – your favourite recipes prepared just how you like them. There's no charge for opening the wine. You can stay as long as you want – nobody will ask you to leave. You can even watch the TV channel of your choice while you eat. There's friendly self-service, of course – and if there isn't, well, you can't complain. But don't forget to do the shopping!

How to compare and discuss preferences

G comparing with *as*   V expressing likes and dislikes   P disagreeing politely

A Vocabulary expressing likes and dislikes

1 Do you agree with these statements? Tell a partner.
John   I can't stand busy, noisy restaurants.
Ali   I don't mind what I eat, I just want a lot of it.
Sue   I absolutely adore Italian food.
Dick   I'm not too keen on curry or hot food in general.

2 Make true sentences for you about restaurants and food using the phrases in red in exercise 1. Tell a partner.
Example   I can't stand restaurants with lots of smoke.

B Read for detail

3 Read **Restaurant Reviews** opposite. Which one is a joke?

4 Work with a partner. Which restaurants would the people in exercise 1 like and not like?
Example   John would hate the Café Paradiso when it's busy.

5 Read the sentences. Write *true, false,* or *doesn't say.*
1 Café Paradiso has the best pizzas in town.   *True*
2 The Chestnut is often full.
3 The service at the Red Lion is fast.
4 The vegetables at the El Paso are very fresh.
5 They don't serve starters at Chez Dominique.
6 The people are nice at the Old Peking.
7 They only serve Indian food at the Bombay Palace.

C Grammar comparing with *as*

6 Underline phrases in **Restaurant Reviews** with these meanings. All the phrases include the word *as.*
1 when it's quieter than early evening
   when it isn't as busy as early evening
2 such tasty vegetarian food
3 slower than some people would like
4 nowhere serves bigger steaks than
5 servings are smaller than you'd expect
6 your meal couldn't be more pleasant
7 I've never had such a hot curry
8 it's cheaper than a restaurant wine price
9 you can stay for any length of time

7 Read the sentences and say if the meanings are *a* or *b.*
1 The Red Lion is as cheap as the Old Peking.
   a The Red Lion is cheaper.
   b You pay about the same at both.
2 The Café Paradiso isn't as big as the El Paso.
   a Both of them are the same size.
   b The El Paso is bigger.

8 Work with a partner and compare your opinions. Use *as ... as* to compare things in these lists. You can use these adjectives or others.
big small cheap expensive sweet tasty
1 Cuisine: Italian French Indian Chinese other
2 Places to eat: take-away cafeteria restaurant
3 Meals: a quick snack a three-course meal dinner
4 Fruit: melons bananas strawberries apples

More practice? **Grammar Bank** >> p.139.

D Listen for specific information

9 **4C.1▶** Listen to Sarah and Tom deciding which restaurant to go to. Which places do they mention?

10 Listen again. Why do they decide *not* to go to the first four places they mention?

11 Look at the audio script on >> p.152. Underline phrases for making suggestions, starting with these words.
Let's ...   Shall we ...?   What about ...?
How about ...?   Why don't we ...?

12 **4C.2▶** Pronunciation Listen and repeat these phrases from the conversation. Copy the tone of voice.

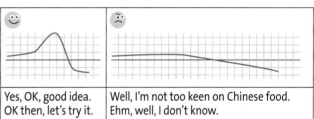

☺	☹
Yes, OK, good idea. OK then, let's try it.	Well, I'm not too keen on Chinese food. Ehm, well, I don't know.

13 **4C.3▶** You will hear Sarah making suggestions. You don't hear the words in Tom's replies, only his tone of voice. Is he agreeing or disagreeing?

ABCD Put it all together

14 Look at **Restaurant Reviews** again and choose two you would love to visit, two you wouldn't mind visiting, and two you wouldn't like. Make notes of your reasons.

15 Work in small groups. You want to go for a meal together on Friday evening. Try to agree which restaurant to go to. Remember to use the phrases from exercises 1 and 11.
Example   A Shall we go to Chez Dominique?
            B I'm not too keen on French food. How about ...

I can compare and discuss preferences.

Tick ✓ the line.   with a lot of help   with some help   on my own   very easily

His film or her film?

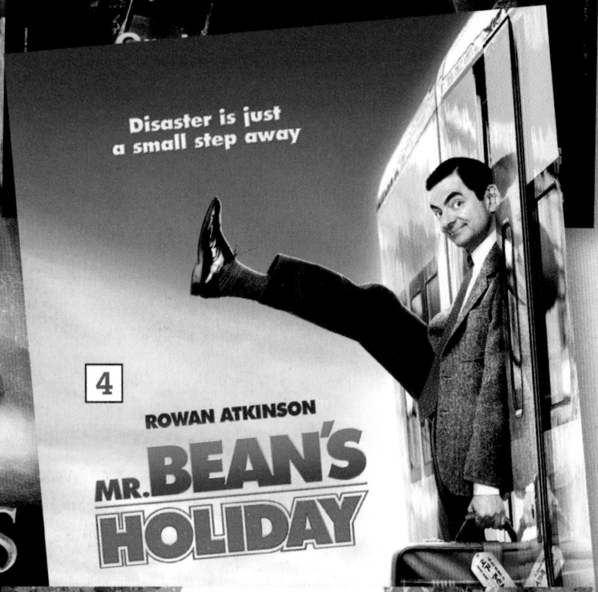

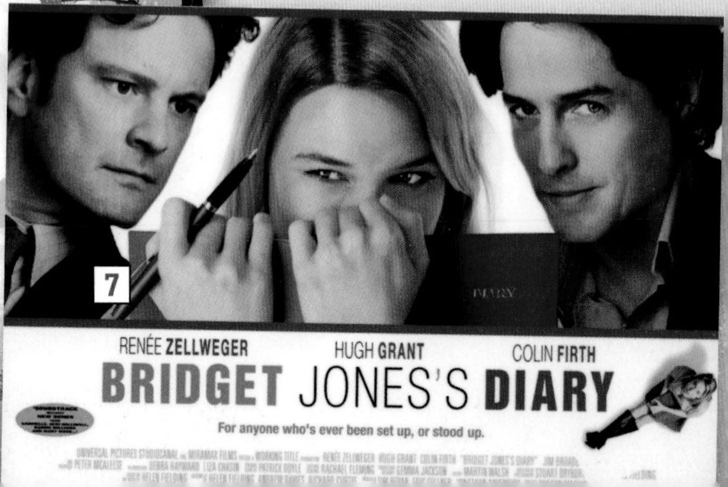

Types of film

an action film   a comedy   a drama
a fantasy film   a musical
a romance   a science fiction film

1 63ᵉᵐᵉ Mostra de Venise Compétition

HELEN MIRREN

THE QUEEN

UN FILM DE STEPHEN FREARS

www.thequeen-lefilm.com

2 MATRIX

3 THE LORD OF THE RINGS
THE FELLOWSHIP OF THE RING

4 Disaster is just a small step away

ROWAN ATKINSON
MR. BEAN'S HOLIDAY

5 TOM CRUISE
M:i:III
THE MISSION BEGINS MAY 5

6 MAMMA MIA!

7 RENÉE ZELLWEGER   HUGH GRANT   COLIN FIRTH
BRIDGET JONES'S DIARY
For anyone who's ever been set up, or stood up.

READERS' REVIEWS

Great fun and so true!
★★★★★

It's a film about a single woman who is looking for the right man to start a relationship with. It's one of my favourites because it's really funny and it shows things that really happen to women. I can really identify with the situations which the woman finds herself in. I LOVE this film!

A load of rubbish!
★★★★★

I can't stand films like this. It's about a woman who is unhappy because she hasn't got a man. She goes out with one guy who is selfish and another guy who is boring, and that's all. End of story. I prefer films which have a plot and a bit of action.

Quite funny
★★★★★

I don't usually like chick flicks, but this one was entertaining. It's about an English woman who wants a relationship but she can't find a man who she likes. She gets into some situations which are really embarrassing. The actress that plays the woman is really good. It's not brilliant, but it's one of those films that leaves you feeling good.

How to explain what a film is about

G defining relative clauses   v films

A Vocabulary films

1 List five or more of your favourite films. Tell your partner why you like them.

2 Match the **Types of film** opposite with film posters 1–7 in **His film or her film?** You can use your dictionary.

3 What types of film do men and women usually prefer? Put them in order from 1–7 for men and women.

4 Look at **Research results** on >> p.128. Does anything surprise you? Tell a partner.

B Listen to a radio programme

5 Work with a partner and decide which of these things men usually want and which ones women usually want.

action   a good story   attractive men
attractive women   dialogue   emotion   excitement
fighting   love   relationships   speed

6 **4D.1▶** Listen to Janet Shaw, a professor of Media Studies, talking about women's films on a radio programme. Which of the things in exercise 5 does she mention?

7 Listen again and answer the questions.
   1 What do women's films focus on?
   2 What does Dr Shaw use the examples below to show?
      a the films *Thelma and Louise* and *Alien*
      b the actors Nicolas Cage, Hugh Grant, and Mel Gibson
      c the book *Pride and Prejudice*
   3 Do women watch only women's films?
   4 Which kind of film does Dr Shaw prefer?

8 Which of the films in **His film or her film?** do you think are women's films? Tell a partner.

C Grammar defining relative clauses

9 Work with a partner. Read **Readers' Reviews** opposite and answer the questions.
   1 Which film are the reviews about?
   2 Do you agree with any of the reviews?
   3 Do you think the writers are male or female?

10 Underline all the examples of the relative pronouns *who*, *which*, and *that* in **Readers' Reviews** and complete the rules.

   Rules _____ refers to people or things.
   _____ refers only to things.
   _____ refers only to people.

11 Read the sentences and answer the questions. The red part of these sentences is called a relative clause.

   a She's found a man who she likes.
   b She's found a man she likes.

   c She's found a man who likes her.
   d She's found a man likes her.

1 One of sentences a–d above is incorrect. Which one? ~~Cross~~ it out.
2 In sentence a, who is the *object* of the verb likes. In sentence c, who is the *subject* of the verb likes. Underline the correct word in this rule.

Rule You can leave out the pronouns *who*, *that*, or *which* if they are the subject / object of the verb in the relative clause.

12 Is it possible to leave out the pronouns *who*, *which*, and *that*? If it *is* possible to cut it, ~~cross~~ it out.
   1 It's about the guys ~~who~~ she goes out with.
   2 It's about a situation which is embarrassing.
   3 It's about the situation that she is in.
   4 The actress who plays Bridget is called Renée Zellweger.
   5 The film is about everything that she writes in her diary.
   6 The first guy who she goes out with is her boss.
   7 The actor who plays her boss is Hugh Grant.

More practice? **Grammar Bank** >> p.139.

ABC Put it all together

13 Choose a film you remember and think of the answers to these questions.

   What type of film is it?   Who's in it?
   What's the story?   Why do you like it?

14 Describe your film to a partner but don't say the title. Listen to your partner's description. Can you guess which film it is? Would you like to see it?

   Example This is an action film about a woman who …

I can explain what a film is about.

Tick ✓ the line.   with a lot of help   with some help   on my own   very easily

Writing A description of a film or book

A Read and order

1 Have you seen this film, or would you like to? Tell a partner.

2 Put the film description in order. Use this structure to help you.

Structure

paragraph 1 title; type of film; setting

paragraph 2 the main star(s); the key characters; how the story begins

paragraph 3 a good moment in the film; a final opinion about the film and actors

- [ ] However, his patients start to die and people in the town think he's a bad doctor.
- [ ] He plays Doctor Jennings, who moves to the town but can't find work because an old man called Doctor Metcalf already works there.
- [ ] But the film is also very amusing, and Jeff Daniels is really funny.
- [ ] When the old doctor is killed by the spiders, Doctor Jennings takes over.
- [ ] I nearly jumped out of my seat!
- [1] I saw a great film recently called 'Arachnophobia'.
- [ ] It's a comedy horror film about deadly spiders who invade a small Californian town.
- [ ] Jeff Daniels is the star of the film.
- [ ] The most frightening moment is when Doctor Jennings finds the queen spider in his own house.

3 Work with a partner. Explain who or what the highlighted words in the text (a pronoun or *the* + noun) refer to.

Example   the town = the town where Doctor Jennings lives

4 The writer of the text decided to cut these sentences. Why is the text better *without* them? Match the sentence and the reason. There may be more than one reason.

1 There are two restaurants in the town.

2 Doctor Metcalf's secretary is woman called Mercedes with a dog called Mary Kate.

3 I went to California once.

4 At the end of the film, the doctor kills the queen spider and everyone in the town is saved.

a [ ] It reveals the end and spoils it for the reader.

b [ ] It is a boring detail.

c [ ] It's long and unnecessary in a brief description.

d [ ] It isn't relevant.

B Content and organization

5 Work with a partner. Read this film description and underline examples of these problems. Write 1, 2, or 3 next to the examples you find.

1 this information is in the wrong order

2 this is an irrelevant or unnecessary detail

3 this should use a pronoun or *the* + noun to refer back

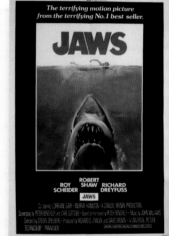

I saw a film from the DVD shop near my house. The DVD was very cheap. The film from the DVD shop was called 'Jaws'. 'Jaws' is a thriller about a killer shark.

A girl goes for a swim in the sea and a shark kills the girl. It's a very frightening film. The most frightening moment is when a shark jumps on the boat.

The chief of police and two other men go out in a boat to hunt for a shark, but a shark hunts them. A shark eats one of the men. In the end, they kill a shark and swim back to the beach.

6 Look at the structure in exercise 2. Is any information missing in the Jaws text? Compare with a partner.

7 Rewrite a better version of the Jaws text.

C Getting ideas to write about

8 Think of a film you have seen recently or a book you have read. Write a description of the story very quickly (five minutes maximum). Don't worry about mistakes or organization for now.

9 Work with a partner. Read your descriptions aloud and discuss any changes which would make it better.

ABC Put it all together

10 Rewrite your description, making changes from your discussion in exercise 9.

11 Now check your grammar and spelling and make corrections.

12 Give your description to another partner. Have you seen the film? Would you like to? Tell your new partner.

I can write a description of a film or book.

Tick ✓ the line.   with a lot of help   with some help   on my own   very easily

Unit 4 Review

A Grammar

1 *-ed* and *-ing* adjectives Finish the words in these sentences.

1 I'm not usually interest*ed__* in history, but this book was quite interest*ing__*.
2 I thought the show was bor____. Everybody else was bor____, too.
3 I used to be really excit____ on New Year's Eve, but now I don't find it excit____ at all.
4 I thought the food was disgust____ but Dad didn't seem disgust____ by it.

2 Comparatives and superlatives Give your opinion using comparatives or superlatives. Use the adjectives given and one of the words below.

a bit   a lot   far   much   slightly

1 Brown or white bread?   good for you/tasty
   I think brown bread is better for you and it's much tastier.
2 Real or instant coffee?   easy to make/taste good
3 Reggae, rock, or jazz?   good to dance to/exciting
4 Films at the cinema or on DVD?   convenient/cheap
5 A weekend break in the country or the city?
   exciting/relaxing
6 Text message, email, or letter?
   quick to write/cheap to send
7 Chess or cards?   learn easily/play quickly

3 Comparing with *as* Put the words in order to make sentences.

1 as as bus isn't quick The the Underground
   The bus isn't as quick as the Underground.
2 as a expensive as hamburger isn't A steak
   _____
3 as cycling Driving for as good isn't you
   _____
4 classical as complicated Folk isn't music
   as music
   _____

4 Defining relative clauses Join the two sentences using relative pronouns to make one longer sentence.

1 It's a story about a poor boy. He falls in love with a rich girl.
   It's a story about a poor boy who falls in love with a rich girl.
2 They're on a ship. It's crossing the Atlantic.
   _____
   _____
3 He meets a woman. She can see the future.
   _____
   _____
4 They say he will never marry the girl. He loves her.
   _____
   _____

B Vocabulary

5 Music Complete the puzzle and find the hidden word.

¹C	O	N	D	U	C	T

Clues

1 To direct an orchestra.
2 A person who plays the drums.
3 A person who plays music.
4 An instrument made of a long, curved metal tube.
5 An instrument like a piano.
6 A person who writes pieces of music.
7 A person who plays the guitar.
8 One song or piece of music on a record or CD.
9 A massive music venue which is normally used for sport.

6 Expressing likes and dislikes Complete the words in this conversation.

A Let's go out to eat.
B OK. ¹How about going to____ a Chinese restaurant?
A I'm ²n____ t____ k____ o____ Chinese food, actually. How about an Indian restaurant? I ³a____ a____ Indian food.
B Oh no, I ⁴c____ s____ it! Do you like Italian food?
A Well, I ⁵d____ m____ pizzas.
B OK, let's go to an Italian then.

7 Films Match the film types and the people.

action   comedy   drama   fantasy
musical   ~~romance~~   science fiction

Kate   I like love films.   *romance*
Jim   I like films set in the future.
Mick   I like films about imaginary, magical worlds.
Sara   I like films with lots of singing and dancing.
Ed   I like films with lots of excitement and adventure.
Liz   I like serious films with good dialogue.
Jo   I like films which make me laugh.

Politics

capital /ˈkæpɪtl/   con**serv**ative /kənˈsɜːvətɪv/   de**moc**racy /dɪˈmɒkrəsi/   e**lect**ions /ɪˈlekʃnz/
head of state /hed əv ˈsteɪt/   **nat**ional /ˈnæʃnəl/   po**lit**ical /pəˈlɪtɪkl/   **pres**ident /ˈprezɪdənt/
repre**sent** /reprɪˈzent/   re**pub**lic /rɪˈpʌblɪk/   **soc**ialist /ˈsəʊʃəlɪst/   U**nit**ed **Nat**ions /juˈnaɪtɪd ˈneɪʃnz/

Symbols *of* Power

An Object

The ballot box has perhaps become one of the great symbols of democracy. It represents the power of the voters to elect their own leaders. The name 'ballot' comes from 'ball'. At one time voters used

a small black ball to vote in elections, instead of paper, or nowadays, an electronic vote. Many ballot boxes are transparent so that people can see that they were empty at the beginning of voting. The idea of transparency, that people can see everything, has become a symbol, too – of honesty.

Directions

The directions left and right are used as symbols for political views. Political parties with more socialist views are called left wing, while parties with more conservative views are

called right wing. This symbolism comes from the French Revolution, where liberal members of parliament sat to the left of the president and conservatives sat to the right.

Colours

Light blue is the colour of the United Nations. It was chosen because it is the colour of the sky above every nation on Earth. The colour is used as a protective sign on the hats of peacekeeping forces so that they are not mistaken for the enemy. Other colours with political meaning are red and green. Red is the traditional colour for socialism and communism, while green is a symbol for parties mainly concerned with the environment.

Buildings

Government buildings are symbols of power and they are often designed to be large and impressive. In the USA, many public buildings were built to look like buildings from ancient Greece and Rome. There was a political message here – like the USA, ancient Greece and Rome were republics, too. Meanwhile, during the time of the Soviet Union, government buildings were massive to remind the public of the great power of the state.

A Shape

The five-pointed star is a very common symbol of military power, and is used on military vehicles and uniforms in many countries. It is also a very common national symbol and is used on the flags of 35 countries. For example, there are 50 stars on the flag of the USA, and they represent the states in that country. The symbol for the European Union also includes stars to represent the member nations.

Animals

Countries often have an animal as a national symbol. Lions and eagles are very popular symbols because they represent strength. For example, Bulgaria, England, and the Netherlands have the lion as the national animal, and the USA, Mexico, and Austria have various kinds of eagle. Other countries use animals which are very characteristic of the region, for example the kiwi in New Zealand or the springbok antelope in South Africa.

How to talk about countries and governments

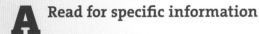

G *the* or no article in names of institutions   V politics   P *the*

A Read for specific information

1 Look at the photos in **Symbols of Power** opposite. Tell a partner what they show.

2 Read **Symbols of Power**. Find two facts you already knew and two facts you didn't. Tell a partner.

3 Read the sentences. Write *true* or *false*.
1 Ballot boxes are all transparent.   *False*
2 Left and right have always been symbols for political views.
3 UN peacekeepers wear blue hats so they are not mistaken for the enemy.
4 US public buildings follow Greek and Roman style because it is impressive.
5 The European Union flag has stars to represent the years since it started.
6 Strong animals are popular as national symbols.

4 Find words with these meanings.
1 a noun from the word *symbol* (para 2)
2 an adjective from *protect* (para 3)
3 an adjective meaning *very old* (para 4)
4 a noun from the word *strong* (para 6)

B Vocabulary politics

5 Look at the words in **Politics** opposite. Are any of them similar in your language? Compare with a partner.

6 Complete the text with the words from **Politics**.

In my country, the ¹*head of state* is the ²_____.
We don't have a king or queen – our country's a
³_____. The people vote to elect the members
of parliament – it's a ⁴_____. We have ⁵_____
every five years. There are two main ⁶_____
parties. The ⁷_____ Party is more left wing and
the ⁸_____ Party is more right wing. The main
government buildings are in the ⁹_____. My
country is a member of the ¹⁰_____ _____.
Our flag has three colours to ¹¹_____ the sea, the
land, and the sky. Our ¹²_____ animal is the eagle.

C Listen for key information

7 5A.1▶ Work in a group. Read and listen to question 1 from a quiz. Choose the correct answer.
1 An election is a system in which the people choose their political leaders. In the past, only men were allowed to vote. Which country, in 1893, became the first nation to allow women to vote in elections?
a The United Kingdom   b Indonesia   c New Zealand

8 Which words in the question <u>must</u> you hear correctly in order to be able to choose the answer? <u>Underline</u> them.

9 5A.2▶ Listen to questions 2–8 and choose *a*, *b*, or *c*.

10 5A.3▶ Listen to the correct answers and count your score. Who has the highest score?

11 Choose two of your correct answers. Look at the questions and answers in the audio script on ≫ p.153 and <u>underline</u> the words which helped you.

D Grammar *the* or no article in names of institutions

12 Write these names in the grammar box. Add *the* if necessary. Then complete the rule.

Australian prime minister   head of state   Irish government
King Richard III   Liberal Party   Queen Elizabeth

individual people	positions	organizations
Princess Diana	the emperor of Japan	the European Union
President Kennedy	the US president	the United Nations

Rule Use *the* with _____ and _____, but not with _____ people.

13 Add the missing *the* to these questions.
1 What's *the* name of *the* president of *the* USA?
2 Who's leader of Conservative Party?
3 Where's headquarters of United Nations?
4 Is Prince William from United Kingdom?
5 Is Czech Republic in European Union?
6 Did President Mandela meet president of Tanzania?

14 Pronunciation *the* is pronounced differently in A and B. Can you see why?

A	B
the president /ðə ˈprezɪdənt/ the European Union /ðə ˌjʊərəˈpiːən ˈjuːnɪən/	the EU /ði iː ˈjuː/ the English /ði ˈɪŋglɪʃ/

15 5A.4▶ Look at the phrases in exercise 12. Is *the* pronounced A or B? Listen, check, and repeat.
More practice? **Grammar Bank** ≫ p.140.

ABCD Put it all together

16 Work with a partner. Write notes about politics in your country, or in another country you know. Try to answer the **Politics** questions on ≫ p.128.

17 Change partners. Tell your new partner about the country from exercise 16. Listen to your partner's description. Is any information surprising?

I can talk about countries and governments.

Tick ✓ the line.   with a lot of help   with some help   on my own   very easily

allow /əˈlaʊ/ *verb* [T] to give permission for sb to do sth

forbid /fəˈbɪd/ *verb* [T] [usually passive] to not allow sth

permit /pəˈmɪt/ *verb* [T] *(formal)* to allow sb to do sth

prohibit /prəˈhɪbɪt/ *verb* [T] *(formal)* to say that sth is not allowed by law

Laws for Paws

A tour of weird and wonderful animal laws in the USA ...

You mustn't take your dog into a barber's!

If you're travelling around the United States with a pet, there are local laws you need to know. For example, if you go for a haircut in Juneau, Alaska, you'll have to leave your dog outside. It's illegal to take a pet into a barber's.

You mustn't travel with an animal on the roof!

Meanwhile, in Sun Prairie, Wisconsin, dogs and cats aren't allowed in cemeteries. In the Californian town of Glendale, you mustn't take a dog in a lift, and in Cathedral City, you can't take one into a school. You can walk your dog in Waterboro, Maine, but the lead must be shorter than 8 feet (about 2.4 metres). And remember, you mustn't travel with an animal on the roof of your car in Anchorage, Alaska.

You mustn't take a skunk into Tennessee!

If you have a pet skunk, you mustn't take it into Tennessee – it's forbidden to enter the state with one of these smelly animals. And remember, pet rats aren't allowed in Billings, Montana.

If your pet suddenly dies, don't forget – you can't leave a dead animal on anybody else's property in Conyers, Georgia.

There are laws about hunting animals, too. While you're in Virginia, don't forget that hunting isn't allowed on Sundays – except for racoons. You can kill a racoon any time before 2 a.m. In Arizona, hunting camels is forbidden. And you must never shoot a fish in Wyoming!

You can kill a racoon any time before two o'clock in the morning.

What about selling animals? Well, if you're planning to sell chicks or ducklings in Kentucky, you mustn't dye them a different colour first. And of course, you mustn't steal animals. In fact, in Louisiana there is a specific law which says it's illegal to steal alligators.

You mustn't dye a chick blue!

You've been warned!

GLOSSARY	
duckling *n*	baby duck
dye *vb*	to change the colour of something
hunt *vb*	to search for and kill animals, for food or sport
smelly *adj*	has a bad smell

How to talk about rules and laws

G modals of obligation   v permission words

A Vocabulary permission words

1 Do you have a pet, or have you had one in the past? Tell your partner about it.

2 Read Signs opposite. What do they mean? Use the dictionary definitions.

3 Write the verbs from the dictionary definitions in Signs in the box.

	you can do it	you can't do it
less formal	allow	
more formal		

4 Write a sentence with the same meaning using the word in green.
1 Smoking is forbidden. allowed *Smoking isn't allowed.*
2 Parking is prohibited. permitted
3 Mobile phones aren't allowed. forbidden
4 Taking photographs is not permitted. prohibited

B Read and interpret

5 Read Laws for Paws opposite quickly. What is the best description of the topic of the text?
a animals in the USA
b funny animal laws
c laws connected with pets

6 Read the text again and decide with a partner which law is the strangest and the funniest. Compare your ideas with other pairs.

7 Can you think of explanations for the laws? Discuss with a partner.
Example A Why do you think dogs are forbidden in hairdressers'?
            B Maybe it's because they aren't clean ...

C Grammar modals of obligation

8 Underline examples in Laws for Paws of *must, mustn't, have to, don't have to, can,* and *can't.*

9 Write *true* or *false*. If the sentence is false, say why.
1 You can leave your dog outside the barber's if you prefer. *False. You haven't got a choice – you have to leave your dog outside.*
2 You don't have to take your dog in a lift in Glendale.
3 You mustn't walk your dog in Waterboro.
4 The lead has to be shorter than 8 feet.
5 You can't take a skunk into Tennessee.
6 You must kill a racoon if you see it before 2 a.m.

10 What can you use the modal verbs for? Write them in the grammar box.

to say it's allowed	to say it's forbidden	to say it's an obligation	to say it's not an obligation
can			

11 Work with a partner and guess what the rules are. Underline the best modal verb.
Dog Ownership in Britain ...
1 Your dog's collar must/can't have your name and address on it.
2 You mustn't/don't have to have a dog licence.
3 You have to/can clean up after your dog.
4 Dogs can/must be kept under control on main roads.
5 Farmers can/must shoot a dog if it chases their cows.
6 If you have a guard dog, you have to/don't have to put up a warning sign.
7 Blind people must/can take guide dogs on buses.

More practice? **Grammar Bank** >> p.140.

D Listen for the general idea

12 5B.1▶ Listen to two friends, Jeff and Sally, talking about one of the questions below. Which question are they talking about?
1 Can you light a fire in your garden?
2 Can you throw an old fridge away?
3 Do you have to buy a licence for a TV?
4 Do you have to wear a seat belt on a bus?

13 Listen again and answer the questions.
1 What is Jeff's answer to the question in exercise 12?
2 Is he sure about it?
3 What happened when he had the same problem?

14 Look at the audio script on >> p.153. Underline the phrases Jeff uses to show that he isn't sure.
Example it isn't allowed, is it?

15 What do you think the correct answers are for the questions in exercise 12 in Britain or your country? Discuss with a partner. If you aren't sure, use some of the phrases you underlined in exercise 14.

ABCD Put it all together

16 Do you know any laws that people coming to live in your country should know? Discuss with a partner.

17 Work in small groups. Explain the laws to the others. Who talked about the most useful laws for a visitor?

I can talk about rules and laws.

Tick ✓ the line.   with a lot of help   with some help   on my own   very easily

SOME STOLEN EARRINGS HAVE BEEN FOUND BY A TREE

A MAN HAS BEEN ATTACKED BY A CASH MACHINE

A WOMAN HAS SHOT A ROBBER WITH A BASEBALL BAT

COW CABS AGAINST CRIME

CHILE – Juan Geraldo has not been robbed since he disguised his car as a cow.

Juan, a 46-year-old taxi driver from Santiago, is tired of being robbed. He has been attacked four times already. The first time, his car was stolen and he was thrown naked into a blackberry bush. The last time, he was attacked with a knife and just managed to drive himself to hospital.

Mr Geraldo got the idea to customize his vehicle from a TV advert showing a sports car lined with cowhide. He went out, bought a roll of cowhide material and covered the inside of his taxi from floor to ceiling. He even covered the steering wheel and changed the sound of his car horn to a cow moo.

The taxi looks very strange, but it is even more impressive at night. Mr

A taxi like this is going to be noticed

Mr Geraldo was thrown naked into a blackberry bush

Geraldo put neon lights on the ceiling, so you can clearly see the black and white cowhide in the bright light as it goes along the street. To complete the picture, Mr Geraldo wears a cowhide jacket and hat.

A taxi like this will be noticed and remembered, and that's exactly the idea. Now, when robbers get in, they get straight out again. 'They don't want to rob me because they'll be seen by everybody,' says Mr Geraldo. Customers like it too, and 80% of Juan's clients are women who

feel safer in the brightly lit cow cabs.

Many customers who call for a cab specifically ask for a cow cab. These clients include government ministers, TV celebrities, and parents organizing birthday parties for their children. They are so popular that Mr Geraldo's business has grown, and now he has seven cow cabs. What's next? Mr Geraldo is keen to develop his idea and is already thinking of making a zebra cab or a lion cab. 'It's a question of using your imagination,' he says.

How to **talk about stories in the news**

A Vocabulary crime verbs

1 When and how often do you read newspapers? What type of stories do you read? Tell a partner.

2 Choose the best verbs to complete the sentences.

steal   rob   attack

1 A young man *robbed* an old lady.
2 A dog _____ the postman.
3 A thief _____ my bicycle.
4 Three men _____ the bank.

shoot   murder   kill

5 The man _____ the victim with a knife.
6 Police _____ the escaping criminal.
7 He _____ himself in the foot.

kidnap   hijack   arrest

8 Some criminals have _____ a politician.
9 Three men tried to _____ a plane.
10 Police _____ the three men.

3 The **Captions** opposite have two meanings. The pictures show the wrong meaning. What do you think the correct meaning is? Compare with a partner.

Example   The tree didn't find the earrings. The stolen earrings were found *next to* the tree.

B Read for detail

4 Look at the headline and photos in **Cow Cabs Against Crime** opposite, but don't read the text. What do you think it will be about? Tell a partner.

5 Read the article. How has Juan Geraldo's life improved since he made his first cow cab?

6 Write *true* or *false*. If the sentence is false, say why.

1 The last time Juan was attacked, his car was stolen.
   False. He drove himself to hospital.
2 He first saw a cow taxi on a TV advert.
3 His taxi horn makes the same noise as a cow.
4 He put neon lights on the outside of the car.
5 Robbers don't attack because everybody notices the taxi.
6 Juan has also made a zebra cab.

C Pronunciation compound nouns

7 **5C.1▶** Listen and write these words in the box according to the stress pattern. Then practise saying the words.

~~baseball bat~~   birthday party   cash machine   earrings
headline   sports car   steering wheel   taxi driver

●●	
●●●	baseball bat
●●●●	

8 Nouns made from two shorter nouns are compound nouns. What is the stress rule for these words?

D Grammar active or passive?

9 Look at the first paragraph of **Cow Cabs Against Crime** and underline these verbs. Then answer the questions.

attack   steal   throw

1 Who did these actions – Juan or the robbers?
2 Why did the writer put these verbs in the passive?
   a To put the focus on Juan, not the robbers.
   b To put the focus on the robbers, not Juan.

10 Active or passive? Underline the correct form of the verb.

1 Oh no! My bike has stolen / has been stolen.
2 While Jade was walking home, a young man robbed / was robbed her.
3 After a fight, the police have arrested / have been arrested three youths.
4 Someone broke into Harry's flat, but nothing took / was taken.
5 A flight to Paris has hijacked / has been hijacked.
6 There was a train crash yesterday, but fortunately nobody killed / was killed.

11 Work with a partner. What happened in this story? Make sentences from the nouns and verbs.

Example   The door was left open.

> A Renoir painting worth three million euros has been stolen from the National Gallery. Police believe it was done with the help of someone who works in the gallery …
> door / leave open   alarms / switch off
> security guards / drug
> film from security cameras / delete
> less valuable paintings / not take
>
> Some news is just coming in. We've just been informed that …
> painting / find in Hong Kong   three men / arrest

12 **5C.2▶** Listen to the radio report of the story. Are there any differences from your version of the story in exercise 11?
More practice? **Grammar Bank** ≫ p.140.

ABCD Put it all together

13 Work with a partner. Choose a true story from the news or one of the **Headlines** on ≫ p.128 and invent the story. Write notes to answer the questions.

14 Work with a new partner or group. Tell your news story. Which story is the most interesting?

I can talk about stories in the news.

Tick ✓ the line.   with a lot of help   with some help   on my own   very easily   51

Mystery in the Tower

The princes disappear

On 9th April, 1483, King Edward IV of England died. He had two sons – Edward, aged 12 and Richard, aged 9. The boys' uncle, also called Richard, was asked to look after them and govern the country until Edward was old enough to be king. This never happened. Uncle Richard put the princes in the Tower of London to 'protect' them, and they were never seen again. They simply disappeared. Meanwhile, their uncle took power and became King Richard III of England.

Richard III is killed

So what happened to the princes? Nobody knows. But later that year, the stories began. People said that Richard had murdered the boys. A lot of people were against Richard and rebelled. Richard's enemy, Henry Tudor, had spent some time in France, but now he returned to England and the rebels joined him. On August 22nd, 1485, their two armies fought at the battle of Bosworth Field. King Richard was killed and Henry became King Henry VII of England.

A forced confession?

Were the boys really dead? Many people thought they were still alive, and perhaps Edward could become king. But King Henry was quite clear: Richard had killed them. In 1502, Richard's friend, Sir James Tyrell, confessed. He had murdered the boys on Richard's orders – although he didn't say what had happened to their bodies.

History is written

In 1674, the bones of two children were found under the stairs of the church in the Tower of London. Now it seemed clear: Richard III had ordered Sir James to kill the princes in the Tower and put their bodies under the stairs. In Shakespeare's play, *Richard III,* Richard was an evil monster, a murderer with a deformed body. The most famous painting from that time shows that Richard had one shoulder bigger than the other. At that time, people thought that a deformed body was a sign of an evil mind. And so history was written. The story was complete. Or was it?

```
King Edward —— brother — Richard —— enemy —— Henry
     IV                                       Tudor
  ┌────┴────┐
Prince   Prince
Edward   Richard
 (12)     (9)
```

How to **talk about past events**

G past perfect   V war and power   P stress in two-syllable nouns and verbs

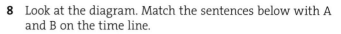

A Read and understand reasons

1 What dates or events in history do people in your country usually remember from school? Tell a partner.
Example   Columbus crossed the Atlantic in 1492.

2 Look at the pictures in **Mystery in the Tower** opposite. What do you think the mystery was?

3 Read **Mystery in the Tower** and discuss the questions after each part.
The princes disappear
1 There are two Edwards and two Richards. How are they all related to each other?
2 Why didn't Prince Edward become king?
Richard III is killed
3 Why were people against Richard?
4 How did Henry become king?
A forced confession?
5 Was everybody sure that the princes were dead?
6 In 1502, people thought the mystery was solved. Why?
History is written
7 Who do you think the bones belonged to?
8 The picture showed Richard was deformed. Why was that important?

B Pronunciation stress in two-syllable nouns and verbs

4 All of these words have two syllables. Put them in the correct box. Use the glossary to help with new words.
~~battle~~   ~~become~~   body   complete   confess   happen   power   protect   rebel *n*   rebel *vb*   return   shoulder

● ●	battle
● ●	become

5 Are the words in exercise 4 nouns or verbs? What is the general rule? Which word breaks the rule?

C Predict before you listen

6 You will hear a historian talking about the murder of the princes. Predict his answers to these questions.
1 The people who first wrote about the princes in the tower were against Richard. Why?
2 Why did Sir James confess?
3 Do we *really* know what happened to the bodies?
4 The painting shows Richard was deformed. But was he really?
5 Who really killed the princes in the Tower?

7 **5D.1▶** Listen to the programme in three parts. After each part, discuss if your predictions were correct.

D Grammar past perfect

8 Look at the diagram. Match the sentences below with A and B on the time line.

1483 Richard took power.   **1485** Henry took power.

A ↑   B ↑

1 ☐ When Henry took power, he killed the princes.
2 ☐ When Henry took power, Richard had killed the princes.

9 Answer the questions about the sentences in exercise 8.
In sentence 1, which happened first?
a Henry took power.
b The princes died.

In sentence 2, which happened first?

10 Complete the grammar box.

+	–	?
He had killed them.	He _____ _____ them.	_____ he _____ them?

11 Underline six examples of the past perfect in **Mystery in the Tower**.

12 Put the verbs in brackets in the past simple or past perfect. Compare with a partner.
1 Henry _took_ (take) power in 1485. His army _____ (kill) Richard in battle.
2 Henry's army _____ (kill) Richard in battle and _____ (take) power.
3 Richard _____ (put) the boys in the Tower in June. Their father _____ (die) in April.
4 Edward IV _____ (die) in 1483 and Richard _____ (put) his two sons in the Tower.
5 Before the rebellion _____ (begin), Henry _____ (spend) some time in France.
6 Experts _____ (examine) the painting with X-rays. They discovered that somebody _____ (change) it.

More practice? **Grammar Bank ▶▶** p.140.

ABCD Put it all together

13 Work with a partner. Tell the **Mystery in the Tower** story together. Use the pictures to help you.
Example   This painting shows the two princes, Edward and Richard, in the Tower. They were put there by …

I can talk about past events.

Tick ✓ the line.   with a lot of help   with some help   on my own   very easily

Writing Narrating a story

A Read and identify narrative strategies

1 Why do people read books? Compare with a partner.
Example To find information …

2 Read this story. What is the purpose of the text? Choose the best answer.
a To give information to the reader.
b To explain something to the reader.
c To entertain the reader.

It was the worst possible moment for my mobile to start ringing.

There was a burglar in the building and I was hiding behind the photocopier. I'd been working late and I was the last person in the office. When I heard the breaking glass, I knew immediately what was happening. I quickly found a dark corner and hid.

Then my phone rang and I heard the burglar stop. He was listening. Then he started walking towards the photocopier! I looked around me for a weapon, but I could only find a ball-point pen. It was blue, I think.

Then he called my name. 'Is that you, Jo?' he asked. It was Tom, my boss. He'd left his keys on his desk and he couldn't get into his house.

3 Put the events in the order they actually happened.

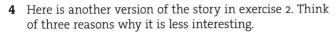

- ☐ Jo heard breaking glass.
- ☐ Jo hid.
- ☐ 1 Tom left his keys on his desk.
- ☐ Jo thought it was a burglar.
- ☐ Jo worked late.
- ☐ Tom asked, 'Is that you, Jo?'
- ☐ Jo's mobile rang.

4 Here is another version of the story in exercise 2. Think of three reasons why it is less interesting.

Tom left his keys in the office and went back to get them. Jo was working late and thought Tom was a burglar.

5 Work with a partner. Find examples of the strategies below in the text in exercise 2.

Narrative strategies

1 Start in the middle of the story to catch the reader's attention quickly.
2 Go back to earlier events to explain the background to the situation.
3 Give details about the most exciting moments to get the reader interested in what's going to happen next.
4 Keep a surprise for the end of the story which explains everything that happened.

B Use narrative tenses to order the story

6 What is the order of the actions? Match a–c with 1–3.

My phone rang … a … and then I left the office.
b … after I'd left the office.
c … while I was leaving the office.

1 ☐ b first green, then blue
2 ☐ first blue, then green
3 ☐ green and blue at the same time

7 What tense are the verbs in green in exercise 6?

8 Order these actions using the three narrative tenses.
1 watch TV have dinner
Example I watched TV and then I had dinner.
I watched TV after I'd had dinner.
I watched TV while I was having dinner.

2 listen to the radio make lunch
3 read the newspaper travel to work

C Think about your reader

9 Work with a partner. Rewrite this story using the strategies in exercise 5 to make it more exciting.

I was staying in a hotel in Barcelona. I went to a concert one night and I took a taxi back to the hotel. It couldn't take me to the door because the hotel was in a pedestrian area, so I had to walk the last 500 metres. I left my bag in the taxi by mistake, got out, and started walking. It was late and I was alone. Then I heard footsteps behind me. I was frightened. I thought it was a robber. I ran to the hotel. The person followed me in. He was the taxi driver and he was returning my bag.

10 Read **Narrating a story** on ›› p.128. Which story is more exciting, yours or the one on ›› p.128? Why?

ABC Put it all together

11 Work with a partner. Choose one of the sentences below to start a story. Make notes on the main events.

The moment I walked into the house, I knew something was wrong.

I'm not usually afraid of dogs, but this one was different.

I'd never ridden a motorbike before and I had no idea where the brakes were.

12 Write a story of about 100 words starting with one of the sentences. Try to make the story entertaining.

13 Work in small groups. Read your classmates' stories. Try to guess the ending before you finish. Which story is the most entertaining?

I can narrate a story.

Tick ✓ the line. with a lot of help with some help on my own very easily

Unit 5 Review

A Grammar

1 *the* or no article in names of institutions Write *the* or nothing in each gap.

Everybody was there – leaders from [1] *the* European Union, [2]_____ Secretary-General of [3]_____ United Nations, [4]_____ King Leopold, [5]_____ Princess Leida, the leaders of [6]_____ Conservative and Socialist Parties, [7]_____ president of [8]_____ United States and [9]_____ Prince Edward.

2 Modals of obligation Write sentences with *must, can't, can,* or *don't have to.*

Instructions when flying

1 The seat belt sign is not switched on.
   You don't have to wear your seat belt.

2 Switch off your mobile phones now.
   _____

3 Put your bags under the seat in front if you want.
   _____

4 Don't leave your seat during landing.
   _____

5 A passport isn't necessary on an internal flight.
   _____

6 Show your ID when you get on the plane.
   _____

7 Don't use electronic equipment during take-off.
   _____

8 Use the overhead light if you want to read.
   _____

3 Active or passive? Which sentence is unlikely in the active? ~~Cross~~ it out and write it in the passive.

1 The boy walked the dog.
   ~~The boy bit the dog.~~ *The boy was bitten by the dog.*

2 The film watched the girl.
   The film amazed the girl.

3 The man has seen the falling rocks.
   The man has hurt the falling rocks.

4 The thief caught the police.
   The thief heard the police.

5 You saw the midday sun.
   You burned the midday sun.

4 Past perfect Put the verbs in the past simple or past perfect.

Dennis [1] *arrived* (arrive) home very late, tired, and wet. He [2]_____ (go) to a party and he [3]_____ (walk) home in the rain. When he [4]_____ (go) into the house, he [5]_____ (be) shocked to find everything in a complete mess. Somebody [6]_____ (broken) in through the window and they [7]_____ (steal) his computer and TV. He [8]_____ (phone) the police immediately.

B Vocabulary

5 Politics Write the words for these definitions.

1 e *l e c t*   To choose your leaders.
2 c_____   City of government.
3 n_____n____   Of the nation. *adj*
4 l_____ wing   Socialist or similar.
5 Leaders r__p_____ the people.
6 p_____   Leader of a republic.
7 d_____c_____   Political system in which people vote.
8 Head of s_____.
9 e_____   Method of choosing governments.
10 c____s_____   Opposite of socialist.
11 p_____c____   Of politics. *adj*
12 r_____b_____   Country without kings or queens.

6 Permission words Complete the sentence for each sign in the passive. Use the verb given.

1 allow   Dogs *aren't allowed* _____.

2 prohibit   Feeding the birds _____.

3 permit   Taking photographs _____.

4 forbid   Bicycles _____.

5 allow   Food _____.

7 Crime verbs Complete the sentences with the correct form of these verbs.

arrest   attack   hijack   kidnap   kill   rob   shoot   ~~steal~~

1 Someone has *stolen* my wallet!
2 I was _____ by a young man with a knife.
3 A gang of criminals _____ the bank and escaped with €20,000.
4 There was a road accident, but nobody was _____.
5 The plane was _____ by a group of terrorists.
6 The boy _____ himself in the foot by accident with his father's gun.
7 The police have _____ two men in connection with the robbery.
8 The criminals _____ Dr Jennings and demanded €150,000 to set him free.

How to express strong feelings

G *so and such*   V extreme adjectives   P high intonation

A Read and follow meaning

1 What are the best tips for driving safely? Discuss with a partner.
Example Watch the other cars carefully.

2 **6A.1▶** Read and listen to **Crash!** opposite and answer these questions.
1 What reasons has Suzi got to be angry at Paul?
2 What does she do about it?

3 Read the story again. Work with a partner and answer the questions. Give reasons.
Do you think …
1 Suzi was responsible for the crash?
2 Suzi is happy to see Paul again?
3 Suzi and Paul used to have a relationship?
4 Suzi really means it when she says 'you're so kind'?
5 Paul understands what Suzi is doing?

4 Work with a partner. What do you think is going to happen next? Compare your answer with other students.

B Vocabulary extreme adjectives

5 Look at **Extreme adjectives** opposite and match one adjective with each of these meanings. You can use a dictionary.

very big *enormous*   very angry
very tired   very surprising*
very frightened
* also often used to mean *very good*

6 Find synonyms for *terrible* and *wonderful* in **Extreme adjectives**. Write them in this diagram.

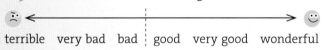

terrible   very bad   bad ┊ good   very good   wonderful

_____   _____
_____   _____

7 Work with a partner. Underline the best word to complete the sentences.
1 He was exhausted/terrified/furious of very high buildings.
2 She was terrified/furious/exhausted after the walk, and needed to rest for a while.
3 I went to see a/an enormous/brilliant/furious film last night.
4 We had such a/an amazing/furious/terrified lunch!
5 She was terrified/furious/exhausted after he damaged her expensive new car.

C Grammar *so and such*

8 Look at the examples and complete the rules.
You were driving so badly.
I'm just so happy.
You always were such an awful driver.

Rules
Use _____ to make a noun* more extreme.
Use _____ to make an adjective or adverb more extreme.
*There may be other words between *such* and the noun.

9 Underline examples of *so* and *such* in **Crash!**

10 Make these sentences more extreme with *so* or *such*.
1 Why was Paul furious?   *Why was Paul so furious?*
2 It's an amazing story.
3 I'm exhausted!
4 Why do you drive an enormous car?
5 Why do you drive fast?

11 **6A.2▶** Pronunciation Listen and repeat the sentences on the audio.

I'm **so** ex**haust**ed!   It's **such** a **brill**iant **film**!

Notice that to express strong feelings, the voice goes high on the main syllables.

More practice? **Grammar Bank** ≫ p.141.

D Listen and identify the topic

12 **6A.3▶** Listen to three conversations. Guess what the people are talking about from the list below.
a restaurant   a shop   a holiday   a film
exam results   a job interview

13 Listen again. Make a note of the words and phrases that helped you identify the topic. Compare with a partner.
Example Conversation 1 – ending, story, music, see

14 Look at the audio script on ≫ p.154. Underline questions and expressions of sympathy which encourage the other person to continue.
Example Really?

15 Choose two of the conversations and practise them with a partner. Use a high voice to express strong feelings.

ABCD Put it all together

16 Prepare to tell your partner a story. Look at **Tell a story** on ≫ p.128.

17 Tell your story to your partner. Listen to your partner's story. Encourage him/her to continue by asking questions and expressing sympathy.

I can express strong feelings.

Lost *and* found

A

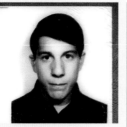

When Doug Schmitt left his wallet at a petrol station in 1967, he didn't expect to see it again.

Mr Schmitt had stopped to buy petrol in Logan, Utah. In those days, he was a student at Utah State University. He forgot to pick up his wallet after paying and drove away. When he noticed, it was too late to go back.

39 YEARS IN A DRAWER

The owner of the petrol station put the wallet in a drawer and hoped that Mr Schmitt would return to collect it. 39 years later, the petrol station owner died and his wife decided to clear out his office. She found the wallet, which contained $5 in cash, some old stamps, a dry-cleaning ticket, Mr Schmitt's university ID card, and some photos of his high school girlfriends. She asked her son-in-law, Ted Nyman, to find the owner of the wallet. Mr Nyman looked on the Internet and discovered that Mr Schmitt runs an antiques business in Lake Ariel, Pennsylvania. He contacted Mr Schmitt and sent him the wallet.

A FULL HEAD OF HAIR

Mr Schmitt was very surprised to get the wallet back and praised the 'good, honest' people of Utah. He said it was strange to receive a little piece of his own history and nice to see the photo on his ID card. 'I had a full head of hair back then,' he said.

DRY CLEANING

Mr Schmitt's wife Vickie decided to contact the local TV station with the story. She said, 'It's wonderful that people are kind enough to do this for a complete stranger.' She added, 'It's great to see how Doug looked when he was at college.'

Mr Schmitt says he must remember to collect his dry-cleaning next time he's in Utah.

B

When Ray Heilwagen lost his wallet in France during World War II, he didn't expect to see it again.

Mr Heilwagen, from Hannibal, Missouri, had fallen into a river after being hurt in the leg by a bomb. While he was waiting for the medics to come, he remembers taking out his wallet to look at the photos. But the next morning, before being moved to hospital, he couldn't find it.

A SURPRISE PHONE CALL

62 years later, he received a phone call from a man who said he had found it. The man, called Stephen Breitenstein, from Illinois, said his father had died recently and he had found the wallet among his things. Mr Breitenstein's dad had been in France during the war and had found the wallet and brought it home hoping to find the owner. However, he didn't know how to do it and finally stopped looking. He left the wallet in a drawer.

'SORRY IT TOOK OVER 60 YEARS'

Mr Breitenstein found the wallet, which contained a few francs, some receipts, some photos, and Mr Heilwagen's social security card. He decided to look for Mr Heilwagen on the Internet, found him, and sent him the wallet. Mr Breitenstein also sent a note saying he was very happy to find Mr Heilwagen, and he apologized for taking over 60 years to return the wallet.

THE KINDNESS OF STRANGERS

Mr Heilwagen was very surprised to get the wallet back. 'I could hardly believe it,' he said. He was amazed that a complete stranger would be kind enough to look for him and return the wallet after so many years, and he really enjoyed seeing his old things again.

Dictionary extracts

GRAMMAR If you **stop to do sth**, you stop in order to do it: *On the way home I stopped to buy a newspaper.* If you **stop doing sth**, you do not do it any more: *I stopped smoking 3 months ago.*

GRAMMAR If you **remember to do sth**, you don't forget to do it: *It's my mother's birthday. I must remember to phone her.* If you **remember doing sth**, you have a picture or memory in your mind of doing it: *Do you remember going to the cinema for the first time?*

Notes from *Oxford Wordpower Dictionary* © Oxford University Press 2006

How to tell and show interest in an anecdote

G infinitives and gerunds

A Read and follow the main events in a story

1 Have you ever lost something valuable? Tell a partner.

2 Work with a partner. Look at **Lost and found** opposite. **Student A** read text A and **Student B** read text B. Write a title for your text.

3 Answer these questions about the article you read.
1 How and where did the man lose his wallet?
2 Who found the wallet first?
3 Where did he keep the wallet all these years?
4 Who found the wallet again?
5 What was in the wallet?
6 How did they find the owner of the wallet?
7 How did the owner feel about getting it back?
8 How long did it take to get his wallet back?

4 Tell your partner about the story you read and make a list of similarities and differences between the stories.

5 Can you remember how these phrases came into the stories? Tell a partner.

after paying   before being moved   expect to see
kind enough to look   remembers taking out
stopped to buy   too late to go back

Example expect to see – The man lost his wallet in the war. He didn't expect to see it again.

B Grammar infinitives and gerunds

6 Find these words in **Lost and found** and write them in the box.

decide   enjoy   expect   forget   hope

use a gerund after ...	use *to* + infinitive after ...
mind fancy finish	want

7 Complete the sentences with the infinitive or gerund of the verbs. You can use your dictionary.
1 I didn't expect _to see_ my wallet again. see
2 We really enjoy _____ out. eat
3 I hoped _____ the man who found my wallet. meet
4 I don't mind _____ you to the station. drive
5 She decided _____ for the owner of the wallet. look
6 Do you fancy _____ to the cinema tonight? go
7 I haven't finished _____ my homework yet. do
8 Don't forget _____ your passport with you. take

8 Read the rules below. Underline examples in the texts.

use a gerund after prepositions	use *to* + infinitive after adjectives (often with *too / enough*)
after being hurt before being moved thanks for helping me	it's great to see too late to go back kind enough to do this

9 Work with a partner. Complete the text with infinitives or gerunds.

bring do go help know ~~leave~~ return

I dropped my wallet on the pavement after [1] _leaving_ a café. When I noticed, it was too late [2] _____ to the place and look for it. I phoned the bank to cancel my credit cards before [3] _____ to bed. The next day, a man came to my house and returned my wallet to me. I thanked him for [4] _____ it back and offered him €20 for [5] _____ me. He refused the money and left. It's nice [6] _____ that there are people honest and friendly enough [7] _____ something like this!

10 *Stop* and *remember* can be followed by an infinitive or gerund, but the meaning is different. Read **Dictionary extracts** opposite and find examples of each meaning in **Lost and found**.

More practice? **Grammar Bank** >> p.141.

C Listen and show interest

11 You will hear Julia telling Ben about losing her handbag. What do you think was in the handbag? Make a list.

12 **6B.1**▶ Listen. Which things on your list do you hear?

13 Listen again and answer the questions.
1 Why did Julia start telling her story?
2 Where did Julia leave the handbag?
3 Did she get it back?
4 What did Julia do after losing the handbag?

14 Ben is an interested listener. Match phrases 1–4 from the audio script with meanings a–d.
1 ☐ What a pain!
2 ☐ Mmm ...
3 ☐ And did you get it back?
4 ☐ Yeah, all the paperwork and everything.

a Ben asks questions to show he's interested.
b He expresses sympathy.
c He adds details to show he can understand what she's saying.
d He makes sounds to show he's still listening.

15 Underline these and more examples in the audio script on >> p.154. Then practise saying them with a partner.

ABC Put it all together

16 Work with a partner. Prepare to tell a story.
Student A Look at **Picture story** on >> p.129.
Student B Look at **Picture story** on >> p.134.

17 Tell your story to your partner. Listen with interest to your partner's story. Use some of the responses that Ben uses in exercise 14.

I can tell and show interest in an anecdote.

Tick ✓ the line.   with a lot of help   with some help   on my own   very easily

Nightmare Neighbours

TBC1 21.30 – 22.00

This is the first of a new documentary series about problem neighbours. In this programme, we follow the lives of the Dicksons – a retired couple in Plymouth, and their next
05 door neighbours, the Lanes – a single mother and her two children.

The Dicksons say that the Lanes are noisy and rough. They say they can't sleep because of the fighting and shouting from next door. Mrs Dickson
10 says she caught Mrs Lane's daughter painting graffiti on their garage wall, and according to Mr Dickson, the Lanes leave rubbish by the front door. He says the smell is terrible and it's a health hazard.

15 But of course, there are two sides to every dispute. According to Mrs Lane, the Dicksons just want to make trouble because she is separated from her husband. She says they enjoy complaining because they're bored and haven't
20 got anything else to do.

There's something fascinating about looking at other people's everyday lives, and this is the secret of reality TV's success. In the series Nightmare Neighbours, we see how tiny disputes
25 can become wars which last for many years. We'll see a woman who set fire to her neighbour's door because he parked his car in the wrong place, and a man who shot his neighbour's dog because it was barking too loudly. We'll see a couple who
30 installed a security camera in their home and pointed it towards their neighbour's front door. At the end of these shows, you come away thinking, 'Why don't these people just talk to each other?!'

PLEASE KINDLY DO NOT LEAVE RUBBISH HERE.

Love Your Neighbours

Mrs Dickson thinks the Lanes
Are noisy and rough
She says the kids are naughty
She says 1_____'s had enough
Mr Dickson says 2_____ leave
Their rubbish by the door
'You can't complain,' says Mrs Lane
'It's not against the law'

Love Your Neighbours ...

Mrs Dickson says their children
Play their music loud
She says 3_____ hears them swearing
It shouldn't be allowed
Mr Dickson says 4_____ hears them
Fighting all night long
'You can't complain,' says Mrs Lane
'We're doing nothing wrong'

Love Your Neighbours ...

Mrs Dickson says 5_____ kick
Their ball along the hall
She says 6_____ saw their daughter
Writing on the wall
Mr Dickson says 7_____ hears them
Talking on the phone
'Don't complain,' says Mrs Lane
'Leave us all alone'

Love Your Neighbours ...

How to talk about people in your neighbourhood

G pronouns in reported speech   V behaviour   P spelling and pronunciation *gh*

A Vocabulary behaviour

1 Look at **Behaviour** opposite. Which words do you think are positive and which are negative? Use a dictionary to help you.

2 Which of these complaints about neighbours are most common? Work with a partner and number them 1–7.

☐ animal problems   ☐ noise
☐ car parking   ☐ rough behaviour
☐ naughty children   ☐ rubbish
☐ walls and fence problems

3 **6C.1▶** Listen to the results of a survey in Britain. What is the order of the complaints in exercise 2?

B Read a TV review

4 Read **Nightmare Neighbours** opposite. Who do you think the people are in the photos?

5 Which of the problems in exercise 2 are mentioned? Say where they are in the text.
Example noise – lines 7–9 and 28–29

6 Find words with these meanings.
1 a thing which may be dangerous
2 an argument or disagreement between people
3 no longer living with your wife, husband or partner
4 the noise made by a dog
5 to fix equipment into position so that it can be used

7 Write *true* or *false*. If the sentence is false, say why.
1 Mr Dickson works in a bank. *False – he's retired.*
2 The Lanes live next door to the Dicksons.
3 There are three people living in the Lane's house.
4 Mrs Dickson says she can't sleep.
5 Mrs Lane isn't married.
6 The Dicksons definitely enjoy complaining.

8 Answer the questions with a partner.
1 Who do you feel more sorry for – the Dicksons or the Lanes?
2 Which do you think is the worst behaviour mentioned?
3 Why do you think the writer recommends this programme?

C Grammar pronouns in reported speech

9 Read **Love Your Neighbours** opposite. Write the missing pronouns in the gaps.

10 **6C.2▶** Listen and check.

11 Write the missing pronouns in the grammar box. Then underline the correct word in the rule.

direct speech (present tense)	reported speech (present tense)
She says, 'They swear.'	She says they swear.
He says, '_____ hear them.'	He says he hears them.
She says, 'I saw their daughter.'	She says _____ saw their daughter.
She says, 'You can't complain.'	She says we can't complain.

Rule
When you change direct speech into reported speech, you always have to/sometimes have to change the pronouns.

12 Work with a partner. Imagine the Dicksons are speaking directly to Mrs Lane. Find more examples of reported speech in the song and say them in direct speech.
Example She says she's had enough. She says, 'I've had enough.'

13 Think of people you know well. What do they often say? Tell a partner.
Example My mother often says she hates the traffic ...

More practice? **Grammar Bank ▶▶** p.141.

D Spelling and pronunciation *gh*

14 Look at this pair of words. What difference do the letters *gh* make to the pronunciation? Choose the best answer.
fit /fɪt/   fight /faɪt/
a They change the sound of the vowel.
b They change the sound of the last consonant.

15 Underline nine words with *gh* in **Love Your Neighbours**. Answer the question.
gh is usually part of a vowel sound. In which two words is it the consonant sound /f/?

16 Practise saying the song lyric.

ABCD Put it all together

17 Look at **Are you a good neighbour?** on ▶▶ p.129. Interview your partner and tick ✓ the answers which are true for him/her.
Example A Who do you know in your neighbourhood?
         B Well, I don't know one of my next door neighbours very well, because they just moved in last month, but I know the other one ...

18 Work with a different partner or group. Tell your new partner(s) what your first partner says about his/her neighbours. Who gets on best with their neighbours?
Example Sonia says she doesn't know her next door neighbours very well because ...

I can talk about people in my neighbourhood.

Tick ✓ the line.   with a lot of help   with some help   on my own   very easily

THE MAN WHO SOLD THE EIFFEL TOWER

1 **Paris, 1925.** World War I had finished and the city was full of people with cash looking for business opportunities. Victor Lustig was reading the newspaper one day and found an article about the Eiffel Tower. It said the tower was being neglected because it was too expensive to maintain. Lustig saw a great 'business opportunity' – he would sell the Eiffel Tower!

2 Lustig wrote to six important businessmen in the city and invited them to a secret meeting in a well-known Paris hotel. He said he was a government official and he told them that he wanted to talk about a business deal. All six of the businessmen came to the meeting.

3 At the meeting, Lustig told them that the city wanted to sell the Eiffel Tower for scrap metal and that he had been asked to find a buyer. He said that the deal was secret because it would not be popular with the public. The businessmen believed him, perhaps because the Eiffel Tower was never planned to be permanent. It had been built as part of the 1889 Paris Expo, and the original plan had been to remove it in 1909.

4 Lustig rented a limousine and took the men to visit the tower. He showed them around. After the tour, he said that if they were interested, they should contact him the next day. Lustig told them he would give the tower contract to the person with the highest offer. One of the dealers, Andre Poisson, was very interested, but he was also worried.

Scrap metal

Why was everything so secret? Why was Lustig in such a hurry?

5 The two men had a meeting, and Lustig confessed that he wasn't looking for the highest offer. He said he would give the contract to anybody – for a price. Poisson understood: Lustig wanted a little extra money 'under the table' for himself. That explained why the deal was secret. This was Lustig's cleverest lie, because now Poisson believed him completely.

6 Lustig sold Poisson a false contract for the Eiffel Tower – and on top of that, Poisson paid him a little extra money 'under the table'. Lustig put

Victor Lustig

Lustig being arrested

Alcatraz

all the money in a suitcase and took the first train to Vienna. Poisson never told the police what had happened – he was too embarrassed. After a month, Lustig returned to Paris and tried to sell the Eiffel Tower again, but this time somebody told the police and he had to escape to America. There, he continued his criminal career and finished his days in the famous Alcatraz prison.

How to report what people said

G tenses in reported speech V *say* and *tell* P *'d*

A Read and understand the main ideas

1 Look at the title and photos opposite. What do you think the story will be about? Tell a partner.

2 Read **The Man Who Sold the Eiffel Tower**. Who sold the tower? Who bought it?

3 Read the text again. Match summaries a–f with paragraphs 1–6. Compare with a partner.
   a ☐ explaining the sale
   b ☐1 a great idea
   c ☐ how to buy the Eiffel Tower
   d ☐ Lustig gets rich
   e ☐ organizing a meeting
   f ☐ reasons why it's a secret

B Vocabulary *say* and *tell*

4 Underline examples of *said* and *told* in the text. Then underline the correct words in these sentences.
   1 I said/told that I had a deal to offer him.
   2 I said/told him to give me the money.
   3 I said/told, 'We will both be rich!'

5 Work with a partner. Complete the text with *said* or *told*.
   In 1924, Arthur Ferguson met an American tourist in Trafalgar Square. He ¹*told*_____ the man that he was an estate agent. He ²_____ that the British Government was short of money and wanted to sell Nelson's Column. He ³_____ they had asked him to sell it. He ⁴_____ the tourist that the deal was secret. The tourist ⁵_____ he would buy it. Ferguson ⁶_____ him he needed a deposit of £6,000. The tourist paid.

C Grammar tenses in reported speech

6 Find these sentences reported in the text in exercise 5 and write them below. What are the differences in tense? Underline the correct word in the rule.

direct speech	reported speech	
'I'm an estate agent.'	*He told the man that he was an estate agent.*	change present simple to *past simple*____
'They asked me to sell it.'		change past simple to _____
'I'll buy it.'		change *will* to _____

Rule
If the reporting verb (e.g. *say* or *tell*) is in the past, you **change/don't change** the tense in the reported speech.

7 Complete the sentences in the box. Note that *had* and *would* can both be reduced to *'d*.

		direct speech	reported speech
1	a	I try to help.	He *said he tried*____ to help.
	b	I tried to help.	He *said he'd tried*____ to help.
	c	I'll try to help.	He *said he'd try*____ to help.
2	a	I need money.	She said she _____ money.
	b	I needed money.	She said _____ money.
	c	I'll need money.	She said _____ money.

8 **6D.1▶ Pronunciation** Can you hear the *'d*? Listen to the difference and repeat.
   he tried to   he'd tried to
   she needed   she'd needed

9 **6D.2▶** Listen to the reported speech sentences from exercise 7 and say if they are *a*, *b*, or *c*. Test a partner.
   Example He said he'd tried to help. = b!

10 The people below tell small lies. These are their actual words. Complete the reported sentences.
   'You'll be fine.' 'Santa Claus brought it.' 'You look lovely.'
   'I bought it.' 'I don't feel very well.' ~~'I'll have a little more.'~~
   1 Beth finished her meal and was full. To be polite, she said *she'd have a little more*.
   2 Edgar's doctor said _____. Edgar was ill for six more months.
   3 Frank found a winning lottery ticket on a train seat. He said _____.
   4 Linda got a new doll for Christmas. Linda's mum told her _____.
   5 Tina looked awful in her new dress. Her friend told her _____.
   6 Tom was fine, but he didn't want to go to school. He said _____.

11 Work with a partner. Do you think the lies in exercise 10 are bad? Put them in order.
   More practice? **Grammar Bank** ≫ p.141.

ABC Put it all together

12 Work with a partner. Read a story carefully and try to remember it. Tell your part of the story to your partner. Use reported speech instead of direct speech.
   Student A Look at **The Violin Story Part A** on ≫ p.129.
   Student B Look at **The Violin Story Part B** on ≫ p.134.

13 Now read **The Violin Story solution** on ≫ p.133.

I can report what people said.

Tick ✓ the line.   with a lot of help   with some help   on my own   very easily

Writing Exchanging news in a personal letter

A Vocabulary responding to news

1 Work with a partner. Match the news and responses. Sometimes more than one answer is possible.

1 ☑ d My birthday is the same day as yours.
2 ☐ My aunt has died.
3 ☐ I can't go on holiday – I've broken my arm.
4 ☐ I've been chosen for the national team!
5 ☐ I've resigned from my job!
6 ☐ We're going to have a baby!

a How terrible! Poor you!
b Oh no, I'm so sorry.
c That's absolutely fantastic! Well done!
d Wow, what a coincidence!
e That's wonderful news. I'm so pleased for you!
f What a surprise!

2 Think of one piece of good news and one piece of bad news. Tell your partner and practise responding.

Example A I've passed my driving test!
B That's absolutely fantastic! Well done!

B Read a personal letter

3 Look at the photo of Ashley's flat. Guess what's happening and how Ashley feels about it. Tell a partner.

4 Read Ashley's letter to Fran and check your guesses.

> Dear Fran,
>
> How are you? I'm fine. I've just moved into my new flat and it's brilliant. It's such a great feeling having a place of my own, although I'm absolutely exhausted after moving all my boxes!
>
> My neighbours Angela and Bruce are nice, although their kids are quite noisy. However, school term starts next week, and Angela says they'll be quieter then. Anyway, I can't complain – I'm quite noisy myself, as you know!
>
> By the way, bad news about me and Gabi. We've split up. It was really hard but I think it was the right thing to do. I'll tell you all about it next time we meet.
>
> Last time we met, you said you were going to move flat as well. Have you moved yet? What's the new place like? Is it a nice area? Do you get on with the neighbours? Write soon and tell me all about it!
>
> Love from Ashley

5 Find the words or phrases below in Ashley's letter. Match them with the meanings in 1–4.

☐ by the way ☐ however ☐ anyway ☐ although

1 A word meaning *but* which isn't followed by a comma.
2 A word meaning *but* which is followed by a comma.
3 A word meaning *also* or *and*.
4 A phrase used to introduce an unconnected topic.

C Connect ideas

6 Write sentences with the same meaning using the blue words. Look at Ashley's letter for help with punctuation. Compare with a partner.

1 They're nice, although their kids are noisy. however
They're nice. However, their kids are noisy.
2 I'm happy. However, I'm very tired. although
3 I don't want it. It's too expensive and I don't even like it. anyway
4 We did it. However, it wasn't easy. although
5 It's boring, although it's very well paid. however
6 I don't take sugar. I don't like it. Also, it's bad for you. anyway

D Think about your reader

7 Look at Ashley's letter again. What is Ashley's relationship to Fran? Choose the best answer.
a Complete strangers.
b Good friends.
c Acquaintances.

8 How does Ashley make the letter like a conversation with a friend? Work with your partner and find examples of 1–4 in the letter.
1 asking the reader questions
2 writing about people and facts the reader knows
3 expressing personal feelings about the news in the letter
4 using written expressions similar to *hello* and *goodbye* in spoken dialogue

9 Imagine Fran and Ashley meet and have the conversation face to face. Role play the conversation. Add more news and use expressions from exercise 1.

ABCD Put it all together

10 You are Fran. Write a reply. Respond to all the news in Ashley's letter and answer his questions. Connect your ideas and add some news about you and people you know.

11 You are Ashley. Read your partner's letter. Does it give you all the news you wanted to hear?

I can exchange news in a personal letter.

Tick ✓ the line.   with a lot of help   with some help   on my own   very easily

Unit 6 Review

A Grammar

1 *so* and *such* Make these sentences more extreme using *so* or *such*.

1 You don't need to speak loudly.
  You don't need to speak so loudly.

2 We ate outside because it was a beautiful day.
  _____

3 Why are fresh vegetables expensive these days?
  _____

4 I didn't know it was a long journey.
  _____

5 I didn't know it was far away.
  _____

2 Infinitives and gerunds Match 1–8 with a–h.

1 [b] It's warm and sunny. Do you fancy …
2 ☐ It's a nice day. Do you want …
3 ☐ After leaving school, I hope …
4 ☐ I'm going to take a year out before …
5 ☐ There were dark clouds, so I decided …
6 ☐ It was raining, but I don't mind …
7 ☐ You can watch TV when you finish …
8 ☐ Please don't forget …

a doing your homework.
b going to the beach?
c going to university.
d to do your homework.
e to go for a picnic?
f to go to university to study economics.
g to take my umbrella.
h walking in the rain.

3 Pronouns in reported speech Report what Holly says about her work using *says*.

'I work in an office. I share the office with a man called Justin. We sometimes have lunch together. I'll introduce you to him one day. I think he's really funny.'

She says she works in an office. She says she shares …

4 Tenses in reported speech Write this conversation in reported speech using *said*.

Anna [1] I'm worried about the maths exam.
  Anna said she was worried about the maths exam.
Ben [2] You'll be fine.
A [3] I didn't study enough.
B [4] You always pass exams.
A [5] I got a C in December.
B [6] There's still time to study.
A [7] I don't understand maths.
B [8] I'll help you.

B Vocabulary

5 Extreme adjectives Complete the sentences with these adjectives.

amazing ~~brilliant~~ enormous
exhausted furious terrified

1 Her first book was good, but her second was _brilliant_ .
2 She's _____ of spiders and snakes.
3 He's _____ because I broke his computer.
4 The Atlantic's big, but the Pacific's _____ .
5 Greg's a magician and he can do some _____ tricks.
6 He was _____ after walking for ten hours.

6 Behaviour Find the answers to clues 1–10. Some letters are used twice.

A	C	N	A	U	G	H	T	Y
E	B	E	H	A	V	E	D	N
F	R	I	E	N	D	L	Y	O
I	R	R	U	D	E	P	U	S
G	N	O	I	S	Y	F	H	Y
H	A	E	S	R	O	U	G	H
T	S	W	E	A	R	L	O	P

Clues
1 Bad behaviour. (adj) *naughty*
2 Opposite of 1. Well-_____.
3 Behaves like a friend. (adj)
4 Opposite of polite.
5 Opposite of quiet.
6 Not polite, may be violent.
7 To use bad words.
8 To attack each other.
9 Likes to help. (adj)
10 Curious about other people's personal life.

7 *say* and *tell* Complete the story with *said* or *told*.

There was a boy with a dog on the train. I [1] _said_ , 'Your dog's nice. What's his name?' The boy [2] _____ me his dog was called Boris. 'He looks like a good dog,' I [3] _____. 'Does he bite?' The boy [4] _____ he didn't. Then I reached over to touch the dog and it bit me. 'Ouch! You [5] _____ me Boris didn't bite!', I [6] _____. 'He doesn't,' [7] _____ the boy, 'That's not Boris.'

DOES YOUR DOG LOOK LIKE YOU?

You often hear people say that dogs look like their owners. It sounds like a crazy idea, but a new study from California suggests that it's true – but only in certain circumstances.

Researchers wanted to find out if people really do look like their dogs, and just how this happens. First of all, they took photos of 45 dogs and their owners. They mixed the photos up and asked a group of people to match them.

The people who took part in the research were able to match most of the owners with their dogs if they were pure-bred – dogs whose parents are both the same type of dog. However, they weren't able to do the matching for mongrels

– dogs with parents of two different types. The researchers have suggested that this may be because people choose dogs which look like themselves, and people who want pure-bred dogs choose their pets more carefully.

The researchers say it isn't clear how the people in their study were able to do the matching. They didn't simply match hairy dogs with hairy people or big dogs with big people. It seems that they used a more complicated method, such as matching friendly-looking dogs with friendly-looking people.

What do you think? Try it for yourself. Can you match these dogs with their owners?

Character	Looks	Age
active **ag**gres**sive am**b**it**ious	**bush**y **eye**brows mou**stache** fringe	in her late teens
ar**tist**ic con**fid**ent **gen**erous	clean-**shav**en round face high **fore**head	in his early twenties
i**mag**inative kind **live**ly **ner**vous	**curl**y hair **ging**er hair straight hair	in his mid thirties around fifty
out**go**ing **ser**ious shy un**friend**ly	**wav**y hair **shoul**der-length hair	in his seventies

How to say how people look

v looks and character; *look* and *look like*   **P** contrastive stress

A Read for detail

1 Which dogs in the photos opposite do you prefer? Why? Tell a partner.

2 Read **Does your dog look like you?** opposite quickly. What is the text about? Choose the best answer.
   a Different types of dog.
   b People who try to look like dogs.
   c Research on the appearance of dogs and their owners.
   d People and their dogs in California.

3 Read the text again. Write *true* or *false*.
   1 Researchers mixed the photos of the dogs and owners.
   2 They asked the dog owners to find their dogs.
   3 All dogs look like their owners.
   4 People are careful when they choose pure-bred dogs.
   5 People simply matched hairy dogs with hairy people.
   6 People matched friendly-looking people and dogs.

4 Work with a partner and match the people in the photos with their dogs. Explain how you did it.
   Example   photo 2 and 11 – the woman and her dog both have the same curly hair and it's the same colour ...

B Vocabulary looks and character; *look* and *look like*

5 Look at the example sentences and underline the correct word in the rules.
   He looks friendly. He looks like his dog.
   1 Use look / look like before a noun, to compare appearances.
   2 Use look / look like before an adjective, to guess a person's character from their appearance.

6 Complete the sentences with the correct form of *look* or *look like*.
   1 He _looks like_ a student.
   2 She _____ very happy.
   3 She _____ her sister.
   4 He doesn't _____ very kind.
   5 She _____ my grandmother.
   6 He doesn't _____ anyone I know.

7 Work with a partner. Look at **Character**, **Looks**, and **Age** opposite. Match the words and phrases with people in the photos. Use a dictionary to help.

8 Make sentences to describe the people in the photos. Compare with a partner.
   Example   She looks generous. She doesn't look aggressive. She's got curly hair. She's probably in her late sixties. She looks like my grandmother ...

C Listen for key words

9 **7A.1▶** Listen and read. Which photo in **Does your dog look like you?** is being described? Underline the key words which helped you.
   This man's in his early twenties, and he's got straight dark hair ... ehm ... it's quite long. He's got quite a long face, and his nose is long and thin too. His eyes are wide open – he looks a bit surprised. He looks a bit shy, nervous perhaps, I don't know.

10 **7A.2▶** Listen to these descriptions and match them with people in the photos. Compare with a partner.

11 Work with a partner. Before you listen again, write down any key words you can remember about each photo. When you listen, tick ✓ your words if you hear them.

D Pronunciation contrastive stress

12 **7A.3▶** Listen to two people playing a guessing game. Say which person in **Does your dog look like you?** they're talking about.

13 **7A.4▶** Which word is stressed? Listen and say *A* or *B*.

	A	B
1	No, **long** fair hair.	No, long **fair** hair.
2	No, curly **ging**er hair.	No, **curly** ginger hair.
3	No, **late** twenties.	No, late **twen**ties.
4	No, big **brown** eyes.	No, **big** brown eyes.

14 Work with a partner. Match the answers in exercise 13 with these questions. Then ask and answer.
   1 ☐B Has he got long dark hair?
     ☐A Has he got short fair hair?
   2 ☐ Has she got curly grey hair?
     ☐ Has she got straight ginger hair?
   3 ☐ Is he in his early twenties?
     ☐ Is he in his late thirties?
   4 ☐ Has she got small brown eyes?
     ☐ Has she got big blue eyes?

   Example   A Has he got long dark hair?
              B No, long **fair** hair.

ABCD Put it all together

15 Work in groups. Look at **Portraits of men** on >> p.129. Take turns to choose a photo. The other students ask closed questions to guess the photo.

Compound adjectives

clean-shaven	loose-fitting	well-known
fashion-conscious /'fæʃn kɒnʃəs/	old-fashioned	well-mannered
good-looking	well-dressed	well-off

The Kings of Cool

Brazzaville, Congo – Bienvenu Mouzieto knows what he likes. Clothes. He's standing in front of his house in the poor and dusty Bacongo neighbourhood, wearing a loose-fitting grey suit, leather shoes, a hat, and a tie. He's even wearing a white scarf. His outfit is possibly worth more than his house. He is elegant in an old-fashioned 1930's style. It's not what you expect to see in one of the world's poorest countries.

But Mouzieto is not the only well-dressed person around here. He is one of a large group of fashion-conscious men called the *sapeurs*. They are mostly poor and unemployed, but they would rather spend their money on clothes than food. For them, looking cool is everything. Style is their identity – they believe in the motto, 'You are what you wear'. The *sapeurs* know what they like, and what they like is expensive. It's Armani. It's Gucci. It's Prada. When they get dressed up and go out, it's a battle of designer labels. The winner is the person with the most elegant and expensive outfit.

The *sapeurs* know how to show off their clothes. They spend hours in front of the mirror practising their own favourite ways of standing. They learn how to walk with style. They know which colours look good together and they only use three colours in any outfit, including the accessories. The socks will match the hat, perhaps, or the belt will match the watch strap. The *sapeurs* are clean-shaven and well-mannered, and they are all well-known in their local neighbourhoods.

Most *sapeurs* can't really afford their lifestyle. They are not well-off, and it's difficult to find the money for such expensive tastes. Sometimes they borrow clothes – after all, only the person who lent the clothes knows where they came from. Sometimes they turn to crime, and many have spent time in prison.

What makes a *sapeur* go to such extremes to look good? Photographer Héctor Mediavilla has been studying the *sapeurs* since 2003. He understands why they like dressing up. 'When they go out dressed up, they walk differently,' he says. They behave as if they are important people – 'They show off. Sometimes they refuse to talk to other people – even their friends. They act as if they really were famous and important. They're stars for that night. It's worth it, isn't it?'

How to talk about fashion

A Vocabulary compound adjectives

1 Describe what another person in the class is wearing, but don't say their name. Your partner must guess who you are talking about.

2 Look at Compound adjectives opposite. Which ones can you use to describe the people in the photos?

3 Can you describe anybody you know with the Compound adjectives? Tell a partner.

B Read for detail

4 Look at the photos in The Kings of Cool opposite. What can you say about the place and the people? Tell your partner.

5 Read The Kings of Cool. What do you find out about Bienvenu Mouzieto? Write *true* or *false*.
   1 He lives in Brazzaville, Congo. *True*
   2 He's part of a group called the *sapeurs*.
   3 *Sapeurs* are rich.
   4 They like expensive clothes.
   5 They've all spent time in prison.
   6 *Sapeurs* behave differently when they're dressed up.

6 Answer the questions and compare with a partner.
   1 Why is Mouzieto's appearance surprising?
   2 What do *sapeurs* do when they go out?
   3 Why do you think they're well-known in their neighbourhoods?
   4 Mediavilla says, 'It's worth it.' What does he mean?

7 Find these words in The Kings of Cool and guess their meanings. Compare with a partner and say how you guessed. Check the words in a dictionary.

   dusty   outfit   designer labels   show off
   accessories   watch strap

C Grammar *wh-* clauses

8 Write the *wh-* words below in the sentences and then check in The Kings of Cool.

   which   why   ~~what~~   what   where   how   how
   1 Bienvenu Mouzieto knows __*what*__ he likes.
   2 'You are _____ you wear.'
   3 The *sapeurs* know _____ to show off their clothes.
   4 They learn _____ to walk with style.
   5 They know _____ colours look good together.
   6 Only the person who lent the clothes knows _____ they came from.
   7 He understands _____ they like dressing up.

9 We often use a *wh-* clause after *know*. Make sentences from the words below beginning with *I know* or *I don't know*.
   1 how much/costs/an Armani suit
     I don't know how much an Armani suit costs.
   2 people/why/designer clothes/buy
   3 is/my UK shoe size/what
   4 my shoes/where/were made
   5 how tall/am/I
   6 jeans/invented/who
   7 what/suit me/colours

10 Make questions beginning *Do you know* from the sentences in exercise 9 and ask a partner.
   Example A Do you know what your UK shoe size is?
              B No, I don't.

   More practice? **Grammar Bank** >> p.142.

D Listen for specific information

11 Look at the photos of Wang Li, Heather, and Marcela. Predict who will say these sentences.
   1 I don't mind what I wear.
   2 I don't care what people think!
   3 I never look at labels.
   4 If you're well-dressed, they treat you differently.
   5 I wear what I'm expected to wear.
   6 My outfit changes how I feel.

12 **7B.1** Listen and check your predictions.

13 **7B.2** Pronunciation Listen and repeat sentences 1–6 in exercise 11. When is the letter t pronounced?

Wang Li

Heather

Marcela

ABCD Put it all together

14 Make notes to answer four or more of these questions.
   1 What do you wear ... at work? at home? to go out in the evenings? on holiday?
   2 Where/How often do you shop for clothes?
   3 How much do you spend on clothes?
   4 Do you have any favourite ... designer labels? outfits?
   5 Do you think clothes are important? Why?
   6 Are you fashionable? What is fashion to you?

15 Use your notes to make a personal 'fashion statement' to a partner. Then make your fashion statement again to another partner or group. Whose opinions are most similar to yours?

I can talk about fashion.

Tick ✓ the line.   with a lot of help   with some help   on my own   very easily

My week of living *differently*

In this new series of articles, we ask different people to change their lifestyle completely for one week and keep a diary of their experiences. This week we follow web-designer **Dwight Miller**'s week of living differently.

Dwight doesn't think much about his body and appearance. He's a scruffy couch potato. So we challenged him to spend a week paying more attention to his image.

Here's Dwight's diary …

Sunday Evening

My week of living differently starts tomorrow. I'm going to do lots of things I've never done before in my life. First of all, I'm having a complete style makeover.

Monday *Makeover day*

I don't normally waste time on my hair. I don't even comb it. For me, a good haircut is a fast haircut – fifteen minutes maximum. But today, I spent two and a half hours in the chair, bored out of my mind. They put red highlights in my hair and then they gave me a funny red jacket to match. When I came out, my girlfriend said I looked like Ronald McDonald.

Tomorrow, I'm going to have a Pilates class. I'm not sure what Pilates is, but I'll check on Wikipedia when I get home …

Tuesday *Pilates day*

OK, so now I know. Pilates is an exercise method where you have to think a lot about breathing. We spent a lot of time breathing deeply. It was quite relaxing, really. I'll go to bed early tonight. Tomorrow's tango day: I'm going to have a dance class.

Wednesday *Tango day*

It was great fun until I stepped on my partner's toe! But I think I'll continue. Tango looks really cool when you can do it well. I'll probably buy some good shoes, though. Trainers don't look right.

Tomorrow, I'm doing something which sounds very exciting and dangerous – Thai boxing!

Thursday *Thai Boxing day*

Thai boxing is called 'The Science of the Eight Limbs' because you use your knees and elbows as well as hands and feet. But for me, it was the science of one limb. I lifted my leg to kick, the instructor kicked my other leg and knocked me over. I fell on my thumb and now it's really painful. I don't think I'll do that again.

Tomorrow's the last day of my lifestyle makeover, and I'm going to do something calm and relaxing – a Turkish bath.

Friday *Turkish Bath day*

Normally, I can't spend more than five minutes doing nothing. I have to be at my computer, or watching the TV, or reading a magazine. But today I sat in a steam bath for two hours doing absolutely nothing and it was fantastic. I got a

massage, too, and I came out feeling brilliant – totally refreshed – a new man! I'll definitely do that again. What a great way to end my lifestyle makeover week!

Next week, read about librarian Linda Smith's week living and working as a fashion model in Tokyo …

How to talk about plans and intentions

G future intentions V body and exercise P silent letters

A Vocabulary body and exercise

1 Write these words in the correct box. Add five more
words of your own. You can use a dictionary.

~~climbing~~ ~~comb~~ ~~elbow~~ gym haircut jogging
knee limb massage shave steam bath
thumb toe walking yoga

parts of the body	exercise activities	body care
elbow	climbing	comb

2 Which words from exercise 1 could go in the gaps?
Complete the questions and ask your partner.
1 Do you ever go _____?
   Example Do you ever go jogging?

2 Have you ever had a _____?
3 How often do you have a _____?
4 Have you ever hurt your _____?

3 **Pronunciation** Some letters in words are not pronounced.
Find words in exercise 1 to add to these lists. Compare
with a partner.
Silent b *climb* ...
Silent k *know, knife* ...
Silent l *calm, half* ...

B Read and infer

4 Read **My week of living differently** opposite. Is
Dwight Miller similar to you? Tell a partner.

5 Answer the questions.
Which activity or activities do you think Dwight ...
1 enjoyed doing? *Tango dancing*
2 would like to do better?
3 had done before?
4 probably won't repeat?

6 Find these words and phrases in the text and guess the
meaning. Underline the best description.
1 scruffy = elegant / untidy / fashionable
2 couch potato = a person who isn't very
   active / attractive / fashion conscious
3 makeover = a complete change of ideas / activity / style
4 bored out of my mind = very interested / quite
   bored / very bored
5 refreshed = the opposite of tired / ill / bored

7 Answer the questions with a partner.
1 Which activities in the diary have you done?
2 Which do you or would you enjoy doing?
3 What activities would your own week of living
   differently include?

C Grammar future intentions

8 Find sentences 1–3 in **My week of living differently**
and match them with sentences a–c.
1 ☐ I'm going to do lots of things I've never done
      before ...
2 ☐ I'm having a complete style makeover.
3 ☐ I'll definitely do that again.

a He probably has an appointment.
b He's probably had this plan for some time.
c He's probably decided this just now.

9 Complete the rules with *will*, *going to*, or *present
continuous*.
Rules
1 Use _____ for arrangements and appointments.
2 Use _____ for plans you've just decided.
3 Use _____ for plans you've had for a while.

10 Underline examples of future forms in **My week of
living differently**. Compare with a partner.

11 Underline the best future forms in this conversation.
A ¹Are you doing / Will you do anything interesting this
   week?
B No, not much. ²I'll do / I'm doing my French exam on
   Monday, so ³I'm going to / I'll stay home and study.
A So ⁴you won't go / you're not going out at the weekend?
B No. Maybe ⁵I'll / I'm going to go out to celebrate after
   the exam! What about you? ⁶Will you do / Are you
   doing anything special?
A Well, ⁷I'm starting / I'll start dance classes on Thursday.
B Really? What sort of dancing?
A ⁸We'll / We're going to study salsa, tango, rumba ... that
   sort of thing.
B Wow, sounds great.

12 **7C.1▶** Listen and check.
More practice? **Grammar Bank ≫** p.142.

ABC Put it all together

13 What do you normally do in a typical week? Write a
Monday–Friday diary and write ideas for each day about
some of the topics below. Give it to a partner.
times (getting up, meals, going to bed) work routines
leisure activities exercise journeys house work

14 Look at your partner's normal week. Prepare a plan for a
'week of living differently' and give it to him or her.

15 Look at your plan and tell a different partner about it. Do
you think you will enjoy the week? Why?
Example I'm going to drive a Formula 1 car. I've always
           wanted to do that!

I can talk about my plans and intentions.

Room Detectives

You can learn a lot about a person by looking at their room. If you look carefully, you will find clues to the person's age and occupation, their interests, habits, and personality. Look at this picture, for example …

It shows a man's bedroom. It must be a man's room because there are men's clothes hanging behind the bed. It doesn't look very comfortable, the furniture is cheap and simple, so he can't have a lot of money. There's a wooden bed, two chairs and a table. I think the man must clean and tidy a lot, because the room is neat and there's nothing on the floor. Or perhaps he tidied the mess for the picture!

The room is quite small, and there are two doors and a window. I guess the shutters of the window must be closed because there isn't much light coming in. There are paintings on the wall – I suppose the man might be an artist, or maybe he just likes pictures. Two of them are portraits of people – they might be members of the man's family or people he knows. There aren't any books in the room, so the man can't enjoy reading much.

The room is old-fashioned. There's no electrical equipment, not even a light. In one corner of the

Room 1

room, there's a jug of water, a bowl, a piece of soap, a mirror, and a towel. I guess this must be a washing area – perhaps there's no bathroom. Maybe this is in a place without electricity or running water, or perhaps it's a long time in the past, before these things were common.

Room 2

How to express guesses

G modals of deduction *must, might, can't*   V adverbs for guessing

A Read and find reasons

1 What's your bedroom like? Describe it to a partner.

2 Read **Room Detectives** opposite. Do you agree with the writer's guesses? Tell a partner.

3 Read the text again and answer the questions with a partner.
   Why does the writer think ...
   1 it's a man's room?
      There are men's clothes hanging behind the bed.
   2 the man isn't rich?
   3 the man's clean and tidy?
   4 the shutters are closed?
   5 the man might be an artist?
   6 the man doesn't read much?
   7 this might be a long time in the past?

4 Read the true information about **The Bedroom in Arles** on ›› p.130. Which guesses in exercise 3 does it confirm?

B Grammar modals of deduction *must, might, can't*

5 Read these sentences from **Room Detectives**. For each sentence, decide how sure the writer is – a or b.
   1 It must be a man's room.
   2 He can't have a lot of money.
   3 The man might be an artist.

   a The writer feels sure about these guesses.
   b The writer thinks this is possible, but isn't sure.

6 Write *must, might*, and *can't* in the diagram.

   ━━━━━━━━━━━━━━━━━━━━━━━━━━▶ **+**
   isn't _____ be _____ be _____ be   is

7 Write sentences with *must, might*, or *can't* about this mystery person. Who do you think it is? Check the answer on ›› p.134.
   1 She's got big houses in the USA and Australia.
      She must be rich. or *She can't be poor.*
   2 She wears a wedding ring.
   3 She travels a lot for work.
   4 She speaks with an Australian accent.
   5 Photographers follow her everywhere.
   6 She's won an Oscar.

8 Look at **Room 2** opposite. Work with a partner and make guesses about the person whose room this is.
   name   age   nationality   occupation   marital status
   hobbies and interests   future plans

   Example   Her name must be Liz, because there's a birthday card to Liz on the wall.

   More practice? **Grammar Bank** ›› p.142.

C Listen for detail

9 **7D.1▶** Listen to a man guessing the information about Liz in exercise 8. Does he talk about the same things as you?

10 Listen again. What does he say about these things? Do you agree? Compare your ideas with a partner.
    birthday   party dresses   graduation photo
    babies   portrait

11 Can you remember the missing words in these phrases? Check the audio script on ›› p.155.
    1 perhaps it's her _____ or _____ birthday
    2 maybe it's a room in her _____ _____
    3 she probably isn't _____
    4 she probably plans to get _____ and have _____
    5 perhaps the girl likes _____

D Vocabulary adverbs for guessing

12 **7D.2▶** The red words in exercise 11 are also used to make guesses. Listen and repeat the sentences.

13 In the sentences below, *he* is the subject of the verb. Underline the correct word in the rules.

Perhaps	he	lives alone.
Maybe		doesn't live alone.
He	probably	lives alone.
		doesn't live alone.

   a We usually put *probably* before / after the subject.
   b We usually put *perhaps* and *maybe* before / after the subject.
   c *Probably* is more / less certain than *perhaps* and *maybe*.

14 Underline the best adverb.
    1 The man perhaps / probably likes the colour blue.
    2 Maybe / Probably he likes living alone.
    3 Probably / Perhaps he's expecting guests.
    4 He probably / maybe wants some peace and quiet.
    5 He probably / perhaps doesn't read much.

ABCD Put it all together

15 Look at the photos of two rooms on ›› p.130 and make guesses about the owners of the rooms. Discuss with a partner. Then check if your guesses were correct.

I can express guesses. ▬▬▬▬▬▬▬▬▬▬▬▬▬▬▬▬
Tick ✓ the line.   with a lot of help   with some help   on my own   very easily

Writing A letter of application

A Read and think about context

1 Read the job ad and answer the questions.
  1 What are they looking for and what are they offering?
  2 How is it different from a more typical job ad?
  3 What should you do if you want to apply?

B Think about the content

2 Read Edith's letter of application (Don't worry about the spelling mistakes). Do you think it will make a good impression? Discuss with a partner.

3 Does Edith's letter follow <u>all</u> the instructions in the ad?

C Check spelling and structure

4 Find six typing errors in Edith's letter. Why do you think the spellchecker on her computer didn't show them? Compare with a partner.

5 Look again at Edith's letter of application. What are the rules of a formal letter? Discuss with a partner.

D Get ideas to write about

6 Complete the information about Edith in this table.

	Edith	me
age and background	20 immigrant from Hong Kong	
appearance		
clothes		
personality		
attitude	like being different don't mind what people think	
availability		

7 Complete the same information about you.

ABCD Put it all together

8 Write a letter of application for the reality show in the advert. Work with a partner and plan what you will include in the paragraphs. Use Edith's letter as a model.
  Example para 1: reason for writing ...

9 Read your partner's letter and comment on the content and accuracy. Do you think your partner will be chosen?

YOUR CHANCE TO APPEAR ON TV!

We are looking for 15 people to take part in a reality show. Participants will spend four months living together on a Pacific island and some will be voted off the island by the viewers every two weeks. There will be BIG CASH PRIZES for the last three people on the island.

We are looking for the widest possible variety of background, appearance, and personality.

Please send a brief handwritten letter (120–150 words) with a photo. Your letter should describe your appearance and personality. We will choose 300 candidates to attend an audition in June.

Please send applications to:
Change Your Life TV, PO Box 2998, Bexhill, Surrey

---

12 Rose Lane
London SE20 9ST

Change Your Life TV   12 February 2009
PO Box 2998
Bexhill, Surrey

Dear Sir or Madam

I'm writing in response to your advert in the Evening Times for participants in a TV reality show. You said you wanted a variety of people of different appearance, personality an background. I think I wood be a good candidate for your programme.

I'm 20 years old and my family moved to this country from Hong Kong when I was too. I'm medium height and slim. I've got a round face and my hair is dyed bright red. I enjoy wearing unusual, imaginative cloths. I'm lively, confident and outgoing. I like being different and I don't mind what people think of me.

I'm working freelance at he moment, so I will be easily available to participate in you're programme. Please find my photograph enclosed.

I look forward to hearing from you.

Yours faithfully

Edith Chan

Edith Chan

I can write a letter of application.

Tick ✓ the line.   with a lot of help   with some help   on my own   very easily

Unit 7 Review

A Grammar

1 *wh-* clauses Find seven sentences with *wh-* clauses.

1 I	2 Does	3 Do	you	know	where
don't	he	know	why	you	Panama
know	what	to	4 I	left	is?
5 I	6 She	wear.	don't	him?	are.
know	knows	how	know	who	you
what	7 I	to	look	after	herself.
happened.	don't	know	where	he	went.

2 Future intentions Underline the correct verb forms.

1 **A** Tea or coffee, sir?
   B I think I'll have/I'm having a tea, please.
2 **A** Have you got any plans for this evening?
   B Yes. I'm going to lie/I'll lie on the sofa and read a book!
3 **A** Have you made any arrangements for Friday night?
   B Yes, I'll go/I'm going out with Sophie – we're going to the cinema.
4 **A** Why are you saving your money?
   B I'm buying/I'm going to buy a saxophone and learn to play it.
5 **A** I can't do my homework!
   B Don't worry, I'm going to help/I'll help you if you like.
6 **A** Do you want to go out tonight?
   B I can't. I've invited Alec and Liz. They'll come/They're coming round at eight.

3 Modals of deduction Read about Louise and complete the sentences about her with *must*, *might*, or *can't*.

Louise Armstrong is from North America. She works as a flight attendant on international flights and she never has time to put away her suitcase. She often visits Ireland in her holidays, and she always stays in other people's homes there. She doesn't want to change her job – even if she could make more money doing something else.

1 She *might* be Canadian.
2 She _____ be from France.
3 She _____ travel a lot for work.
4 She _____ spend much time at home.
5 She _____ have family in Ireland.
6 She _____ enjoy her work.

B Vocabulary

4 Looks and character Do the puzzle and find the hidden word.

Clues
1 Wants to be very successful, rich, etc.
2 He's in his _____ thirties.
3 Always busy doing things.
4 Opposite of *shy*.
5 Feeling sure about your abilities.
6 Gives people a lot of money, help, etc.
7 Hair: not curly, but not straight.
8 Character like an artist.
9 Hair colour: red or orange.
10 Afraid of things, not confident.
11 Behaving in an angry way.

1 A M B I T I O U S

5 Compound adjectives Match the two parts of the compound adjectives.

1 [b] well-   a conscious
2 ☐ well-   b ~~dressed~~
3 ☐ old-   c shaven
4 ☐ loose-   d fashioned
5 ☐ good-   e fitting
6 ☐ fashion-   f mannered
7 ☐ clean-   g looking

6 Body and exercise Label the pictures.

1 thumb
2
3
4
5
6
7
8
9

On the Phone

1 Look, I'm with a client and I can't get away right now. Can I ring you back tomorrow?

2

3

a Hi, Lucy. It's me. I'm calling from the hospital. Gloria has had the baby. It's a beautiful boy! Hang on, I'll hand you over to Gloria ...

b Look, I've tried that number already, but I can't get through. I either get cut off or I just get the engaged signal. Is there another number I can call? Please don't hang up!! Hello?

c Hello, can you put me through to the emergency rescue service, please. My car's broken down ... Thanks.

d Extension 483? Who's calling please? ... Hold on. I'll put you through ... I'm sorry, the line's busy right now. Would you like to leave a message or call back in five minutes?

e Hello, it's Mike calling from Bike World. I'm calling to let you know the spray paint you ordered has arrived, so you can call by and pick it up some time ...

f Have you got her mobile number, please? ... Great. Hang on, I'll just get a pen to write it down ... OK, go ahead.

4

5

6

7

Phrasal verbs in the dictionary

☐ **break down**
☐ **call by** (*informal*)
☐ **cut sb off** [often passive]
☐ **get away (from …)**
☐ **get through (to sb)**
☑*a* **hand (sb) over to sb**
☐ **hang on** (*informal*)
☐ **hang up**
☐ **put sb through**
☐ **ring (sb) back** (*Brit**)
*call back is an alternative for *ring back*

a (used at a meeting or on the phone) to let sb speak or listen to sb
b to end a telephone conversation and put the phone down
c (used about a vehicle or machine) to stop working
d to stop or interrupt sb's telephone conversation
e to telephone sb again or to telephone sb who has telephoned you

f to succeed in speaking to sb on the telephone
g to make a short visit to a place or person as you pass
h to succeed in leaving or escaping from sb or a place
i to wait for a short time
j to make a telephone connection that allows sb to speak to sb

How to talk on the phone

8A

G phrasal verbs (2)   V phrasal verbs; telephone words and phrases   P stress in phrasal verbs

A Read and think about the situation

1 How much do you use the phone, and what do you use it for? Tell a partner.

2 Look at photo 1 in **On the Phone** opposite. Discuss the questions with a partner.
   1 Who are the people and where are they?
   2 Who do you think the man is talking to?
   3 Do you think he's lying? Why? Why not?

3 Match photos 2–7 in **On the Phone** with texts a–f. Say which words helped you decide.
   Example 2 = f pen; write it down

4 **8A.1▶** Listen and check.

5 Work with a partner. Match photos 2–7 with these descriptions.
   This person …
   1 is giving some good news to a friend or relative. *photo 4*
   2 has tried to phone already, but without success.
   3 is definitely speaking to a customer.
   4 has called a person who she doesn't know.
   5 is trying to get in touch with a woman.
   6 is responding to a caller – she definitely didn't phone the other person.

6 Find phrases in **On the Phone** with these meanings.
   1 I'm phoning from …   *I'm calling from …*
   2 I can't connect to that phone number
      I can't g_____ _____
   3 get the signal that means that someone is on the phone   *get the _____ signal*
   4 What's your name?   *Who's _____, please?*
   5 someone's talking on the line already
      the line's _____
   6 Would you like me to tell him/her?   *Would you like to _____ _____ _____?*
   7 I'm calling to tell you …   *I'm calling to _____ _____ _____ …*
   8 collect it   *_____ it _____*

B Grammar and vocabulary
phrasal verbs (2)

7 Look at **Phrasal verbs in the dictionary** opposite. Find the phrasal verbs in **On the Phone**. Match the phrasal verbs and the definitions.
   Example hand over = a

8 Complete the text with verbs from exercise 7. Compare with a partner.
   Stephanie's car [1] *broke* down on the way to work, so she had to ring a garage for help. A recorded message said, 'I'm sorry, all our lines are busy. Please [2]_____ back in five minutes.' When Stephanie called a second time, a secretary answered and said, '[3]_____ on, I'll [4]_____ you through.' Then she got [5]_____ off so she had to call back a third time. Finally, she [6]_____ through to a mechanic. He said he was busy and [7]_____ her over to a colleague. The colleague said, 'If you [8]_____ by, I'll check your car and see what the problem is.' She explained that she couldn't move her car. 'Then I can't help you,' replied the mechanic, and he [9]_____ up.

9 **8A.2▶** Pronunciation Listen to the examples and read the rules.
   a I **called** by **public phone**.
   Rule *by* isn't part of a phrasal verb. We don't usually stress prepositions.

   b I **called by** this **morn**ing.
   Rule *by* is part of a phrasal verb. We stress the particles in phrasal verbs.

   More practice? **Grammar Bank >>** p.143.

C Listen for detail

10 **8A.3▶** Listen to Stephanie's phone calls to the garage from exercise 8. You will hear some extra information. Tick ✓ the information you hear.
   1 the name of the garage ✓
   2 where Stephanie is
   3 the time
   4 the problem with the car
   5 the names of the mechanics

11 Listen again and make notes about the new information in exercise 10. Read the audio script on **>>** p.155 and check.

12 Work with a partner. Role play the phone call.
   Student A Say Stephanie's lines.
   Student B Say the lines of the other characters.

ABC Put it all together

13 Work with a partner. Look at **Phoning Frank** on **>>** p.130. Choose the Caller or the Answerer role and read it. Plan what you are going to say before you start. Change partners and do the role play again.

I can talk on the phone.
Tick ✓ the line.   with a lot of help   with some help   on my own   very easily

Intelligent Animals

Smart Alex

An African grey parrot called Alex has amazed scientists with his language abilities. This clever bird can identify 50 different objects using English words, and he can also answer questions about their shape, colour, and number. But it's not just words – Alex can even make sentences in requests like 'I want X' or 'I wanna go Y'.

Alex is Irene Pepperberg's star pupil

African grey parrots have enjoyed popularity for thousands of years. They've been popular pets since ancient Egypt, perhaps because they're sociable and fun. They are able to repeat words and phrases they hear, and they can even copy the sound of laughter or a ringing phone. However, Alex's abilities show that parrots can actually use language, not just repeat it.

Training a parrot to speak

Animal psychologist Dr Irene Pepperberg has studied parrot intelligence since 1977. Alex is her star pupil and he's able to answer complicated questions like 'What object is green and has three corners?' Through her work, Pepperberg has made Alex famous. She's been able to show that parrots can actually think.

Birds get bored too

Because they are so intelligent, parrots can get bored easily. They're very active and they need things to stimulate their curiosity. Pepperberg created a computer program for Alex, so he could choose from four activities – watching a video, listening to music, seeing pictures, or playing a game. To begin with, Alex was curious and played with the system for an hour a day, but then he got bored with it. However, Pepperberg managed to get him interested again by changing the content of the program.

'You have to put this bird on the camera!'

A sense of humour?

Another African grey parrot who has been in the news is N'kisi, from New York. Apparently, N'kisi has a vocabulary of 950 words and can even make jokes. Once, when he saw another parrot hanging upside down, he said they should 'put this bird on the camera'.

Clever Rico

Rico, a border collie from Germany, is a surprisingly clever dog. Although Rico can't speak, he can understand more than 200 words, and he's able to learn the names of new toys easily. What's more, Rico can remember the new vocabulary weeks later.

Border collies can be trained as rescue dogs

Border collies are well-known to be intelligent animals. They are used as sheepdogs and can respond to many different whistles. They can also be trained as rescue dogs, for finding people lost under the snow, for example. However, Rico's abilities show that collies are even cleverer than we thought.

Famous on TV

Professor Julia Fischer of the Max-Planck Institute in Leipzig first saw Rico on television, on a popular German TV programme called 'Wetten Dass?' Millions of viewers were amazed to see how Rico could understand his owner's instructions and fetch things. He could go and get the correct toy from among many in his collection.

Rico's abilities have amazed TV viewers

A mathematical horse?

Fischer was suspicious because she remembered the case of the horse called Clever Hans. Hans was able to answer mathematical problems by tapping his foot the correct number of times. However, a psychologist discovered that in reality, the horse's owner was giving signals to Hans with his eyebrows. Fischer decided to test the possibility that Rico's owner was doing the same thing.

Rico passes his exams

Fischer put Rico and his owner in one room and placed Rico's toys in a different room. She asked the dog's owner to request different toys in a random order. It wasn't possible for Rico's owner to point to the toys, but Rico was able to fetch the correct toy 37 times out of 40. In one test, he also managed to learn the name of a new toy after hearing it once. A new toy was placed in his collection, and when Rico heard the name, he was able to correctly fetch the toy. 'This tells us he can do simple logic,' says Fischer, 'He's actually thinking.'

How to talk about ability

G ability *can, could, be able to, manage to*   P stress in words ending *-ity*

A Read and summarize

1 Which animals do you think are the most intelligent? Discuss with a partner.

2 Work with a partner. Look at **Intelligent Animals** opposite. What is the most interesting fact in your text?
   Student A Read **Smart Alex**.
   Student B Read **Clever Rico**.

3 Complete the notes about your text in the box.

	Smart Alex	Clever Rico
animal	African grey parrot	border collie dog
human use of animal	_____ since Ancient Egypt	sheepdog and _____
language ability	can identify _____ can _____ complicated questions	can understand _____
Why famous?		
Who studied it?	Dr _____ _____	Prof. _____ _____
other animal in text		

4 Use your notes. Tell your partner about your text. Listen and complete the notes in the box.
   Example My text is about an African grey parrot ...

5 Decide with a partner which animal is more amazing.

B Grammar ability *can, could, be able to, manage to*

6 Look at the examples in the box and then match rules 1–4 with a–d.

present simple	Rico can understand ... Parrots are able to repeat ...
past simple	Rico could understand ... Rico also managed to learn ... Hans was able to answer ... Rico was able to fetch ...
other tenses and modals	Irene's been able to show ...

Rules
1 ☐ For ability in the present simple,
2 ☐ For general ability in the past simple,
3 ☐ For ability on one occasion in the past simple,
4 ☐ In other tenses or after modal verbs,

a use *was/were able to* or *managed to*.
b use *be/been able to*.
c use *can* or *is/are/am able to*.
d use *could* or *was/were able to*.

7 Complete the sentences with the forms in exercise 6. Compare with a partner.
   1 Yesterday, my dad _was able to_ (or _managed to_) finish the crossword for the first time ever!
   2 When I was a child, I _____ sing very well.
   3 My cat's very clever. I think she _____ understand me.
   4 In the future, we will _____ communicate with dolphins.
   5 I lost my key this morning, but I _____ open the door with a credit card.
   6 Some dinosaurs _____ fly.
   7 I've never _____ to do maths very well.

   More practice? **Grammar Bank** ≫ p.143.

C Pronunciation stress in words ending *-ity*

8 Complete the table. The words you need are in **Smart Alex** or **Clever Rico**.

adjective	noun
able	ability
popular	
	activity
	curiosity
real	
possible	

9 8B.1▶ Listen and repeat the words in exercise 8. Be careful to put the stress on the correct syllable.

10 The stress is in a different place in the adjective and noun. Choose the correct ending to the rule.
   able   a**bi**lity

   In words ending with *-ity*, always put the stress on ...
   a the last syllable.
   b the second-to-last syllable.
   c the syllable before *-ity*.

11 Test a partner. Choose an adjective for your partner to say the noun. Is the stress correct?

ABC Put it all together

12 Think of a time you were or weren't able to do something. Look at **Ideas** on ≫ p.130. Write notes about your story. Tell your story to your partner.

I can talk about ability.

Tick ✓ the line.   with a lot of help   with some help   on my own   very easily

Two Guys in BBC surprise

In the waiting room

When Guy Goma went for an interview for an IT job at the BBC, he didn't expect to become a TV celebrity. Mr Goma, a business studies graduate from Congo, was sitting in a waiting room with the other candidates for the job. At the same time, Guy Kewney, a British technology expert, was sitting in another room waiting to be called for a live TV interview on the subject of online music downloads.

Mistaken identity

Five minutes before the start of the programme, the producer went to the receptionist and asked where Guy Kewney was. She pointed to Guy Goma, so the producer approached him and asked him if he was Guy Kewney. Mr Goma thought that perhaps the man couldn't pronounce his surname and answered yes.

Mr Goma was taken to a TV studio where they put make up on his face and a microphone on his shirt, and sat him down in front of the cameras. This was a very strange job interview, he thought, but he decided to do his best. Finally, the live broadcast began.

The interview

The topic of the programme was a famous court case involving Apple Computers. The results of the court case had come out that day. The interviewer, Karen Bowerman, asked Mr Goma what he thought about the results of the case. She wanted to know if he was surprised at what had happened. Thinking that perhaps she was talking about the job interview, Guy replied that yes, he was very surprised.

The court case had been about downloading music from the Internet, and Ms Bowerman asked Guy if more people would download music online in the future. Guy thought this was another strange question, but he said yes, they would. However, by now it started to become clear that there had been a mistake and Ms Bowerman was surprised that Mr Goma had so little to say. He was obviously not an expert on the subject, and the interview ended shortly afterwards.

TV celebrity

The programme was seen all over the world and Guy Goma quickly became a celebrity.

Since his hilarious interview on the BBC, he has been invited to appear on Channel 4 News, CNN International, and other TV channels. So what about his interview for the IT post at the BBC? Unfortunately, he didn't get the job.

GLOSSARY
IT *n* information technology
BBC *n* British Broadcasting Corporation

How to report an interview

G reported questions

A Read and predict

1 What questions do people usually ask at a job interview? Discuss with a partner.

2 Look at **Two Guys in BBC surprise** opposite. Read the first paragraph **In the waiting room** and answer the questions with a partner.
   1 What are the names of the two people?
   2 Why are they waiting?
   3 Can you guess what will happen later in the story? What are the clues?

3 Read **Mistaken identity**. What are the two misunderstandings? What do you think happens?

4 Read **The interview** and answer the questions with a partner. Then read the final part of the story.
   1 How do you think Mr Goma felt when the interview began?
   2 How did the interviewer begin to understand that there had been a mistake?
   3 What will happen to Mr Goma? Will he get the job he's applying for?

5 Work with a partner. Choose four of these words in the text and guess the meaning. Say how you guessed. Then check in a dictionary.

   expert approach microphone broadcast case
   download afterwards hilarious post

B Grammar reported questions

6 Look at the examples and answer the questions.

	open question	reported question
A	Where's he from?	I asked him where he was from.
B	Where does he live?	I asked him where he lived.

   1 In **A**, does the verb to be come before or after the subject?
   2 In **B**, which sentence has an auxiliary verb?
   3 Is the word order the same in the questions and the reported questions?
   4 Is the tense the same in the questions and the reported questions?

7 Imagine a female receptionist asked you these questions. Later, you tell a friend about it. Write the questions in reported speech.
   1 What's your name? *She asked me what my name was.*
   2 What do you do?
   3 Where do you work?
   4 What's your nationality?
   5 Who do you want to see?

8 Work with a partner. Complete the grammar box with sentences from **Two Guys in BBC surprise**. How are open and closed questions reported differently?

closed question	reported question
Are you Guy Kewney?	He asked him _____.
Are you surprised at what happened?	She wanted to know _____.
Will more people download ...?	She asked Guy _____.

9 Here are some unusual questions which *candidates* have asked at job interviews. Work with a partner and report the questions from the interviewer's point of view.
   1 **Woman** 'What does your company do?'
      She asked me what our company did.
   2 **Man** 'Why do you want my CV?'
   3 **Woman** 'What is your star sign?'
   4 **Man** 'Can I bring my dog to work?'
   5 **Woman** 'Will I have to wear shoes?'
   6 **Man** 'Are you happily married?'
   7 **Woman** 'Do you have a sauna in the building?'
   8 **Man** 'Where's the company golf course?'

More practice? **Grammar Bank** >> p.143.

C Listen for detail

10 **8C.1▶** Listen to Ricardo and Cath talking about a job interview. Do you think Cath will get the job?

11 Listen again and write *true* or *false*.
   1 Cath thinks the interview went well. *False*
   2 They asked why Cath wanted to work for them.
   3 They asked about Cath's language abilities.
   4 They said the salary was £30,000 a year.

12 Look at the audio script on >> p.155. What did Cath and the interviewers say? Role play the interview.
   Example **A** Why do you want to work for us?
              B I need the money.

ABC Put it all together

13 Work with a partner. Choose one of these jobs and think of five questions which an interviewer might ask.

   accountant computer technician graphic designer
   interpreter lifeguard nurse reporter taxi driver

14 Change partners. Interview your new partner using your questions from exercise 13.

15 Tell your first partner about your interview. Guess what job your partner was interviewed for.
   Example **A** What did the interviewer ask you?
              B She asked me what languages I spoke ...

I can report an interview.

Tick ✓ the line.   with a lot of help   with some help   on my own   very easily

Vikram's Story

I quite often travel to France for work. One time, I was in the Gare du Nord in Paris. I'd just arrived on the Eurostar train from London and while I was walking towards the exit, a man approached me. He looked very tired and hungry and I thought maybe he was homeless. He asked me whether I spoke English, and I told him I was English. He told me he was English too and he asked me to help him.

He said he'd been robbed and only had 80 euros cash to get home – but the ticket was 90 euros. He asked me to give him the 10 euros. He even promised to post it back to me when he got home. I agreed to give him the money, but when I looked in my pocket, I only had a couple of 50 euro notes.

I told him to wait while I went to get change. Then I gave him the money and invited him to join me for a coffee. While we were drinking the coffee, he advised me to be careful – he'd been robbed by a thief working in the station. Before he said goodbye, he asked me to give him my address so he could send me the money. I told him not to worry – he could keep it. I offered to give him five pounds for when he arrived in London, but he refused to take the money. He thanked me and walked away towards the ticket office. I left the station feeling I'd done something good.

The next day, I was in the station again. Another London train had just arrived and a crowd of passengers was leaving the station. Then I saw him – the same man from yesterday. He was asking a woman to give him money. I was so angry that I went over and warned the woman not to give him anything.

Vikram Shenoy
Leicestershire, UK

Reporting verbs

- ☐ agree (not) to
- ☐ advise sb (not) to
- ☐ invite sb to
- ☑ offer to
- ☐ refuse to
- ☐ promise (not) to
- ☐ warn sb (not) to

a to ask if sb would like sth or to give sb the chance to have sth
b to ask sb to come somewhere or do sth
c to say yes to sth
d to say definitely that you will do or not do sth or that sth will happen

e to say or show that you do not want to do, give, or accept sth
f to tell sb about sth unpleasant or dangerous, so that they can avoid it
g to tell sb what you think they should do

How to report a conversation

A Read and follow a story

1 Look at the photos opposite. What do you think the story is about? Discuss with a partner.

2 Read **Vikram's Story** opposite. What happened? Choose the best answer.

  a He was robbed. b He was tricked. c He got lost.

3 Answer the questions with a partner.
1 Why did the man ask Vikram if he spoke English?
2 Why did the man refuse the five pounds?
3 Why did the man walk towards the ticket office after saying goodbye?
4 How did Vikram know the man had tricked him?
5 Would you do the same as Vikram in this situation? Why? Why not?

B Grammar reported imperatives and requests

4 Find the reported form of these sentences in **Vikram's Story**. Then answer the questions below.

	direct speech	reported speech
request	'Can you help me?'	
imperative	'Don't worry!'	

Which verb do we use …
a for reported requests? b for reported imperatives?

5 Put these sentences in reported speech.
1 I/her 'Can you wait, please?' *I asked her to wait.*
2 She/me 'Don't wait!'
3 I/him 'Don't go!'
4 He/me 'Will you go, please?'

6 **8D.1▶ Pronunciation** Listen and repeat the answers to exercise 5. Notice that you don't hear the past tense endings in ask<u>ed</u> and tol<u>d</u> before *me*.

7 Work with a partner. Report these mini-conversations.
1 **Me** Can you help me?
  Woman Could you wait a moment, please?
  I asked her to help me and she asked me to wait a moment.

2 **Me** Can you show me the way to the station, please?
  Man Follow me.

3 **Man** Be careful!
  Me Don't worry!

4 **Woman** Can you give me €10, please?
  Me Leave me alone.

More practice? **Grammar Bank** ≫ p.143.

C Vocabulary reporting verbs

8 Look at **Reporting verbs** opposite and <u>underline</u> examples of the verbs in **Vikram's Story**.

9 Match the reporting verbs with the definitions. Compare with a partner.

10 <u>Underline</u> the best option in these sentences.
1 They advised/warned/offered me to take the bus because it was cheaper.
2 Tom offered/promised/invited me to stay in his flat during the holidays.
3 I invited/offered to lend her €20, but she offered/refused to take it.

11 Report these sentences using all of the reporting verbs.
1 I'll come, I promise. *He promised to come.*
2 If you go, there will be trouble! *She warned me not to go.*
3 I'll come, if you want. *He …*
4 No, I'm not coming! *She …*
5 Would you like to come? *He …*
6 Yes, OK, I'll come. *I …*
7 You should come. *She …*

D Listen and show interest

12 **8D.2▶** Listen to Vikram telling his story to his friend Anita and answer the questions.
What does Anita think about …
1 Vikram telling the man to keep the money?
2 Vikram warning the woman about the man at the end of the story?

13 Anita is an interested listener. She asks a lot of questions and makes comments. Look at the audio script on ≫ p.155 and <u>underline</u> them.
Example Why? What happened?

14 Work with a partner and practise the conversation.

ABCD Put it all together

15 Think of a time you had a conversation with someone you didn't know, for example on a train, in a café, etc. Look at the **Questions** on ≫ p.131 and write notes.

16 Tell your partner about your encounter. Listen to your partner's story and be an interested listener.

I can report a conversation.
Tick ✓ the line. with a lot of help with some help on my own very easily

Writing A report

A Listen to a survey question

1 Which is the best way to do these things? Tick ✓ one or more boxes in each row. Compare your answers with a partner.

	face to face	phone	text	email	post
arrange to meet					
invite to a wedding					
apologize					
say 'happy birthday'					
say 'I love you'					
pass on a quick message					
give important information					

2 Sandra is doing a class survey and she has asked a question about communication habits. Read her notes. Which of the five forms of communication in exercise 1 could it be about?

Why?
— quick to send info: no conversation
— convenient: if busy, can read later

3 **8E.1▶** Listen and check.

4 Listen again and answer the questions with a partner. Then check your answers in the audio script on **»** p.155.
1 What four questions does Sandra ask?
2 What does the other person answer?

5 Imagine you are doing a survey on one of these topics. Choose a topic and think of three questions to ask.
1 What do people do when they receive a phone call from a company selling things?
2 When do people switch off their mobile phones?
3 When do people prefer to speak face to face?
4 What do people use email for?
5 Why do people still use the post?

B Read a report

6 Work with a partner. Complete Sandra's class report with these words and phrases.

so   however   if   because   such as

Why do people send text messages?

For me, writing a text message on a mobile phone isn't very easy. 1_____, text messages are very popular these days. I decided to find out why.

I asked five people why they sent text messages. One person said she never sent them 2_____ they were too difficult. The other four said they often used them to send short pieces of information, 3_____ arranging a place to meet. One person said that text messages were convenient because the other person doesn't have to answer immediately. 4_____ they aren't able to answer now, they can answer later.

5_____ text messages are popular because they are convenient. Perhaps in the future, new technology will make them easier to write.

7 Match the words and phrases in exercise 6 with these uses.
1 to give a reason
2 to give an example
3 to introduce a conclusion
4 to introduce a contrasting fact
5 to introduce a possible situation

8 How is Sandra's text divided into paragraphs? Use the topics below to complete the description.

~~introduction to the topic~~   results
conclusion   the question

paragraph 1 = *introduction to the topic*
paragraph 2 = _____, _____
paragraph 3 = _____

AB Put it all together

9 Choose a topic and some questions to ask from exercise 5, or use your own survey ideas. Ask people around the class and take notes of their answers.

10 Write a report of your survey. Follow the same paragraph structure as Sandra's text in exercise 6.

11 Read other students' reports. Are any of the results surprising?

I can write a report.
Tick ✓ the line.   with a lot of help   with some help   on my own   very easily

Unit 8 Review

A Grammar

1 Ability: *can, could, be able to, manage to* Complete the sentences with *can, could, able to* or *managed to*.

1 I _could_ swim when I was five.
2 Tom woke up late, but he _____ get to work on time.
3 I've never been _____ do calculations in my head.
4 These days, my son _____ run faster than I can.
5 Irene was _____ communicate with her parrot.
6 Some people _____ remember everything they see.
7 Hillary and Tenzing _____ reach the top of Mount Everest in 1953.
8 I _____ speak Arabic in the past, but I've forgotten it now.

2 Reported questions Report the questions in these short conversations.

1 **Man** Where are you from?
  He asked her where she was from.
  Woman Do you really want to know?
  She asked if he really wanted to know.

2 **Man** Are you married?
  _____
  Woman Why are you asking?
  _____

3 **Man** Where did you get your bag?
  _____
  Woman Do you like it?
  _____

4 **Man** How did you make the cake?
  _____
  Woman Would you like a piece?
  _____

3 Reported imperatives and requests You are in a taxi. Who said these sentences – you or the (male) taxi driver? Report the sentences.

1 Can you take me to 21 West Street?
  I asked him to take me to 21 West Street.
2 Can you fasten your seat belt, please?
  _____
3 Don't smoke in the taxi, please.
  _____
4 Go a bit slower, please.
  _____
5 Can you tell me the address again?
  _____
6 Stop at the corner, please.
  _____

B Vocabulary

4 Phrasal verbs Match 1–8 with a–h.

1 [f] A woman answered but she hung ...
2 [ ] Do you want to speak to Jo? I'll hand ...
3 [ ] I rang before, but I couldn't get ...
4 [ ] I'm in a meeting and I can't get ...
5 [ ] Sorry I'm late – the bus broke ...
6 [ ] Sorry, I'm busy – can you ring ...
7 [ ] Yes, he's in. Hang on and I'll put ...
8 [ ] Your new camera is here – call ...

a away at the moment.
b back in about half an hour?
c by and pick it up any time.
d down on the way here.
e through – all the lines were busy.
f ~~up as soon as I spoke.~~
g you over to her right now.
h you through to his office.

5 Telephone words and phrases Complete the phrases in this conversation.

A Hi, I'm ¹*calling* from ACM Insurance. Can I speak to Ms Soames, please?
S Yes. ²W_____'s c_____, please?
A Mr Ackroyd.
S I'm sorry, Mr Ackroyd, the ³l_____ b_____ at the moment – I'm just getting the ⁴e_____ s_____. Would you like to ⁵l_____ a m_____?
A Yes, can you tell her I called to ⁶l_____ her k_____ about her claim. She's got my number.
S OK, Mr Ackroyd. I'll tell her to call you back. Goodbye.
A Bye.

6 Reporting verbs Complete the stories with the verbs in the correct form.

agree ~~invite~~ offer warn

Grandma ¹*invited* Rose to go to her cottage for lunch. Rose ²_____ to visit and ³_____ to bring a basket of fruit. Grandma ⁴_____ her not to take the path through the woods because it was dangerous. 'And you must promise not to talk to any strangers!' said Grandma.

advise promise refuse

Rose ⁵_____ not to. On the way to Grandma's cottage, Rose met a stranger and he ⁶_____ her to take the path through the woods because it was shorter. Fortunately, Rose remembered her promise to Grandma and she ⁷_____ to listen to the stranger.

...ther
...ing   boiling
...ud   floods
freezing   gales
heat wave   lightning
mild   pouring
shining   showers
snowing   soaking
stormy   windy

Four good reasons to ...

Talk about the Weather

by Josh Elliot

'It's a lovely day, isn't it?'
'Yes, it's so mild for the time of year!'

Why do we talk so much about the weather? I mean, we don't really do it for practical reasons, do we? I can understand farmers or sailors being interested in the weather, but most of us live and work inside. And anyway, a lot of what we say are things that everybody knows already. On a cold day, why do I need somebody to say to me, 'It's freezing out there, isn't it?' I know that already! But there are some good reasons to talk about the weather.

Reason 1

It's a good way to start a conversation. Everybody knows something about it. Think of the alternatives. Try starting with something like, 'Picasso's early works are marvellous, aren't they?' It'll probably be a very short conversation! Everybody has different interests and opinions, but the weather is something which we share. We all have to live with the same weather. There's nothing we can do about it so we just celebrate it or complain about it together.

Reason 2

We all have lots to say about the weather. We have a lifetime of experience of it – or more. Ideas about the weather are given to us by our grandparents and great-grandparents. Think of old sayings like 'Red sky at night, sailor's delight'. In the days before weather forecasts, people had to predict what was coming by looking for clues around them. For example, there were clues in animal behaviour: 'If crows fly low, winds will blow'.

Reason 3

Weather is important to us. It can change our moods. We know that weeks without sunshine can cause winter blues, or seasonal affective disorder, as doctors call it. Statistics show that heat waves in New York cause more crimes. Also, it seems that many of us are fascinated by the weather. The weather forecast is one of the most popular programmes on TV. We don't just watch it for information, it's entertainment too – especially when it gets extreme, with snowstorms, gales, floods, and tornados.

Reason 4

We can talk about the weather to communicate other things. A character in an Oscar Wilde play says, 'Whenever people talk to me about the weather, I feel quite sure they mean something else.' It's true. When we say, 'Lovely day, isn't it?' perhaps we are really saying, 'I feel cheerful and I'd like a chat.' People enjoy chatting – it makes them feel part of a group. Monkeys pick insects from each other's hair for the same reason. But I'd prefer to talk about the weather!

Red sky at night, sailor's delight

If crows fly low, winds will blow

How to make small talk

G tag questions   V weather   P tag questions

A Vocabulary weather

1 Look at the words in **Weather** opposite. Decide if they are nouns, verbs, or adjectives. You can use a dictionary. Work with a partner and think of other weather words.

2 **9A.1▶** Guess which words normally go together. Match the words in the two columns, then listen, check, and repeat.

1	[e] heavy	a cold
2	[ ] blowing	b hot
3	[ ] boiling	c a gale
4	[ ] freezing	d rain
5	[ ] pouring	e ~~showers~~
6	[ ] soaking	f wet

3 Complete the sentences with words from **Weather**.
1 The day will start quite _mild_ and dry, but heavy _____ are expected in the afternoon.
2 We walked home in the _____ rain and got _____ wet.
3 We have an extreme climate, with _____ hot summers and _____ cold winters.
4 As a child, I hated _____ nights because I was afraid of thunder and _____.
5 It was _____ a gale last night but when I woke up, the sun was _____.

4 Describe the weather in different parts of the picture in **Weather**.
Example The sun's shining in the city.

5 What's your favourite weather? Does the weather change your mood? Why? Tell your partner.

B Read and understand reasons

6 Read **Talk about the Weather** opposite. Match summary sentences a–d with reasons 1–4.
a [ ] Most people are interested in the weather, and it can change how we feel.
b [ ] We sometimes talk about the weather just to be sociable, not because we're interested in it.
c [ ] Weather has always been a popular topic.
d [ ] Weather is a good conversation starter because it's a subject we all have in common.

7 Answer the questions with a partner.
According to the writer ...
1 why would sailors and farmers be interested in the weather?
2 why is talking about art not a good conversation starter?
3 why did our great-grandparents have a lot of sayings about the weather?
4 why is the weather important to us?
5 why do we say things like 'Lovely day, isn't it?'

C Listen to conversations about the weather

8 **9A.2▶** Listen to four conversations between Susan and Tom. What is the weather like in each conversation?
Example winter – cold wind; freezing

9 Listen again and tick ✓ the things they do in each conversation. Write the number of the conversation.
a Talk about extreme weather in other places. ✓ *1, 3*
b Say how nice the weather is.
c Complain about the weather.
d Talk about the weather forecast.
e Say what the weather will be like at the weekend.
f Agree with each other.
g Say how typical the weather is for the time of year.

D Grammar tag questions

10 Read Susan's sentence and say if 1–3 are *true* or *false*.
Susan It's a lovely day, isn't it?
1 Susan thinks it's a lovely day.
2 She isn't sure if it's a lovely day.
3 She invites Tom to agree with her.

11 **9A.3▶** Pronunciation Listen and repeat the sentences from Susan and Tom's conversation. Notice that although *isn't it?* has a question mark, it isn't really a question, so you pronounce it like a statement.

12 Match the sentences with their tag questions.
aren't they?   do we?   is there?   ~~isn't it?~~   don't we?

1 It's amazing, *isn't it?*
2 The days are getting shorter,
3 I guess we need it,
4 There's no wind at all,
5 We don't want floods,

13 Answer the questions with a partner.
1 When is the tag question positive or negative?
2 When do we use *be* or *do*?

14 Add tag questions to these sentences.
1 The nights aren't very long, *are they?*
2 It's a beautiful evening,
3 It isn't very warm,
4 You don't like hot weather,
5 You like cold weather,

More practice? **Grammar Bank** >> p.144.

A B C D Put it all together

15 Work with different partners. Start a conversation about the weather, and continue making small talk for as long as possible. Who did you have the longest conversation with?
Example Hi. It's freezing cold today, isn't it?

I can make small talk.

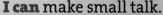

Tick ✓ the line.   with a lot of help   with some help   on my own   very easily

My Body in Five Years

1 I was at a job interview recently and they asked, 'Where will you be five years from now?' I didn't know what to say. Where will I be in five years' time? Perhaps I'll have a new job or maybe I'll be in another country, I've no idea. But one thing I DO know is – my body will have changed. How? Well, let's start from the top. All the hair which I have today will have gone and I'll have a completely new head of hair. It takes about five years from when a new hair starts growing to when it falls out.

2 Five years from now, my eyebrows and eyelashes will have changed between 15 and 20 times. My eyelashes are there to help me blink and keep my eyes clean, and over the next five years I'll blink about 30 million times. What about my nails, which are made from the same stuff as my hair? Well, in five years' time, I will have grown about ten new sets of fingernails – but only five sets of toenails. That's because fingernails grow twice as fast as toenails. Did you know your fastest-growing fingernail is on your ring finger?

3 Then there's the skin, which is the body's largest organ. My skin will have changed too, and during the next five years, I will lose about 10 kilograms of the stuff. The human body grows a new outer layer of skin every month.

4 I'll need to work to maintain my body over the next five years. For example, I'll probably eat about 2,500 kilograms of food, I'll breathe about 40 million times, and my heart will beat about 175 million times. The body never stops working and renewing itself. But it's not all good news. Unfortunately, some parts of my body won't get replaced. Hopefully, I'll still have the same teeth in five years' time, because I definitely won't grow any new ones. And my brain will get lighter by one gram each year as a small part dies, never to be replaced.

5 So next time I'm in a job interview and they ask, 'Where will you be in five years' time?' I'll know what to say!

My future

a Five years from now, I'll be sixty-six, but I'm not going to retire until I have to.

b In five years' time, I'll be 14. Hopefully, I'll have my own room by then.

c I've no idea where I'll be in five years, but I hope I'll have bought my own place to live.

d In five years' time, I'll have found a job. I'd like to be a fashion designer.

How to talk about your future

G future perfect V parts of the body; attitude adverbs P stressed and unstressed words

A Read for detail

1 Work with a partner. Look at the photos opposite. How many body parts can you name?

2 Read **My Body in Five Years**. What kind of text is it?
   a medical text   c popular science
   b fashion and beauty   d science fiction

3 Read the text again and find the following things.
   1 five things that grow
   2 three other things the body does automatically
   3 two parts of the body that don't get replaced

4 In the first paragraph, underline two predictions which the writer is sure about and two which the writer isn't sure about. Compare with a partner.

B Grammar future perfect

5 Read the sentence and decide when the change happens – A, B, or C. Then choose the best ending for the rule.
   In five years' time, my body will have changed.

   A Between now   **B** 5 years   **C** More than 5
   and 5 years' time   from now   years in the future

   ←-------------------→ ↓ -------------------→

   ---|------------------------------|----------------→
   now

   Rule Use the future perfect to show that something …
   a will start at a certain time in the future.
   b will be finished by a certain time in the future.
   c will happen at a certain time in the future.

6 Underline five examples of the future perfect in the text and compare with a partner. Complete the rule.
   Rule The future perfect = will (or won't) + _____ + past participle

7 Use these words to make true sentences for you.
   By this time tomorrow,
   1 I/have/meals   *I'll have had three meals.*
   2 I/sleep/for/hours
   3 I/have/cups of coffee
   4 I/watch TV/for/hours

8 **9B.1▶** Pronunciation Listen to these sentences and underline the stressed words.
   1 My hair will have grown.
   2 I'll have cut my nails.
   3 Things won't have changed much.
   4 I'll have passed the exam.

9 Listen again and check. Practise saying the sentences. Which kinds of words are *not* stressed?

10 Tell your partner the following.
   1 Three things you will/won't have done by the time you go to bed tonight.
   2 Three things you think will have happened in the world five years from now.

   More practice? **Grammar Bank** ≫ p.144.

C Vocabulary attitude adverbs

11 Look in paragraph four of **My Body in Five Years**. Find sentences with these adverbs and answer the questions.
   probably   un**fort**unately   **hope**fully   **defin**itely
   1 Which sentences tell you something which the writer …
      a wants to happen?   c is very sure about?
      b isn't happy about?   d is not 100% sure about?
   2 Which adverbs go at the beginning of the sentence?
   3 In negative sentences, do *probably* and *definitely* come before or after *won't*?

12 Add adverbs to the sentences to give your attitude. Compare with a partner.
   One year from now …
   1 I'll be older.   *I'll definitely be older.*
   2 I will have learnt a lot more English.
   3 I will have grown a new set of toenails.
   4 there will be more people in the world.
   5 there will be less ice at the North Pole.

D Listen to people talking about their future

13 Look at the photos in **My future** opposite and match the sentences and the people.

14 **9B.2▶** You will hear two of the people giving more details. Who's talking? How do you know?

15 Listen again and tick ✓ the topics they talk about.

	age	family	health	home	marriage	people at work	studies	transport	work
1	✓								
2	✓								

16 Can you remember what they said? Tell a partner.

ABCD Put it all together

17 Imagine yourself in five years' time. What will you have done by then? Make notes about the topics in exercise 15.

18 Work with a partner. Tell your partner about your future. Find at least three things you have in common.
   Example In five years' time I'll have left home …

I can talk about my future. ▬▬▬▬▬
Tick ✓ the line. with a lot of help   with some help   on my own   very easily

...on of movement

...ackwards downhill downwards forwards
...outside towards you uphill upwards

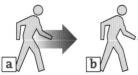    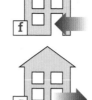

gills

NATURE'S NIGHTMARES

WHAT'S THE *WORST* THING YOU CAN DO ...?

1 if a bear comes towards you?
a   Make a noise.
b   Turn and run.
c   Climb a tree.
d   Walk slowly backwards.

2 if you're stuck in quicksand?
a   Lie down.
b   Move a lot.
c   Stay calm and wait.
d   Hold a tree root.

3 if you're caught in an avalanche?
a   Open your mouth.
b   Drop your pack.
c   Hold on to a tree.
d   'Swim' upwards through the snow.

4 if a current pulls you out to sea?
a   Float with it.
b   Swim parallel to the beach.
c   Swim directly to the beach.
d   Swim under the waves.

5 if you see a tornado coming towards you?
a   Lie in a bath with a mattress over you.
b   Get in a car and drive fast.
c   Go into a basement and sit under a table.
d   Lie in a ditch.

6 when you're in a lightning storm?
a   Sit inside a car.
b   Get out of the swimming pool.
c   Stand under a single tall tree.
d   Go inside.

7 if you're attacked by a shark?
a   Play dead.
b   Hit it in the eye.
c   Take hold of its gills.
d   Fight it.

8 if you're near a volcano and it erupts?
a   Go inside and close the windows.
b   Drive out of the area.
c   Lie on the ground near a stream.
d   Move uphill away from a stream.

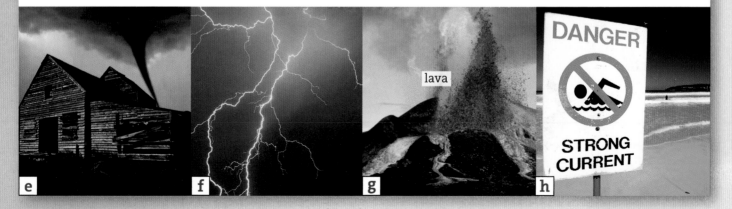

lava

DANGER
STRONG CURRENT

How to give advice

A Vocabulary direction of movement

1 Look at **Direction of movement** opposite. Match the words and pictures.

2 Discuss these questions with a partner.
   1 Which is more tiring – walking uphill or downhill?
   2 Which is more fun – having meals inside or outside?
   3 Which is more difficult – walking backwards or walking along a rope?

B Read and respond

3 Look at the photos in **Nature's Nightmares** opposite. Answer these questions with a partner.
   1 Have you ever been near any of these things?
   2 Which ones do you think are the most frightening?

4 Read quiz questions 1–8 and match them with photos a–h.

5 Underline new words in the quiz and try to guess their meanings. Discuss with a partner.
   1 How did you guess the meaning? Choose one option.
      a From the photo.   c It's similar in my language.
      b From the context.   d other …
   2 Are there any you can't guess or you are not sure about? Check them in a dictionary.

6 Do the **Nature's Nightmares** quiz with a partner. Circle the worst option for each situation and say why.

7 **9C.1▶** Listen and check your answers.

8 Listen again and complete these sentences.
   1 If you run, the bear will probably … *run after you.*
   2 If you disturb the quicksand a lot, it'll …
   3 If your mouth is open, it'll get …
   4 If you try to swim against the current, you'll probably …
   5 If any lava comes from the volcano, it will flow …

C Grammar 1st conditional; *if* clauses

9 Look at the grammar box and answer the questions with a partner.

1st conditional	
if clause	main clause
If you run,	the bear will probably run after you.

   1 What tenses are used in the *if* clause and main clause?
   2 Which part of the sentence makes a prediction?
   3 What is the sentence being used for?
      a to invite
      b to give advice
      c to warn of a danger

10 Put the verbs in the correct tense in these 1st conditional sentences.
   1 If you _don't take_ (not take) your coat, you _'ll get_ (get) wet.
   2 If he _____ (not be) careful, he _____ (hurt) himself.
   3 If it _____ (get) foggy, I _____ (not be able) to find my way down.
   4 If we _____ (not hurry up), it _____ (get) dark.

11 Match the beginnings and endings of the sentences in the grammar box and answer the questions.

other *if* clauses	
if clause	main clause
1 ☐ If you meet a bear,	a don't stand under a tall tree.
2 ☐ If it's foggy,	b walk slowly backwards.
3 ☐ If you're not a good swimmer,	c you should stay near the beach.
4 ☐ If there's lightning,	d you shouldn't drive fast.

   1 What verb forms are used in the *if* clause and main clause?
   2 What are these sentences being used for?
      a to give advice
      b to predict
      c to ask a question

12 Work with a partner. Give advice for these situations.
   1 If you drive your car into a river, …
      you should open the windows to get out.
   2 … if you can't swim.
   3 If you meet an aggressive dog, …
   4 … if you don't have a good map and some warm clothes.
   5 When it's dark, …

   More practice? **Grammar Bank** >> p.144.

D Read and paraphrase

13 Work in pairs.
   Student A Read **Safety Leaflet A** on >> p.131.
   Student B Read **Safety Leaflet B** on >> p.135.

14 Use your notes. In your own words, give your partner advice about what to do in your dangerous situation.

ABCD Put it all together

15 Think of a dangerous situation. Look at these examples.
   cycling in the city   driving on the motorway
   skiing   swimming in the sea   walking home at night
   walking in the mountains

16 Work in small groups. Give advice about what to do in your dangerous situation. Was all the advice good?

I can give advice.

HIGH-TECH

For this edition of *High-Tech*, Marion Brent travelled around the country and visited three technology fairs. She describes six of the most interesting devices she saw on display, and reports the reactions of some of the visitors.

◖ Personal Helicopter

This personal helicopter will take off and land vertically, like a normal helicopter, and it will be able to fly for over two hours at around 100 km per hour. It has been available on eBay for several years already.

Inflatable Computer ◗

This computer weighs less than a loaf of bread and it can fit in your pocket, but when you inflate it, it's the size of a normal laptop computer. It's waterproof too, so now you can surf the Internet in the swimming pool.

◖ Memory Recorder

This is the prototype of a device to help you remember names. It continually monitors your conversation. When it hears the words 'Nice to meet you', it permanently saves the previous and next 10 seconds of the conversation. Later on, if you can't remember the names of the people you have spoken to, you can listen to the recording again.

Walking Chair ◗

This is a robot with legs and a seat on top, and it is able to carry people. It can walk along level ground, but it can also go up and down stairs. This prototype has been developed at Waseda University in Japan.

◖ Dream Programmer

This is a device designed to help you to choose your own dreams. Before sleeping, you look at a picture of what you want to dream about and record yourself talking about it. During the night, when you start a period of rapid eye movement (REM) sleep, the machine plays the recording along with music, lights, and smells.

Brain Keyboard ◗

This is a prototype of a cap designed to read electrical signals from your brain and translate them into commands for a computer. With this cap, you will be able to control your computer without moving any part of your body.

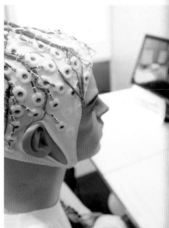

GLOSSARY
prototype *n* the first design which other models are copied from
device *n* an object or machine designed for a particular purpose
rapid *adj* very quick

VISITOR COMMENTS

1 This would be fantastic for disabled people in wheelchairs. If they had one of these, they would be able to go to places where they can't go now. They could even go for a walk in the country. I wouldn't mind having one myself, actually – it would be great for walking the dog!

2 I think this would be really interesting. I'd love to know how it feels to look completely different. If you wore it on your face, your friends wouldn't recognize you, so you could hear what they talk about when you aren't there. I would wear it at parties!

3 If you had one of these, you'd have to be careful what you think! For example, what would happen if I was writing an email to Fred and I secretly think that he's an idiot? How would it begin? 'Hi Fred, you idiot'? I think you'd have to practise a lot to use this device, but it would probably be good for disabled people.

4 It would be nice to have one of these, but if we all had one, there would be traffic chaos. There would be people flying in all directions, bumping into each other and crashing into buildings. The traffic on our streets is bad enough already – imagine it in three dimensions!

5 This is like something from a James Bond film. If I had one of these, I'd go somewhere hot so I could see all the tropical fish and the coral. I'd be able to see the sharks and if they attacked, I'd be safe inside it. But where would I keep it? I don't live near the sea, and there isn't enough space in my garage – so it's not a very practical idea!

6 If I had one of these, I'd sleep for entertainment. It would be like going to the cinema, but better. However, there's a problem. I never remember my dreams, so I wouldn't know if the machine was working.

How to talk about unreal situations

G 2nd conditional   V compound nouns   P linking in questions

A Vocabulary compound nouns

1 Which of the following things do you have? How important are they to you? Tell a partner.

an alarm clock   a DVD player   an Internet connection
a mobile phone   an MP3 player

2 Make compound nouns by putting the words below before or after *phone*.

book box call car card cell mobile number public

Example   phone book

3 Work with a partner. Make compound nouns using the words in **bold**. Check in your dictionary.

Example   laptop computer, computer technology ...

1 **computer**   laptop, technology, programmer, desktop, keyboard, personal, graphics
2 **alarm**   fire, clock, burglar, smoke, bell
3 **science**   fiction, computer, teacher, faculty, medical
4 **service**   room, charge, station, health
5 **book**   shop, address, exercise, fair, text, phrase, club

B Read for general meaning

4 Read **High-Tech** opposite. Which device is a joke?

5 Read **Visitor Comments** opposite and match four of them with the objects in **High-Tech**. Can you guess what the other two devices in **Visitor Comments** are?

6 Which device would you like to have? Tell a partner.

C Grammar 2nd conditional

7 Read the 2nd conditional sentences in the grammar boxes. Then choose the best option to describe their meaning.

if clause	main clause
If we all had a personal helicopter,	there would be traffic chaos.

main clause	*if* clause
What would happen	if we all had a personal helicopter?

a They are about situations which will happen in the future.
b They are about situations which are true now.
c They are about situations which are not true now and probably won't be true in the future.

8 What tenses are used in the *if* clause and main clause of 2nd conditional sentences?

9 <u>Underline</u> seven more examples of 2nd conditionals in **Visitor Comments**.

10 Put the verbs in the correct tense.
1 If I _didn't have_ (not have) a TV, I _would be_ (be) very bored in the evenings.
2 Public transport _____ (be) much better if people _____ (not have) cars.
3 What _____ you _____ (do) if a shark _____ (attack) you?
4 If you _____ (can have) one of the devices, which one _____ you _____ (choose)?

11 Complete the sentences with true information and tell a partner.
1 If I had more free time,   *I'd learn the piano.*
2 If I was rich,
3 If I was the president,
4 If I could live anywhere in the world,

More practice? **Grammar Bank** >> p.144.

D Pronunciation linking in questions

12 **9D.1**▶ Listen to Kurt and Nicola talking about the devices in **High-Tech**. Who sounds more sure about what they say? Compare with a partner and say why.

13 **9D.2**▶ Listen and repeat these questions. Notice how *would you* is linked with a /dʒ/ sound.

would you = /wʊdʒuː/
Which one would you **choose**?
What would you **do** with it?
Where would you **go**?
What would you **do** if you had **that**?

14 Say this rhyme a few times. Start slow, then go faster and faster. Remember to link *would* and *you*.

Where would you go?
Who would you meet?
What would you do?
What would you eat?

ABCD Put it all together

15 Think of three things which you would like to have. Choose from this list or think of something else.

a famous work of art   a good quality camera
a massive diamond   a private jet   an unusual pet
a very powerful computer   a year-long holiday

16 Ask your partner questions about the things he or she would like to have. Then change partners and ask again. Has anybody chosen the same things as you?

I can talk about unreal situations.

Tick ✓ the line.   with a lot of help   with some help   on my own   very easily

Writing An opinion

A Read opinions on an Internet page

1 How much do you use the Internet? Tell a partner.

2 Read these opinions from an Internet page. Do you agree with any of the points of view?

If you want to stop global warming, ban private cars!	
green_star	📄 June 1st
	If you want to stop global warming, ban private cars! Obviously, private cars are convenient, but they also destroy the planet. Only the owners of cars enjoy the benefits, but everybody has to suffer the consequences, including people without cars. In global terms, that's a lot of people. Clearly, this is unfair.
Add a comment	
mickey says:	📄 June 3rd 9.30 p.m.
	That's just crazy – how would I get from A to B if I didn't have my car? Unfortunately, public transport is not an option for me because I live outside the city. There are no buses where I live. What should I do – buy a horse?
green_star says:	📄 June 3rd 9.55 p.m.
	If we banned private cars, public transport would get better. There would be more trains and buses because more people would want them. Also, buses would be faster because there would be less traffic. But also I think the government would have to pay for public transport in rural areas.
easy_rider says:	📄 June 4th 3.05 a.m.
	Global warming? I love my big car, and I'm looking forward to surfing in Greenland!
peggy_sue says:	📄 June 4th 7.15 a.m.
	I agree with green star that cars are a problem, but I don't think we should ban them. Unfortunately, the solution is not so simple. What about people who need to move around a lot for work, or people who need to transport heavy equipment? What about disabled people? What do you do if you need to travel in the middle of the night, when there are no buses? I think we should find other solutions such as tax benefits for cleaner cars.

3 Discuss these questions with a partner.
   1 Why do you think people often use false names on the Internet?
   2 Which comment is probably not serious? Why? Why do you think the writer sent it?

B Organize information in a paragraph

4 Read this description of how to write an opinion paragraph. Find examples on the Internet page.
   1 Start with a topic sentence which gives a brief summary of your point of view.
      Example If you want to stop global warming, ban private cars!
   2 Add two or three more sentences to do one or more of these things:
      a support your point of view
      b give examples
      c ask questions to the writer who you are addressing

5 Write a comment to add to the Internet discussion in exercise 2. Use the structure in exercise 4.

6 Read your partner's comment. Is the point of view clear?

C Use adverbs of attitude

7 Underline examples of *clearly*, *obviously*, and *unfortunately* on the Internet page. What do these adverbs mean? Choose the best answer for each one.
   a it is not difficult to see or understand
   b this is a fact which I'm not very happy about

8 Add attitude to this passage using the adverbs in exercise 7.

> Plane fares are much cheaper these days. This is good for travellers. But it's bad for the environment. We can't continue enjoying so many holidays abroad. We must fly less and use cleaner forms of transport such as the train.

ABC Put it all together

9 Work in small groups. Choose a different issue related to science and nature and write, briefly, what you think we should do about it. Start with a topic sentence and use adverbs of attitude. Here are some ideas.
   A healthy life is a boring life.
   There are some things which science can't explain.
   It's too late to stop global warming.
   Technology controls us.
   Nature is our enemy.

10 Give your page to another student. Read the problem and opinion and add your comment. Use a new name.

11 Continue passing around the pages. Add a comment to each problem, until everyone in the group has written one comment for each topic.

12 Find your comments and check your writing. Take turns to read out the discussions to the group. Which points of view are the clearest?

I can write about my opinion.

Tick ✓ the line.   with a lot of help   with some help   on my own   very easily

Unit 9 Review

A Grammar

1 Tag questions Write the tag questions at the end of the sentences.

are you? aren't you? do you? don't you? is it? ~~isn't it?~~

1 Your name's Laslo, _isn't it?_
2 You're Italian, _____
3 Your name isn't Italian, _____
4 You're not from Venice, _____
5 You work in a car factory, _____
6 You don't work on Saturdays, _____

2 Future perfect Put the verbs in the future perfect.

1 Hi Gina! Listen, we're having dinner right now. Can you call back in half an hour? We _'ll have finished_ by then.   finish
2 The house isn't really ours yet. We borrowed all the money from the bank. I _____ paying until I'm 65!   not finish
3 I guess by the time I'm 50 I _____ bald, like my dad.   go
4 I'm still a student, but in five years' time I _____ university and hopefully I _____ a good job.   leave/find
5 A few years from now we _____ all the oil reserves. Hopefully, by then the scientists _____ a new, clean source of energy.   use/find
6 There's no point going to the cinema now. We _____ the start of the film.   miss

3 1st and 2nd conditional; *if* clauses Put the verbs in the correct form.

1 If we don't hurry, we_'ll be_ late.   be
2 If you _____ a bear, you shouldn't run away.   meet
3 If I won a lot of money, I _____ working.   stop
4 If you _____ Jeremy, tell him to call me.   see
5 What would you do if you _____ your passport?   lose
6 If I had more free time, I _____ to play an instrument.   learn
7 If the plane is delayed, we _____ our connection.   miss
8 If you go to the beach, _____ to use some sun cream.   not forget
9 I would go to the shops with you if I _____ so busy.   not be

B Vocabulary

4 Weather Do the crossword.

```
1 C O L D       2           3
        4
              5
6              7
8       9
```

Across
1 Opposite of *hot*.
4 Very hot. _____ hot.
5 Short periods of rain.
6 Winter weather: it's _____.
8 Opposite of *wet*.
9 Very cold. _____ cold.

Down
1 White things in the sky.
2 The wind is _____.
3 Thunder and _____.
5 Weather with 3 down.
7 Very strong wind.

5 Attitude adverbs Order the words to make sentences.

1 be good Hopefully the tomorrow weather will
   Hopefully, the weather will be good tomorrow.
2 It on probably rain Saturday will
3 bus I my left on the umbrella Unfortunately
4 be at dark definitely It five o'clock won't
5 won't the Hopefully late train be

6 Direction of movement Match the words and pictures.

along backwards downhill downwards
forwards towards you uphill ~~upwards~~

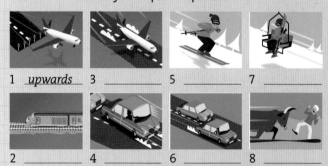

1 _upwards_   3 _____   5 _____   7 _____
2 _____   4 _____   6 _____   8 _____

7 Compound nouns Make compound nouns by matching one word from each line.

~~alarm~~ credit DVD mobile room computer text
book card ~~clock~~ programmer phone player service

1 _alarm_   _clock_   5 _____ _____
2 _____ _____   6 _____ _____
3 _____ _____   7 _____ _____
4 _____ _____

95

Death of the High Street

The butcher on the high street
Listens with alarm
They say that Farmer Jones
Is going to sell the farm
05 The greengrocer was driving past
And saw the land for sale
The cashier in the bank thinks
They're going to build a jail

The chemist tells the optician
10 The optician tells the nurse
The people on the high street
Say there's nothing worse
The newsagent saw an engineer
Walking on the land
15 The grocer on the corner
Saw a lorry full of sand

The baker saw a bulldozer
Driving through the town
'Did you hear about the farm house?
20 They've knocked the old place down!
They're building roads and walls
A big new shopping mall
We're going to lose our customers
The mall will take them all!'

25 **The mall kills the high street**

Have your say!

More and more big shopping malls are being built outside Britain's towns and cities, and traditional town-centre shopping streets are losing business. The old high-street shops are closing as shoppers abandon town centres and go to the malls instead. Is this a bad thing or is it modernization and progress? **What do you think? Opinions please!**

Amrita *25*

I think big shopping centres are much more convenient than high-street shops. You can get everything in one place, so it's much quicker. I've got a full-time job, so I don't have time to go around lots of little shops. It's much easier to park the car, and it's all indoors so you don't have to walk around in the rain. Shopping centres have more up-to-date stuff and more to choose from, and I think they're cheaper, too. So yes, for me, shopping centres are definitely progress.

Jerry *31*

In my opinion, high-street shops are much better than big shopping malls. The shopkeepers are friendlier and they give you better service. You can get fresh produce in small shops – local fruit and vegetables, and it's different from season to season. It's not all imported stuff from all around the world. Also, shopping malls are usually a long way outside town – that's no good for people who don't have cars, like me. I think local shops are the heart of our communities and if the shops close, our town centres will die.

How to exchange opinions

G articles *the, a, an*   V shops; agreeing and disagreeing   P agreeing and disagreeing intonation

A Read and infer

1 Do you like small, local shops or big shopping malls? Why? Think of two or three reasons and tell a partner.

2 **10A.1▶** Read and listen to **Death of the High Street** opposite. What opinion of the shopping mall do the shopkeepers have?

3 Answer the questions with a partner.
1 Line 3: Who are 'they'?
2 Line 5: 'The greengrocer was driving past' ... past what?
3 Line 7: What does the cashier think?
4 Line 12: 'Say there's nothing worse' ... worse than what?
5 Line 14: 'Walking on the land' ... what land?
6 Lines 19–24: Why are these lines in 'quotation marks'?
7 Was the cashier right? Did they build a jail?
8 How does the mall 'kill' the high street?

B Vocabulary shops

4 Work with a partner. Add more words to the lists of shops. Use **Death of the High Street** to help you.
a object + shop   *shoe shop; clothes shop ...*
b job + *'s* (shop)   *butcher's ...*
c other   *supermarket ...*

5 Work with a partner. Underline the correct word and explain why the other is not correct. You can use a dictionary.
1 You can buy milk at a grocer's / greengrocer's. *A greengrocer's sells fruit and vegetables.*
2 You pay at the checkout in a market / supermarket.
3 You don't have to go inside to buy a paper at a news-stand / newsagent's.
4 You don't pay to take books from a bookshop / library.
5 There are lots of shops with different owners inside a shopping mall / department store.

C Grammar articles *the, a, an*

6 Read these two conversations and answer the questions.
a **A** I'm going to the greengrocer's. Do you want anything?
   B Yes, can you get some apples, please?
b **A** Excuse me, is there a greengrocer's near here?
   B Yes, over there on the corner.

1 In which conversation do both people know the shop they're talking about?
2 Why does one speaker say *the greengrocer's* and the other *a greengrocer's*?

7 Work with a partner. Complete this summary of **Death of the High Street** with *the, a,* or *an.*
[1] *The* people on [2]_____ high street all know each other. Everybody knows who [3]_____ butcher is and who [4]_____ greengrocer is. But there are some strange people and vehicles in town – [5]_____ engineer, [6]_____ lorry and [7]_____ bulldozer. Nobody knows what they're doing here. [8]_____ cashier in [9]_____ bank thinks they're building [10]_____ jail. But finally, everybody discovers the truth: they're building [11]_____ shopping mall.

More practice? **Grammar Bank ≫** p.145.

D Listen to people exchanging opinions

8 Read **Have your say!** opposite. Who do you agree more with, Amrita or Jerry? Tell a partner.

9 Underline five or six key points in each opinion text.
Example I think big shopping centres are much more convenient than high-street shops.

10 **10A.2▶** Listen to Amrita and Jerry's conversation. Which of your underlined key points do they mention?

11 Listen again. Who uses these phrases, Amrita or Jerry?
1 I don't think so.   *Jerry*
2 Yes, maybe, but ...
3 Not really, no.
4 OK, that's true, but ...
5 Alright, but ...
6 Well, OK, you're right, I suppose.
7 I'm not so sure about that.
8 Yes, I agree, but ...

12 Match the phrases from exercise 11 with a–c.
a agree
b agree, but not completely
c disagree   *1*

13 **10A.3▶** Pronunciation Listen and repeat the parts of the conversation. Copy the intonation.

ABCD Put it all together

14 Work with a partner. Make a list of *for* and *against* points for each topic.
1 'Shopping with friends is better than shopping alone.'
2 'Internet shopping will kill traditional shopping.'
3 'Life in a small town is better than life in a big city.'

15 Work in groups. Choose one of the topics and exchange your opinions. Are your opinions similar?
Example **A** I think shopping with friends is more fun.
          B I'm not so sure about that ...

I can exchange opinions.
Tick ✓ the line.   with a lot of help   with some help   on my own   very easily

ving
e box can carton jar
acket pot tin tub tube

The RUBBISH Revolution

The average person in Britain produces seven times their own weight in rubbish every year. But perhaps this is not surprising when you look at the amount of packaging on supermarket food. And most of it is unnecessary. Think, for example, of four plastic pots of yogurt sold in a cardboard packet. The cardboard packet goes straight in the bin. Think of six plastic bottles of water packaged together in plastic packaging and carried home in a plastic bag. That's a lot of plastic. Only a few years ago we drank water out of the tap, and how much rubbish did that produce? None at all!

A lot of the rubbish we produce can be recycled of course, but that uses valuable resources too. It's better to buy food with as little packaging as possible. Some of the biggest supermarket chains in the country

have agreed to cut unnecessary packaging. However, government minister Ben Bradshaw says this is not enough and he is advising consumers to take direct action. He suggests that we take unnecessary packaging off our food at the supermarket checkout tills and leave it there.

Well, perhaps there are few people who are brave enough to leave rubbish at the till, but there are plenty of other things we can do to reduce waste:

- Say no to supermarket plastic bags. Take a few bags with you when you go shopping.
- If there is a choice, choose a product with less packaging.
- Buy a bigger packet if you think you will use it all. One big packet is better than lots of smaller ones.
- Try not to use plastic cups and plates.
- Choose food sold in environment-friendly packaging.
- If you find a product with too much packaging, complain to the manager.

But perhaps consumer action is not enough, and in fact some governments are taking stronger action. In 2002, Bangladesh became the first country to ban the plastic bag. Taiwan has gone a step further and banned plastic plates and cutlery as well as bags. But would consumers in Britain accept such a ban? The answer is yes. In the town of Modbury in Devon, they decided to ban the plastic bag for six months as an experiment. The ban was so popular that they have decided to keep it, and other towns are planning to follow their example.

How to talk about your shopping habits

G quantifiers V packaging P *of*

A Vocabulary packaging

1 Work with a partner. How many things in **Packaging** opposite can you find in the photos?

2 **10B.1▶** Complete the phrases with some of the words from **Packaging**. Listen and check.

1 a j*ar*____ of coffee
2 a p_____ of biscuits
3 a b_____ of eggs
4 a c_____ of milk
5 a p_____ of yogurt
6 a t_____ of tomatoes
7 a b_____ of ketchup
8 a b_____ of potatoes
9 a t_____ of toothpaste
10 a t_____ of margarine

3 Work with a partner. Think of other products which could complete the phrases in exercise 2.
Example a jar of baby food

4 Pronunciation Listen again and repeat. Notice that *of* is always unstressed and is pronounced /əv/.

5 Read the small pieces of text. Where do you think you would find them and what do they mean? Tell a partner.

Best before end ... see lid   Store in cool dry place
Keep out of reach of children   May contain nuts
Suitable for vegetarians   Smoking kills
Do not exceed stated dose   Avoid contact with eyes

Example Best before end ... see lid   *On a pot of yogurt.*

B Read for general meaning

6 Read **The Rubbish Revolution** opposite. What do you think the author is worried about?
a unhealthy eating habits
b the environment
c supermarkets killing the small shops
d high prices

7 Work with a partner. Write *true* or *false*. If the sentence is false, say why.
1 Food wrapping isn't necessary.
 False. Most of it, but not all of it, is unnecessary.
2 Drinking bottled water produces more rubbish.
3 All rubbish can be recycled.
4 Some supermarkets have agreed to use less food wrapping.
5 Consumers can take action to produce less rubbish.
6 You shouldn't buy bigger packets because they produce more rubbish.
7 Plastic bags have been banned in some places.
8 Plastic bags are so popular in Modbury that they've decided to keep them.

C Grammar quantifiers

8 Are these words countable or uncountable?
bottle   cardboard   packet   jar   packaging
plastic   plastic bag   rubbish   rubbish bin
water   yogurt   yogurt pot

9 Match 1–8 with a–h. Do the quantifiers in blue go with countable nouns, uncountable nouns, or both?

1 [f] There's
2 [a] There are
3 [ ] There's
4 [ ] There are
5 [ ] There isn't
6 [ ] There aren't
7 [ ] Is there
8 [ ] Are there

a a few bottles.
b many bags.
c any rubbish bins?
d a little yogurt.
e any rubbish?
f a lot of packaging.
g much water.
h a lot of jars.

10 Underline the best answer, according to **The Rubbish Revolution**.
1 Britain produces a lot of/a little/very little rubbish.
2 Supermarkets use enough/too much/a lot of packaging on food.
3 A lot of/Not much/No packaging is unnecessary.
4 Supermarkets are doing too little/too much/enough to reduce packaging.
5 Bottled water produces lots of rubbish but tap water produces some/no/hardly any rubbish.
6 We take home a few/too few/too many plastic bags from supermarkets.

11 Tell your partner about problems in the world today, using quantifiers.
Example There are too many cars on the road.

More practice? **Grammar Bank** >> p.145.

D Listen for specific information

12 Look at Linda's shopping (photo 1) and Mark's shopping (photo 2) opposite. Guess their answers to these questions.
1 What's in your shopping basket today?
2 What do you normally buy?
3 How often do you go shopping?
4 Do you write a shopping list?
5 Do you pay by card or in cash?

13 **10B.2▶** Listen. Were your guesses correct?

ABCD Put it all together

14 What are your shopping habits? Write notes to answer questions 2–5 in exercise 12.

15 Ask other students about their shopping habits. Whose shopping habits are most similar to yours?

I can talk about my shopping habits.
Tick ✓ the line.   with a lot of help   with some help   on my own   very easily

THE SALESPEOPLE

1

Ms SAYLES We haven't been selling many of these sunshades lately. I want you to try harder. The one who sells the most over the next month or so will get a bonus.

2

ONE MONTH LATER
Ms S Right. What have you been doing to sell more sunshades, Winston?
WINSTON I've been offering two for the price of one, Ms Sayles.

3

Ms S And how many have you sold?
W I haven't sold many recently. People don't want sunshades with pink rabbits on.
Ms S How many, Winston?
W Well, none, in fact.
Ms S None. And how long have you been working here?
W Almost six months.
Ms S Nearly six months and you haven't learnt anything. It's not good enough!

4

Ms S What about you, Janet?
JANET I've been advertising in the daily paper, Ms Sayles. I've also been phoning people at home.
Ms S And how many have you sold?
J About five. It's been raining for weeks. Nobody wants a sunshade.
Ms S You're a saleswoman, Janet. It's your job to sell things that nobody wants.

5

Ms S And you, Charlie? How many have you sold?
CHARLIE Two thousand, more or less. People have been queuing to buy them.
Ms S That's amazing! What have you been doing?

6

C I've been selling them outside the station as umbrellas.

How to talk about recent activities

G present perfect continuous V approximate times and amounts P when to stress *have/has*

A Read and follow an explanation

1 What's the best way to sell something? Discuss with a partner.
   a Offer your product to the customer at just the moment they need it.
   b Tell your customer that your product is the best quality.
   c Offer your product at a price which seems cheaper than normal.
   d Give information about your product to as many people as possible.

2 **10C.1▶** Listen and read **The Salespeople** opposite. Match *Winston*, *Janet*, and *Charlie* with a–d in exercise 1.

3 Answer the questions.
   Who has been …
   1 contacting lots of people? *Janet*
   2 selling lots of sunshades?
   3 wasting his time?
   4 trying to sell sunshades cheap?
   5 waiting to see who sold most sunshades?
   6 working hard with poor results?

4 Work with a partner. Explain why each salesperson was or wasn't successful.

B Vocabulary approximate times and amounts

5 Underline these words and phrases in **The Salespeople**. Write them in the correct box. Then decide which of them can complete sentences 1–3.
   lately or so recently ~~almost~~
   nearly about more or less

a little less than	in recent times	approximately
almost		

   1 I bought this computer _____ nine months ago.
   2 Have you bought any music CDs _____?
   3 I've been working here for ten years _____.

6 Complete these sentences to give true information about yourself. Compare with a partner.
   1 I've been studying this page for *15 minutes or so./ almost 15 minutes.*
   2 I've been sitting in this room since _____.
   3 I've been awake since _____.
   4 I haven't _____ lately.

C Grammar present perfect continuous

7 Complete the sentences in the grammar box.

+ ●●●●●	− ●●●●●●	? ●●●●●
It's been raining.	It hasn't been raining.	
I've been sleeping.		Have I been sleeping?
		Have you been waiting?

8 **10C.2▶** Pronunciation Listen, check, and repeat the sentences in exercise 7. Copy the stress pattern. When do we stress *have/has*?

9 Compare the sentences and answer the questions.
   present perfect simple   I've sold two thousand.
   present perfect continuous I've been selling them for a month.

   1 Which sentence answers the question *How long*?
   2 Which sentence answers the question *How many*?
   3 Which sentence focuses on a completed achievement?
   4 Which sentence focuses on continuing actions?

10 Underline the best form of the verb. Compare with a partner.
   1 I've sold/been selling five umbrellas today.
   2 I've sold/been selling them outside the station all day.
   3 Winston's sat/been sitting behind the counter in his shop all morning.
   4 Janet's phoned/been phoning about 50 people.
   5 It's rained/been raining for three hours.
   6 I've seen/been seeing this advert three times already.
   7 Have you waited/been waiting for long?

   More practice? **Grammar Bank** >> p.145.

D Listen for detail

11 **10C.3▶** Two friends, Simon and Teresa, have been out of contact. Listen to their conversation. What have they been doing recently? Make notes.
   Example Simon's been saving money.

12 Practise the conversation with a partner. Use your notes.

ABCD Put it all together

13 Write a list of activities you've been doing recently.
   Example reading books; going to the gym; travelling for work …

14 Work with a partner and do a role play. Have a conversation about what you've been doing lately.
   Example A I haven't seen you for ages! What have you been doing lately?
            B Oh, I've been travelling a lot for work …

I can talk about recent activities.

Tick ✓ the line. with a lot of help with some help on my own very easily

ersonality Quiz!
What kind of shopper are you?

Which of the options best describes what you do in these situations? If you can't decide, choose two – or none!

1 You see a nice pair of shoes in a sale. They're good value and they're the last pair available. What do you think?

- a 'I'll buy them as long as there's no queue in the shop.'
- b 'I'll buy them if they're good quality.'
- c 'I won't buy them unless I really need them.'
- d 'I'll buy them quickly before someone else decides to buy them.'

2 You need a new printer. What do you do?

- a I won't buy one unless I know it's one of the best available.
- b I won't buy one until I've compared the prices in five different shops.
- c Buy the first one I see, as long as it can print!
- d Look around the shops until I see one which looks nice.

3 You decide to learn the guitar. How do you get your first instrument?

- a Borrow one from a friend until he or she wants it back.
- b Buy a guitar and perhaps buy a few other things while I'm in the shop.
- c Find out what the professionals use before I buy one.
- d Get the cheapest and upgrade when I know I'm going to continue.

4 You get a €15 book voucher for your birthday. What do you think?

- a 'I'll check if there's anything I want in the bargain section.'
- b 'I'll go to the shops and take my credit card in case I want to buy something else, too.'
- c 'I'll read the book reviews in the paper before I go to the bookshop.'
- d 'I'll wait until someone else's birthday comes round and I'll give it to them.'

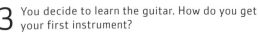

BOOK TOKEN €15 Book Token The gift or reading

5 You buy a fridge. When they deliver it, you notice it isn't the same colour as the one in the shop. What do you do?

- a Ask them to replace it – unless it matches the colour scheme of my kitchen.
- b Nothing. I don't mind as long as the fridge works.
- c Complain even if I like the colour because I might get some money back!
- d I go to the shops as soon as I can to buy more things which match the colour.

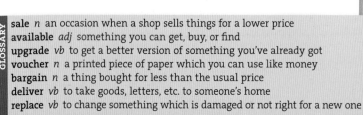

GLOSSARY

sale *n* an occasion when a shop sells things for a lower price
available *adj* something you can get, buy, or find
upgrade *vb* to get a better version of something you've already got
voucher *n* a printed piece of paper which you can use like money
bargain *n* a thing bought for less than the usual price
deliver *vb* to take goods, letters, etc. to someone's home
replace *vb* to change something which is damaged or not right for a new one

Buying a camera

Tina Oops, I've taken a photo of my foot!

Dan It's all right. We can delete it unless …

A   **D** Yes, all included. And there's a six-month guarantee. If you have any problems with it, we'll repair it free of charge. Here, try it …

     T Mmm. Oops, I've taken a photo of my foot!

B   **D** A digital camera? OK. How much do you want to spend?

     T £100 or so …

C   **D** Sorry, we don't sell batteries, but you can buy them at any supermarket.

     T How much do they cost?

D   **D** Well, this one is normally £120, but it's reduced at the moment to £99.99.

     T Does that include the batteries, the memory card, and everything?

E   **D** Can you enter your PIN number, please … Thanks. And here's your receipt. Keep it in case you need to bring the camera back.

     T OK. Thanks. Goodbye.

     D Bye.

F   **D** Can I help you?

1   **T** Yes, I'm looking for a cheap digital camera.

G   **D** £2.50, more or less. Would you like to buy a leather case for your camera? Brown, to match your shoes!

     T Ha ha. No, thanks. That's all, thanks.

H   **D** OK. How would you like to pay – by cash or card?

     T I'll pay by credit card, please.

I   **D** It's all right. We can delete it unless you want to keep it!

     T No, thanks. I hate these shoes! OK, I think I'll take the camera. And I'll buy some spare batteries while I'm here.

How to ask about products in a shop

G time and conditional clauses   V words connected with buying and selling

A Read and respond

1 You're buying one of these things. What do you do before you buy? Tell a partner.

a camera   a car   a flat   a jacket   a package holiday   shoes

Example   Try it on …

2 Read **Personality Quiz!** opposite with a partner. Choose your answers for yourself.

3 Look on >> p.131 to calculate your score and read your shopping personality. Do you agree with the description?

B Grammar time and conditional clauses

4 Look at the sentences and choose the correct answer to the questions.

Anne   I'll buy the shoes if they're good.

Beth   I'll buy the shoes when I've got the money.

1 Will Anne buy the shoes in the future?
   a No.   b Maybe.   c Yes, definitely.

2 Will Beth buy the shoes in the future?
   a No.   b Maybe.   c Yes, definitely.

5 These sentences mean the same as the sentences in exercise 4. Put the words and phrases in blue in the box.

Anne   I'll buy them as long as they're good. I *won't* buy them unless they're good.

Beth   I'll buy them as soon as I've got the money. I *won't* buy them until I've got the money.

	if	when
synonym	as long as	
opposite		

6 Underline clauses in **Personality Quiz!** beginning with the words and phrases in exercise 5. What tense is the verb in the clause?

Example   as long as there's no queue in the shop
   present simple tense

7 Make true sentences from the box and tell your partner. Say if you agree with your partner's sentences.

Example   **A** I won't buy a jacket unless it's cheap.
   B Oh, really? I don't mind paying more as long as it looks nice.

I'll	buy	a jacket	as long as	it's cheap.
I won't		a computer	as soon as	there's a guarantee.
		other	unless	I think it looks nice.
			until	*other*

More practice? **Grammar Bank** >> p.145.

C Vocabulary words connected with buying and selling

8 Read **Buying a camera** opposite and put the conversation in order. Compare with a partner.

9 **10D.1▶** Listen and check.

10 What is the difference between these pairs of words from the conversation? Use your dictionary.

buy – pay   spend – cost   reduced – included
guarantee – receipt /rɪ'siːt/

11 Complete the questions with these words and phrases.

cost   free of charge   guarantee
~~included~~   pay   price   spend

1 Is the software   _included_ ?
2 How much does it _____?
3 Do you deliver _____?
4 How much do you want to _____?
5 How would you like to _____?
6 Does it come with a _____?
7 What's the reduced _____?

12 What are the steps of the conversation in **Buying a camera**? Work with a partner and find the path from *Start* to *Finish*.

salesperson   customer

START offer to help	say what you want	offer extra goods	refuse extra goods
say how much you want to spend	ask how much customer wants to spend	explain about spares	ask about way of paying
offer product	accept product	ask for spares	choose way of paying
ask what's included	say what's included	say goodbye **FINISH**	take payment + give receipt

13 Practise the conversation with a partner. Don't read it – use the conversation map in exercise 12.

ABC Put it all together

14 Work with a partner. Role play shop conversations. The customer is buying the products in the pictures on >> p.131.

Example   **A** Can I help you?
   B Yes, I'm looking for a camera.
   A What make are you looking for?
   B I don't mind as long as it's good quality …

I can ask about products in a shop.

Tick ✓ the line.   with a lot of help   with some help   on my own   very easily

A Read a letter of complaint

1 Do you ever buy things from catalogues, from the Internet, or over the phone? What are the possible problems? Tell a partner.

2 Read the letter of complaint. Why do you think the company sent the wrong book?

3 Answer the questions with a partner.
  1 How does Marcus know the name of the person he's writing to?
  2 What's the name of the company he's writing to?
  3 Why doesn't he want to keep the book?
  4 Why didn't Marcus return the book immediately?

B Think about the reader

4 What do you think about Marcus Page from his letter? Choose the best description.
  a He seems aggressive and negative.
  b He seems angry and impatient.
  c He seems firm but friendly.

5 Read the tips for writing a letter of complaint. Do you agree? Do you think it is better to be more aggressive? Tell a partner.

6 Work with a partner and underline examples of the four tips in the letter of complaint.

7 Marcus divides his letter into paragraphs to make it clearer for the reader. What information does he give in each paragraph?

C Get ideas to write about

8 Brainstorm with a partner and write possible answers.
  You ordered a product:
  1 What did you order?
  2 What was the problem with the product?
  3 Have you contacted anybody about the problem yet? What did they say?
  4 How did you order (e.g. over the phone)?
  5 When did you place the order and when did it arrive?
  6 What would you like them to do about the problem?

9 Use Marcus's letter to put the information in order.

ABC Put it all together

10 Write a letter of complaint using some of your ideas from exercise 8. Follow the tips.

11 Check your writing and then pass it to a partner.

12 Read your partner's letter and imagine it is addressed to you. Does it make you want to help the person?

April 1st 2010

Dear Ms Parchment

I'm writing to explain a problem I have had with your telephone ordering service. I recently ordered a book called "Lords of Things" – a history of modern Thailand by Maurizio Peleggi, but your company sent a different book.

I placed the order on February 29th and I received the package from your company about two weeks ago. I was away at the time, so I wasn't able to open it until this morning. Unfortunately, it was the wrong book; it was "The Lord of the Rings" by JRR Tolkien. It's a good book, but I've already read it! I rang your telephone service to explain the problem, but they said it was too late to change the book. Then they suggested I wrote to you.

I have ordered books from Paperbooks Express in the past and I have always found the service to be excellent. I'm sure this misunderstanding can be easily solved. Please could you send me the book I originally ordered? I will be happy to return the Tolkien book as long as you refund the postage costs.

I look forward to hearing from you.

Yours sincerely

Marcus Page

Marcus Page

TIPS FOR WRITING A LETTER OF COMPLAINT

How do you feel when you spend money but don't get what you want? Most of us feel angry and we want to shout at the people who sold us the goods or services. However, being aggressive is not usually the best way to get a positive response. If you really want to solve the problem, calm down and think about what you are going to say – or write. Try to give a firm but friendly impression:

1 Explain your problem **briefly**. Let your reader know quickly why they're reading your letter.

2 Give detailed **facts**. This will give the reader a chance to check their records.

3 Say what you'd like the reader to do. This will show the reader **a way forwards**.

4 Be **friendly**. A compliment or a touch of humour helps to create a positive feeling.

Tick ✓ the line. with a lot of help   with some help   on my own   very easily

Unit 10 Review

A Grammar

1 Articles *the*, *a*, *an* Write *the*, *a*, or *an* in each gap.

A Have you got ¹*a* road map?

B Yes, but it's in ²____ car.

A Oh. I didn't know you had ³____ car.

B Yes – I've got ⁴____ Opel.

A Where do you keep it? Have you got ⁵____ garage?

B No. I park it in ⁶____ street, in front of ⁷____ flat.

2 Quantifiers Complete the sentences with these quantifiers.

a few   ~~a little~~   a lot of   few   little   many   much

1 I always keep _a little_ water in a glass by the bed.

2 There's too _____ packaging on supermarket food, and most of it isn't necessary.

3 There's been very _____ rain this year and the river's dried up.

4 There are _____ packets of nuts in the kitchen – help yourself!

5 There are too _____ people in the world and not enough food to feed them.

6 Unfortunately, there are very _____ places to buy fresh fish in my town.

7 _____ the rubbish we produce ends up in the sea.

3 Present perfect continuous Put the verbs in the present perfect continuous.

A I haven't seen you for ages. What ¹_have you been doing_ (do) recently?

B Oh, I ²_____ (not go) out much. I ³_____ (try) to save money.

A ⁴_____ you _____ (watch) a lot of TV, then?

B Yes, TV and DVDs. And I ⁵_____ (read) a lot, too. And you – ⁶_____ you _____ (do) anything interesting?

A No, not really. Mum's not been very well so I ⁷_____ (look) after her.

4 Time and conditional clauses Write a sentence with the same meaning.

1 I'll buy it as long as it's cheap.   unless
I won't _buy it unless it's cheap_ .

2 I'll buy it as soon as I get paid.   until
I won't _____ .

3 Start when you're ready.   as soon as
Start _____ .

4 Buy it if you like it.   unless
Don't _____ .

5 You can't leave until it finishes.   as soon as
You can _____ .

B Vocabulary

5 Shops Write the words for these definitions.

1 b_o_o_k_s_h_o_p   You buy books here.

2 b_____'__   You buy meat here.

3 s_____ m_____   An enormous building full of shops.

4 n_____-s_____   You can buy a newspaper here without going inside.

5 l_____   You borrow books here.

6 m_____   People sell things in the street here.

7 n_____a_____'__   You can go inside and buy a newspaper.

8 b_____   You get money here.

9 g_____g_____'__   You can buy fruit and veg here.

10 d_____ s_____   An enormous shop with different departments.

6 Packaging Find the words for these items of packaging.

P	A	C	K	E	T
T	R	A	A	Y	U
U	P	R	U	N	B
B	O	T	T	L	E
A	T	O	P	I	R
G	E	N	I	D	N

7 Approximate times and amounts <u>Underline</u> the correct time expression in these sentences.

1 Fifty-five minutes is <u>almost</u>/or so/lately an hour.

2 Have you seen the news more or less/recently/about?

3 I've been waiting for half an hour about/or so/lately.

4 It's nearly/recently/or so three o'clock.

5 It takes lately/about/or so an hour to get to the station.

8 Words connected with buying and selling Complete the text with these words.

cost   guarantee   included   prices   receipt   ~~spend~~

Tips for shoppers

– Decide how much you want to ¹_spend_ before you begin.

– Compare the ²_____ in at least three different shops.

– Check that the product comes with a ³_____.

– Check if batteries are ⁴_____ in the price.

– Find out how much the extras ⁵_____, e.g. ink for printers.

– Keep your ⁶_____ in case you need to return the product.

The Shakespeare Trail

A guided tour of the most important places in Shakespeare's home town ...

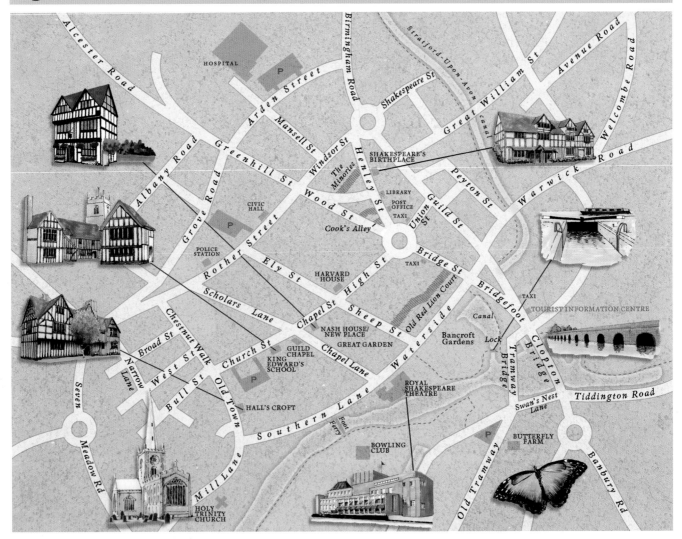

The town made famous as the birthplace of the great playwright, William Shakespeare, Stratford-upon-Avon is one of Britain's most popular tourist destinations. Here you can visit the house where the great poet was born, his old school, the place where he got married, and the house where he died. The best way to see everything is on foot, and on this two-hour walking tour, our expert guides will show you all the points of interest.

The tour will take us past the various homes where Shakespeare and his family lived in Stratford-upon-Avon. The route begins at Shakespeare's parents' home in Henley Street. Shakespeare was born in this house on April 23rd, 1564, and he spent his childhood years here.

From Shakespeare's birthplace, we go down Henley Street, turn right at the roundabout, and go along High Street. At the crossroads, we go straight across and then along Chapel Street, and we come to Nash's House on the left. This was the home of Shakespeare's granddaughter Elizabeth, and it is built next to the site of Shakespeare's own house, New Place. The house is no longer here, but we can still see the Great Garden which belonged to it. Shakespeare bought New Place when he got married and left his parents' house. He died here on April 23rd, 1616.

After visiting Nash's house, we continue along Chapel Street to the crossroads and then go along Church Street. We pass the Guild Chapel and the old grammar school. At the end of Church Street, we turn left and go along Old Town, and we come to Hall's Croft on the left. This was the home of Shakespeare's daughter Susanna.

From Hall's Croft, we continue down the road to Mill Lane and carry on until we reach the Holy Trinity Church. Shakespeare was baptized and also buried at this church. The end point of the Shakespeare trail is our visit to his grave.

How to give and ask about directions

G indirect questions   V the street

A Vocabulary the street

1 Work with a partner and decide how to give these directions. What other words and phrases do you know for giving directions?

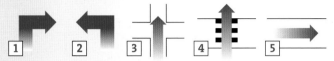

Example 1 turn right

2 Work with a partner. Look at the map opposite and find these things.
an alley   a bridge   a canal   a car park   a crossroads
a dead-end street   a path   a pedestrian street
a roundabout   a taxi rank   a T-junction

B Read and follow directions

3 Read **The Shakespeare Trail** opposite. Who do you think the text was written for?

4 Read **The Shakespeare Trail** again and draw the route on the map. Compare with a partner.

5 Work with a partner. Explain the route in the opposite direction – from the Holy Trinity Church to Shakespeare's birthplace. Compare with another pair.
Example   Go along Mill lane. Then continue along Old Town, past Hall's Croft ...

C Listen and follow directions

6 Follow these directions from the tourist information centre. Where do they take you? Underline the key words with a partner.

Go out of the door and turn right. Keep left, along Bridgefoot until you come to a crossroads. Go straight across, and straight along Bridge Street and you'll come to a roundabout. If you go straight across, there are two streets – one on the left and Henley Street on the right. Go up Henley Street, past the post office and the library and you'll see the house on the right.

7 **11A.1▶** Three tourists have asked for directions. Listen and find out where they want to go.
1 Paola's at the Royal Shakespeare Theatre. She wants to go to ...
2 Ignacio's at Harvard House. He wants to go to ...
3 Laura's at the Bowling Club. She wants to go to ...

8 Read the audio script on ≫ p.157 and check your answers.

D Grammar indirect questions

9 Complete the grammar box and underline the correct words in the rules.

	direct question	indirect question (more polite)
open	Where's Chapel street?	Can you tell me where Chapel Street is?
		Do you know where Mill Lane is?
closed	Is there a taxi rank near here?	Can you tell me if (or whether) there's a taxi rank near here?
		Do you know if there's a shopping centre near here?

Rules
1 Use *if* in open / closed questions.
2 To be more polite, use direct / indirect questions.

10 Make these questions more polite with *Can you tell me* or *Do you know*.

1 Where's the Royal Shakespeare Theatre?
2 Is there a bus stop near here?
3 Where's the town hall?
4 Is there a shopping centre near here?

11 Work with a partner. Ask about places on **The Shakespeare Trail** map.
Student A   Ask politely where a street or place is.
Student B   Answer and point to it on the map.
Examples **A** Excuse me, can you tell me where Chapel Street is?
  B Yes, it's here.
  A Excuse me, do you know if there's a taxi rank near here?
  B Yes, there's one here.

More practice? **Grammar Bank** ≫ p.146.

ABCD Put it all together

12 Work with a partner. Above your map, there is a list of six places you want to find. Ask your partner for directions. For each turn, start from a different number on the map.
Student A   Look at the map on ≫ p.132.
Student B   Look at the map on ≫ p.135.

I can give and ask about directions.
Tick ✓ the line.   with a lot of help   with some help   on my own   very easily

Accommodation adjectives

comfortable /'kʌmftəbl/ delicious /dɪ'lɪʃəs/ delightful /dɪ'laɪtfl/ efficient /ɪ'fɪʃnt/
elegant /'elɪɡənt/ friendly /'frendli/ magnificent /mæɡ'nɪfɪsnt/ secluded /sɪ'kluːdɪd/

Punta Paloma
Resort

1 *Punta Paloma* is a luxury nature resort, located on Honduras's Caribbean coast only one hour from La Ceiba International Airport. It is set in the magnificent rainforest of the Punta Paloma National Park. At *Punta Paloma* we offer service with a smile from the moment you arrive. You will be greeted with a welcome cocktail while your luggage is collected from your car. Then you will be taken to your secluded guest cabin hidden among the coffee and cacao trees.

2 In *Punta Paloma*, **you** decide. Enjoy delicious Central-American cuisine in our elegant restaurant with views of the Bay Islands, or have your dinner served in the garden. Relax in our comfortable terrace bar, or have your drinks served by the pool. Choose from a delightful selection of fresh food at our breakfast buffet, or have breakfast brought to your room.

3 There's plenty to do during your stay at *Punta Paloma*. Follow forest paths through the hotel grounds and into the national park. Our guides will help you identify the exotic local birds and wildlife. Go riding, whitewater rafting, or snorkelling on the coral reefs. Take a day trip to the ancient ruins of Copán and have your photo taken beside a Mayan temple. Or simply relax by the pool!

4 At *Punta Paloma*, you will find the hotel staff friendly, efficient, and ready to help in any way. You only have to ask! Have your hair cut and styled by a qualified hairdresser. Have your clothes washed and ironed overnight. Have international newspapers brought to your room. Or simply hang out the 'Do not disturb' sign and enjoy the peace and quiet.

5 *Whether you're looking for sport, nature, peace, or comfort,* Punta Paloma *is your ideal holiday choice.*

Fish Head Inn

The **Fish Head Inn** is a run-down old guest house, located on the coast of Cumbria in north-west England, only four hours from Manchester International Airport. It is set in a desolate seaside resort only a couple of miles from the Sellafield Nuclear Power Station. When you arrive at the **Fish Head Inn**, you will have to ring five times at reception before anybody notices you. Then you will be given a key and you will have to carry your own bags up the narrow stairs to a room in the attic.

At the **Fish Head Inn**, you eat what you're given. Usually, it's a slice of pork with cold mashed potato. If you don't like it, there is a fish and chip shop just down the road. Breakfast is served from 7.30 until 8.00, and don't be late or you'll get nothing. You can have it in your room, but you'll have to fetch it yourself.

There's very little to do during your stay at the **Fish Head Inn**. Walk on the windy beach, visit the abandoned church, or have your photo taken in front of the nuclear power station. Or simply stay in bed and wait till it's time to leave!

At the **Fish Head Inn**, don't expect any help from the hotel staff. If you want anything, you'll have to do it yourself. We don't employ any cleaning staff, so we ask guests to wash their own sheets before leaving. And if anyone can fix the dripping taps, that would be much appreciated!

Whether you're looking for bad weather, desolate scenery, greasy food, or polite self-service, the *Fish Head Inn* is your perfect choice.

How to **talk about holiday accommodation**

G *to have something done* **v** describing holiday accommodation

A Vocabulary describing holiday accommodation

1 Work with a partner. Make a list of words connected with holidays and tourism.
Example seaside resort; sightseeing; youth hostel ...

2 Look at **Accommodation adjectives** opposite. What things could these adjectives describe? You can use a dictionary. Compare ideas with another pair.
Example comfortable – room, lounge, bed ...

B Read holiday accommodation adverts

3 Read **Punta Paloma Resort** opposite. Match the paragraphs with these titles.

☐ activities   ☐ service
☐1 introduction   ☐ meals
☐ summary

4 Answer the questions with a partner.
1 Who is the text written for?
2 What is the purpose of the text?
3 How does the writer make the place sound attractive? Underline positive words and phrases.

5 Read **Fish Head Inn** opposite. How do you know it's a joke? Compare with a partner.

6 How does the writer make the place sound bad? Find one or more phrases in each paragraph.
Example They say 'it's only four hours from Manchester'.

7 Talk to a partner. Compare the **Punta Paloma Resort** and the **Fish Head Inn**.
Example The Punta Paloma Resort is in a rainforest, but the Fish Head Inn is in a seaside resort.

C Grammar *to have something done*

8 Match these pictures with the sentences. Underline the correct word in the rule.

a
b

1 ☐ I took my photo.
2 ☐ I had my photo taken.

Rule to have something done = subject + *have* + object + infinitive / past / past participle

9 Underline seven examples of the *to have sth done* form in **Punta Paloma Resort**. Compare with a partner.

10 In this advert, the text is mixed up. Match beginnings 1–8 with endings a–h.
Example 1 – c

WE OFFER THE BEST SERVICE

1Have your meals	aput in the hotel safe.
2Have your breakfast	bparked by our driver.
3Have your valuables	ccooked by Paris's finest chefs.
4Have your hair	dtranslated into perfect French.
5Have your clothes	etaken on top of the Eiffel Tower.
6Have your documents	fcut by a qualified hairdresser.
7Have your photograph	gwashed and ironed overnight.
8Have your car	hbrought to your room.

THE HOTEL PARIS

ENJOY YOUR STAY!

11 Rewrite these sentences using the *to have sth done* form. Keep the same tense as the original sentence.
1 My parents are paying some builders to decorate their house. *My parents are having their house decorated.*
2 I pay a mechanic to service my car once a year.
3 A dentist took out my back teeth when I was a child.
4 Ask room service to bring breakfast to your room.
5 I'm going to pay a technician to repair my computer.

More practice? **Grammar Bank** >> p.146.

D Listen for detail

12 **11B.1▶** Listen to a conversation between Claire and Ian. Why does she mention the Punta Paloma Resort?

13 Listen again and answer the questions with a partner.
1 What things in the **Punta Paloma Resort** text does Claire mention? Underline them.
2 What thing in the text does she disagree with?
3 Do you think Ian will go to the hotel?

14 Work with a partner. Look at the audio script on >> p.158. Have a similar conversation about the **Fish Head Inn**.

ABCD Put it all together

15 Choose a hotel or other holiday accommodation where you have stayed – good or bad. Make notes about the location, the meals, the activities, and the service.

16 Work in groups. Describe your accommodation and the services offered to the others. Listen to the others in the group. Which hotel would you like to visit?

I can talk about holiday accommodation. ▮▮▮▮▮▮▮

Tick ✓ the line.   with a lot of help   with some help   on my own   very easily

Health Precautions

THINK BEFORE YOU TRAVEL!

- Are there any **injections** that you need to have?
- Will you have to show any **vaccination certificates**?
- Are there any **pills** that you need to take?
- Do you need to take out **medical insurance**?
- Should you drink the **tap water**?
- Are there any **local foods** that you ought to avoid?
- Do you need to take **sun block**?
- Should you carry a **first aid kit**?
- Will you need to take **insect repellent**?
- Should you carry a **mosquito net**?
- What should you do in an **emergency**?

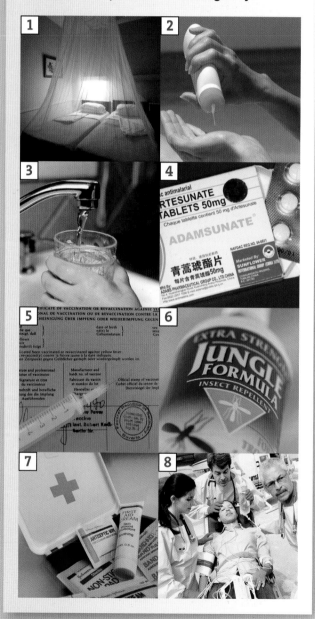

Ask the doctor

Dear Dr Sharma

I've just been to Ibiza for a week. I'd been very busy at work and I really needed to relax. But when I was there, I had a really bad cold. I had to stay in bed and my boyfriend had to look after me! I think I caught my cold on the flight. I've heard that people often catch colds on planes. Is that true, and if so, what can we do about it?

Tracey Williams

Dear Tracey

Yes, it's true. You have 100 times more chance of catching a cold on a plane than in your normal life. We're not sure why, but it's probably because the air is very dry on board. You can catch a cold more easily when your nose and throat are dry. And of course, there are a lot of people in a small space so germs don't have to travel far from one person to the next. But don't worry, you don't need to cancel your next holiday. Here are some simple things you can do to avoid aeroplane colds:

- DRINK WATER. In dry air, your body loses water so you need to replace it. You don't have to drink a lot, but you should drink little and often to keep your throat wet. Tea is also good because the steam goes up your nose and makes it less dry. But you shouldn't drink coffee or alcohol because these make your body drier.

- WASH YOUR HANDS. You catch more colds from touching than breathing. A cold or flu virus can live for several hours on an aeroplane seat or tray table. From there, the virus can pass to your hand and then your mouth. So ideally, you ought to wash your hands before eating snacks and meals. If you can't get out from your seat, you should clean your hands with disinfectant tissues.

- CLEAN YOUR MOUTH. Ideally, you ought to use a mouthwash to kill the germs before they act. However, you will need to go to the bathroom to use the mouthwash – not very convenient if you're in a window seat. Also, you'll need to check the rules for hand luggage – you won't be allowed to take a large bottle of mouthwash onto the plane.

- WEAR A FACE MASK. If you are really worried, you should think about wearing a mask. These can stop germs reaching your mouth and nose – but of course, people may look at you strangely!

Finally, remember that if you are travelling with a cold, you shouldn't pass on your germs to the other passengers. Cover your mouth when you cough and don't touch people – by shaking hands, for example. But hopefully, you won't have a cold the next time you fly!

How to give health advice

G *have to, need to, should, ought to* V health and travel P the main stress in a sentence

A Vocabulary health and travel

1 Answer the questions with a partner.
1 What are the main health risks when you travel?
2 Have you ever been ill on holiday?

2 Read Health Precautions opposite. What do you think *precautions* are? Discuss with a partner.

3 Find the words for photos 1–8.
Example 1 = mosquito net

4 Which of the precautions should visitors to your country follow? Compare your answers with a partner.

B Pronunciation the main stress in a sentence

5 11C.1▶ Listen and repeat the questions in Health Precautions. Remember to put stress on the word or phrase in **bold**.

6 Look at Health Precautions again. Read 1–3 and write *true* or *false*.
The main stress in the sentence is …
1 always at the end of the sentence.
2 usually at the end of the sentence.
3 on the most important word or phrase in the sentence.

7 11C.2▶ Where do you think the main stress will be in these questions? Underline the word or phrase. Then listen, check, and repeat.
1 Do you need to carry your passport?
2 Are there any documents that you need?
3 Are there any guide books I should buy?
4 Should you take travellers' cheques?

8 Work with a partner. Take turns to read the sentences in Health Precautions. Does your partner use main sentence stress?

C Read for the main points

9 Do you often travel by plane, and do you enjoy it? Why / Why not? Tell a partner.

10 Read Ask the doctor opposite and find two reasons why flying is unhealthy.

11 Choose the best summary of the doctor's reply to Tracey.
a Yes, there is a problem, and there's nothing you can do about it.
b Yes, there is a problem, but there are things you can do about it.
c No, there's no problem, and you shouldn't worry about it.

12 Write notes to complete the table. Compare with a partner.

action	Why?	problems and difficulties
drinking	keeps nose, throat wet	alcohol, coffee – dry out body
washing your hands		
using a mouthwash		
wearing a mask		

D Grammar *have to, need to, should, ought to*

13 Find sentences or phrases in Ask the doctor with the same meaning as these.
1 It was necessary for me to stay in bed.
   I had to stay in bed.
2 It was necessary for me to relax.
3 It isn't necessary to cancel.
4 It's a good idea to drink.
5 It isn't a good idea to drink coffee.
6 It's a good idea to wash your hands.
7 It'll be necessary to go to the bathroom.
8 It isn't a good idea to pass on your germs.

14 Work with a partner. Answer the questions.
1 What's the difference between these pairs of sentences? (Clue: look at the phrases in green in exercise 13.)
   a You need to wash your hands. / You ought to wash your hands.
   b You don't have to drink a lot. / You shouldn't drink a lot.
2 What are the negative forms of these verbs?
   a You have to   *You don't have to*
   b You need to
   c You should
3 Look at your answers to exercise 13. Which of the verbs have past tense forms and what are they?

15 Write travel tips with these words.
1 not / have / get a visa   *You don't have to get a visa.*
2 not / need / print your ticket
3 ought / buy / guide book
4 should / not / carry lots of cash
5 have / take / passport
6 not / have / take a lot of luggage

More practice? **Grammar Bank** ≫ p.146.

ABCD Put it all together

16 Look at **Travel advice** on ≫ p.132. Work in pairs or small groups and give each other holiday advice.

I can give health advice.

Tick ✓ the line.   with a lot of help   with some help   on my own   very easily

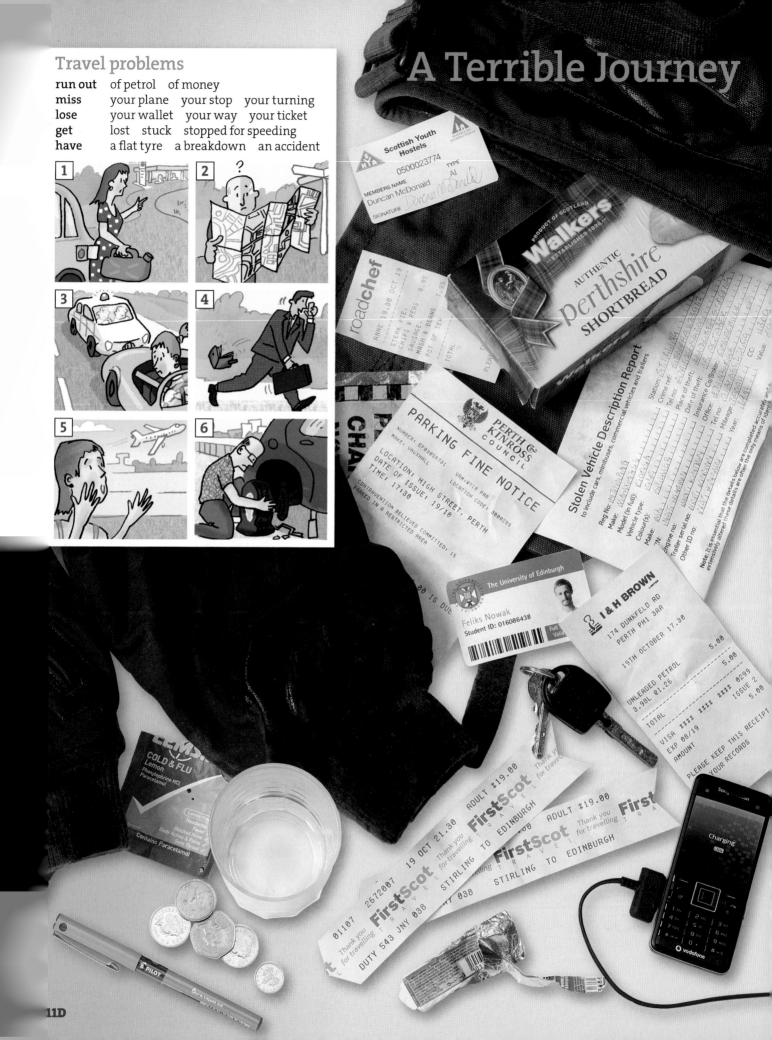

Travel problems

run out	of petrol	of money	
miss	your plane	your stop	your turning
lose	your wallet	your way	your ticket
get	lost	stuck	stopped for speeding
have	a flat tyre	a breakdown	an accident

How to give extra information

G non-defining relative clauses V travel problems P non-defining relative clauses

A Vocabulary travel problems

1 Describe the pictures in **Travel problems** opposite. Use phrases from the box.

Example 1 = She's run out of petrol.

2 Which problems are connected with car travel? Have you ever had any of these problems? Tell your partner.

B Listen for factual information

3 Look at **A Terrible Journey** opposite and guess what happened in the story. Work with a partner and write notes about these topics.

places people weather problems

4 **11D.1▶** Feliks tells Fiona about his terrible journey. Listen and tick ✓ the words and phrases you wrote in exercise 3.

5 Listen again. What happened in each of these places? Make notes and compare with a partner.

The Highlands → Perth → Stirling → Edinburgh

6 Feliks doesn't know how to say the sentences below in English. What does he say instead? Check the audio script on **>> p.158**.

1 We ran out of petrol.
2 The car was missing.
3 His batteries were flat.

7 Imagine you are telling your partner the things below but you don't know the words in green. Use other words with a similar meaning and ask for help like Feliks did.

1 I got stopped by the police for speeding.
2 I had a breakdown while I was driving to London.
3 I took the wrong turning off the motorway and got lost.
4 I got stuck in traffic on my way to work.

C Grammar non-defining relative clauses

8 Look at the grammar box and answer questions 1–3.

	question	When was it?
a	defining	It was during the time when (or that) I was living in Scotland.
b	non-defining	It was four years ago, when I was living in Scotland.

Note: you can't use 'that' for non-defining relative clauses.

1 In which sentence is the clause in blue very important for the meaning of the sentence? In which sentence is it simply extra information?
2 If you remove the clause in blue, which sentence still answers the question *When was it?*
3 Which relative clause has a comma before it?

9 Complete the sentences with these words. Compare with a partner.

~~where~~ which whose when who

1 It was in Edinburgh, *where* I was a student.
2 It was four years ago, _____ I was studying at university.
3 It was with Duncan, _____ was my flatmate.
4 I got petrol on my coat, _____ was new.
5 It was worse for Duncan, _____ car it was, because he never got it back.

10 **11D.2▶ Pronunciation** Listen and say A or B.

A defining	B non-defining
I changed the tyre which was flat.	I changed the tyre, which was flat.
They stopped the driver who was speeding.	They stopped the driver, who was speeding.
The man who was lost asked for help.	The man, who was lost, asked for help.

11 Read the information about Feliks. Add non-defining relative clauses to the sentences to give extra details.

Feliks is from Katowice. He's a nurse in London. He's coming to Edinburgh next weekend. He bought a new car last month. I once stayed with Feliks's parents – their house is by the seaside.

1 When I was at university, I shared a flat with Feliks, *who's from Katowice.*
2 Feliks moved to London,
3 I'm going to see him next weekend,
4 He's coming in his new car,
5 I once stayed with Feliks's parents,

12 Work with a partner. Look again at **A Terrible Journey**. Take turns telling the story from memory and ask your partner questions if they miss any details.

More practice? **Grammar Bank >> p.146**.

ABC Put it all together

13 Think of a bad journey you've made. Write notes about the times, places, people, and objects in the journey.

Example times   *four years ago ...*

14 Think of extra details which you could give about some of your notes. Write the end of the sentence.

Example ... four years ago, when I was living in Scotland.

15 Work in small groups. Tell the others about your bad journey. If you don't know how to say something in English, explain in other words and ask the others for help. Whose journey was the worst?

I can give extra information.

Tick ✓ the line.   with a lot of help   with some help   on my own   very easily

Writing   A website recommendation

A Read for general information

1 How do you decide which places to visit while you're on holiday? Choose from the list and discuss your answers with a partner.

guide books   recommendations from friends
organized tours   the Internet   asking local people   other …

2 Read the travel recommendation. Match the paragraphs with these questions.

a ☐ What do I need to take?
b ☐ Where is it and what is it?
c ☐ Are there any problems?
d ☐ What will I be able to see and do?

3 Look at the words and phases below with a partner. Which paragraph would you use them in? Which words and phrases tell us the order of events? Which introduce a contrasting idea?

group 1   first, then, after that, finally
group 2   unfortunately, however

B Brainstorm ideas

4 The writer of the travel recommendation brainstormed ideas by drawing a mind map. Tick the ideas on the mind map which were used in the final text.

5 Read these tips for drawing a mind map. Which two are probably not good ideas?
1 Put the main topic in a circle in the middle.
2 Think of words connected with the topic and write them around it.
3 Make a list of words, and then copy them in the correct place in the mind map.
4 Try to put words which are connected with each other in the same area of the map.
5 Use your best handwriting.

6 Work with a partner. Think of a good place for an excursion which you both know. Draw a mind map.

AB Put it all together

7 Your friend is going to visit an area you know. Write a website recommendation about an excursion in that area. Use your mind map from exercise 6, or draw a new one. Use the paragraph and text building ideas from exercises 2 and 3.

8 Read your partner's recommendation. Can you find the answers to the questions in exercise 2 easily?

A travel recommendation

e   _ ☐ ✕

1 If you're going to Crete, you ought to see the Samariá Gorge, which is in the west of the island. It's a really spectacular gorge and it passes through some enormous mountains.

2 It's a 16-kilometre walk from the head of the gorge to the sea, and it takes about five to seven hours. You need to wear some strong walking shoes and a sun hat. You don't need to carry a lot of water because there are springs along the path, but you need to carry enough food for the day.

3 First of all, you take a bus to the head of the gorge. You have to pay €5 to enter, and then you just follow the path, which is clearly marked. About halfway along, you pass an abandoned village, and after that you pass through a narrow gap between massive walls of rock. This is the most spectacular part of the walk. Finally you reach a village on the coast called Agía Rouméli, where you can have a swim and a snack. There are no roads, so you have to catch a ferry out.

4 Unfortunately, hundreds of tourists visit the gorge and it gets quite crowded. However, I think it's worth it, because it's so spectacular.

(mind map)

west
Crete
Greece — where
mountains   beach — see — wildlife   abandoned village   walls of rock
bus
ferry — transport
Samariá Gorge
problems — tired legs   hot   crowds
good shoes
food   need   rucksack   sun hat
swim   do — walk 5-7 hrs   take photos   picnic

I can write a website recommendation.

Tick ✓ the line.   with a lot of help   with some help   on my own   very easily

A Grammar

1 Indirect questions Put the words in order to make questions.

1 Can is me office tell the ticket where you
   _Can you tell me where the ticket office is_____?

2 Do four is know platform where you
   _____?

3 a bank Can here if me near tell there's you
   _____?

4 Do know open shops the tomorrow whether you are
   _____?

2 to have something done Complete the sentences with the *to have something done* form of the verb. Then change the sentences to make them true for you.

1 I _haven't had my teeth checked_ for nearly two years.
   my teeth/not check

2 I _____ about once a month. my hair/cut

3 I don't like _____. my photograph/take

4 I'd like _____ by a professional. my nails/cut

5 I've never _____ to me in bed. my breakfast/serve

3 have to, need to, should, ought to Complete the text with these words. Note that *have* and *need* are both possible in some of the gaps.

have   have   ~~need~~   need   ought   should   should

If you're planning to go to Ethiopia, you [1] _need_ to get a visa. You'll [2] _____ to take your passport to the nearest consulate to get one. You'll [3] _____ to have some injections too – you [4] _____ ask about this at your health centre. You don't [5] _____ to take malaria pills in the mountains, but you [6] _____ carry some pills in case you decide to go to the lowlands. You [7] _____ to take some water purification tablets too.

4 Non-defining relative clauses Copy the sentences and add the extra information in the brackets as a non-defining relative clause.

1 I met Annie in Turkey (I was working there as a teacher).
   I met Annie in Turkey, where I was working as a teacher.

2 I shared a flat with John (he was from Portsmouth).
   _____

3 We lived in Izmir (it's on the west coast of Turkey).
   _____

4 I left Turkey two years later (my contract finished then).
   _____

B Vocabulary

5 The street Look at the map and complete the missing words in the directions.

Go straight on to the [1]_T-junction_. Then walk across the [2]b_____ over the [3]c_____. Walk along the [4]p_____ to the car [5]p_____. Go along the street, past the taxi [6]r_____. Go straight over the [7]cross_____ and along the pedestrian [8]s_____, past the town hall. Finally, go straight across at the [9]r_____.

6 Describing holiday accommodation Match 1–8 with a–h.

1 [g] an elegant   a rooms
2 [d] some delightful b meal
3 [ ] a delicious   c waiters
4 [ ] a secluded   d ~~views~~
5 [ ] comfortable   e service
6 [ ] efficient   f countryside
7 [ ] magnificent   g ~~building~~
8 [ ] some friendly   h location

7 Health and travel Circle the words that go together to make compound nouns.

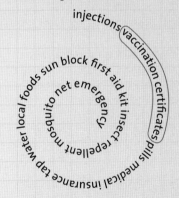

injections / vaccination certificates / pills / medical insurance / tap water / local foods / sun block / first aid kit / insect repellent / mosquito net / emergency

8 Travel problems Write the correct form of these verbs in the gaps.

~~get~~   get   lose   miss   miss   run out

What a terrible journey! First of all, we [1]_got_ lost. Then we [2]_____ our turning off the motorway and had to turn back. Then we [3]_____ of petrol and had a flat tyre. After that, we [4]_____ stopped for speeding. In the end, we arrived at the airport too late and we [5]_____ our plane. And just to complete the disaster, when we got back to the car, I discovered that I'd [6]_____ my keys!

African Stories

The Bread Seller's Trick

Once upon a time, there was a dishonest bread seller at the village market. She arrived early to get a good place and put her basket of bread under the market tree. Then she went to hide in the bushes.

A little while later, a meat seller arrived and sat down. She was hungry because she hadn't had time to eat that morning. She noticed the basket of bread and wondered who it belonged to. 'Whose bread is this?' she shouted. Nobody answered, so she repeated the question a few times. Finally, she decided that there was no owner so she took some of the bread to eat.

After seeing this, the bread seller came out of her hiding place. She said, 'You've taken some of my bread so you must give me some meat to pay for it.' The meat seller refused so the bread seller called the other sellers to support her.

The other sellers came and stood by the two women. They listened to their stories in order to decide who was right and who was wrong. Finally they decided that the bread seller had left the bread there to trick the meat seller. She didn't deserve to be paid because she had wanted the meat seller to take some bread.

The Smell of Soup

Once upon a time, there were two neighbours. One of the neighbours was a poor woman. She couldn't afford to make soup, so she had to eat just dry bread. One day, her richer neighbour was cooking soup. It smelt delicious, so the poor woman went to ask for a little. The richer woman refused. She sent the poor woman away with nothing because she thought she was lazy and didn't deserve any soup. However, the poor woman didn't go away. She sat outside the richer woman's house in order to enjoy the smell of the soup. Even the smell was better than nothing.

After that, the poor woman sat outside her neighbour's house every day because she liked smelling the soup. The richer woman became angry, so she went to the chief to complain. She explained the problem to him. 'My neighbour is stealing the smell of my soup,' she said. 'She is a thief so she must be punished!'

The chief said, 'I agree. She must be punished, and you must punish her. Take this stick and beat her shadow.' The richer woman did this and felt really stupid. From that day on, she gave her poor neighbour some soup to go with her bread.

How to explain your point of view

G *so, because, (in order) to*   P **keeping your turn**

A   Read and follow

1   Look at the photos opposite. What are the stories about?

2   Work in pairs. Look at **African Stories** opposite. Write a list of the characters in your story.
   Student A   Read **The Bread Seller's Trick**.
   Student B   Read **The Smell of Soup**.

3   Read your story again and complete the notes in the box.

structure	The Bread Seller's Trick	The Smell of Soup
1st woman	bread seller	poor neighbour
2nd woman		
1st woman's action	left basket of bread under tree and hid in bushes	
2nd woman's action		refused to give soup
1st woman's response		
2nd woman's response	asked other sellers to support her	
final result		rich neighbour allowed to beat poor neighbour's shadow

4   Tell your story to your partner from your notes. Listen to your partner's story and complete the notes in the box.

5   Work with a partner. Answer the questions.
   1   The moral of **The Bread Seller's Trick** is *If you trick someone into taking something, you don't deserve to be paid for it.* What do you think is the moral of **The Smell of Soup**?
   2   Do you completely agree with the morals?
   3   Do you think both stories could be true?

B   Grammar *so, because, (in order) to*

6   Read the grammar boxes and complete the rules.

result	cause	result
She was hungry	because she hadn't eaten.	
	She hadn't eaten	so she was hungry.

action	purpose
She arrived early	(in order) to find a good place.

Rules
1   Use *because* to give a cause.
2   Use _____ to give a result.
3   Use _____ to give a purpose.

7   Underline examples of *so*, *because*, and *(in order) to* in **African Stories**.

8   Work with a partner. Make sentences with *so*, *because*, and *(in order) to* from the information.
   1   I'm tired. I didn't sleep well. I want to go home. I need to rest.
      Example   I'm tired because I didn't sleep well.
      I didn't sleep well so I'm tired.
      I want to go home to rest.
   2   I passed the exams. I'm happy. I'm going out. I want to celebrate.
   3   I'm running. I'm late. I want to catch the bus.

   More practice? **Grammar Bank >>** p.147.

C   Listen for points of view

9   **12A.1▶** Listen. Serge and Lucia are discussing **The Smell of Soup** story. What are Lucia's opinions about the rich woman, the chief, and the idea of stealing a smell? Does Serge agree?

10   **12A.2▶** Listen. What is the next part of Serge and Lucia's conversation about?

11   Do Serge and Lucia have the same point of view on the topic? Do you agree with them? Tell a partner.

12   **12A.3▶ Pronunciation** Listen and read these phrases from the conversation. Why do the speakers make the words in blue long? Choose the best option.
   ... the chief's very clever, b-e-c-a-u-s-e e-h he shows her ...
   ... stealing a smell is l-i-k-e like hitting a shadow ...
   ... you know s-o e-h-m so it's like the smell of soup ...
   ... people use your Internet connection in order t-o to get free Internet ...

   They pronounce the words longer ...
   a   to give themselves time to think what to say.
   b   to make their opinion stronger.

13   Listen again and repeat the phrases, including the long pronunciation.

14   Look at audio scripts **12A.1** and **12A.2** on **>>** p.158. Underline sentences with these phrases to give opinions.
   I think ...   I don't think ...   To me, ...   In my opinion, ...

ABC   Put it all together

15   Read **Is it stealing?** on **>>** p.132 and decide your answers to the questions. Then discuss your point of view in pairs or small groups. Do you agree or disagree?

I can explain my point of view.

Three Wishes

1 I wish people would stop fighting and I wish there were no more wars. I hope there will be peace in the world one day in the future.
David, 7

2 I wish I had a genie. I would call him Aladdin. If I wanted anything, I could just call for Aladdin and make a wish.
Timothy, 5

3 This is me and my best friend Zoë. I wish she lived in my house. Then we could play together all day. I'm glad she's coming to my birthday party. I can't wait!
Grace, 6

Desert Island Joke

How to talk about hopes and wishes

G *wish*   V *wish, hope, be glad*   P contrastive stress

A   Vocabulary *wish, hope, be glad*

1 Work with a partner. Read **Three Wishes** opposite.
Match pictures a–c with texts 1–3.

2 Match the blue words with the definitions.

I'm glad she's coming ...
I hope there will be peace ...
I wish she lived in my house ...

1 to want something which is possible for the future (vb)   *hope*
2 to want something which is impossible for now or the past (vb)
3 happy about a situation (adj)

3 Make true sentences from the box. Tell a partner.

I wish I had a	million dollars car mobile phone
I'm glad I've got a	child dog new computer
I hope one day I'll have a	home of my own friend like you! *other*

B   Listen and predict

4 Look at **Desert Island Joke** opposite. What can you guess from the pictures about the story?

5 Guess who says these sentences with a partner.
1 I wish I was somewhere far away from here.   *Lofty*
2 Oh, it's not so bad.
3 I hope a passing ship rescues us.
4 I hope I never see another coconut again in my life!
5 I'm glad I've got my guitar.
6 I wish you hadn't saved the guitar. It's driving me crazy.
7 Look what I've found.

6 **12B.1▶** Listen to part 1 of the joke and check your answers. Then predict what will happen next.

7 **12B.2▶** Listen to part 2 of the joke and check your predictions. Then predict the end of the joke.

8 **12B.3▶** Listen and check. Do you think the joke is funny?

C   Grammar *wish*

9 Underline sentences with *wish* in audio scripts **12B.1▶** – **12B.3▶** on **>>** p.158–159. Is *wish* a noun or a verb?

10 What is the meaning of this sentence? Underline the correct word in the explanations.

Shorty   'I wish I had a new guitar.'
1 Shorty has/hasn't got a new guitar.
2 Shorty wants a new guitar now/in the past.
3 The verb *had* is in the past tense but the meaning is past/present/future.

11 Complete the grammar box. What are the rules for the tense of the verb after *wish*?

real situation	wish
I'm not rich.	I wish I was* rich.
I don't have a car.	
	I wish I didn't work in a shop.
I can't speak German.	
	I wish they would listen to me.

*or *were*

12 Fill the gaps in these short conversations with positive ⊞ or negative ⊟ forms of verbs. Compare with a partner.
1 **A** I wish I ⊞ *lived*   in a big city.
   B Really? I wish I ⊟ *didn't live*   in a big city.
2 **A** I wish I ⊞ _____ an office job.
   B Really? I wish I ⊟ _____ an office job.
3 **A** I wish I ⊞ _____ speak Arabic.
   B Really? I wish I ⊞ _____ speak Chinese.
4 **A** I wish I ⊞ _____ older.
   B Really? I wish I ⊟ _____ so old!
5 **A** I wish people ⊞ _____ drive more carefully on the motorway.
   B Really? I wish people ⊞ _____ drive more carefully everywhere!

More practice? **Grammar Bank >>** p.147.

D   Pronunciation contrastive stress

13 **12B.4▶** Listen. Explain why B stresses the words in **bold**.
A I wish I lived in a big city.
B Really? **I** wish **I** **did**n't live in a big city.

14 Which words make a contrast? Underline the two stressed words in each of B's lines in exercise 12.

15 **12B.5▶** Listen, check, and repeat.

16 Work with a partner. Say your sentences from exercise 3 again. Respond with a contrasting sentence.
Example   **A** I wish I had a dog.
         B Really? I'm glad I haven't got a dog.

ABCD   Put it all together

17 Look at **Wish box** on **>>** p.133 and complete the sentences about yourself.

18 Show your **Wish box** to your partner. Ask and answer about the words and names.

I can talk about hopes and wishes.   ■■■■

Tick ✓ the line.   with a lot of help   with some help   on my own   very easily

///THE BOOKSHELF DETECTIVE///

What can you learn about people from their book collections? Here are some questions to consider …

1 How many books are there?
2 Is there a wide variety, or are all the books similar?
3 What genres of fiction are there?
4 Are there any textbooks? What subjects are they?
5 Are there other kinds of books – cookery, computer manuals, and so on?
6 How 'used' do they look?
7 Have they been bought as sets, or one by one?
8 What languages are they in?
9 Are there a lot of best-sellers?
10 How are they kept and organized?

Antique Book Covers

1 What will people read in history textbooks in the year 2106? Dr Phillip Raven sees the book in his dreams and writes down all that he can remember. First of all, there is a world war which lasts nearly 30 years. Civilization is almost destroyed by a killer virus, and after that, the world is controlled by a dictatorship. This book, written in 1933, is full of predictions, and many of them have already turned out to be true. Perhaps the pages contain the shape of more things to come?

2 Two wagons leave Kansas heading along the Oregon Trail for a new life in the west. One of the wagons is driven by Sam, a violent man, and the other is driven by a charming captain called Will. Both men compete for the love of the same woman. She is a pretty passenger called Molly. Their journey is full of difficulty and dangers, including dry deserts and high mountains. They are also attacked by Indians. But who will Molly choose to be with when they reach their journey's end?

a   b   c   d

3 Eighteenth-century London; in a dark, narrow alley off Fleet Street there is a barber's shop. The owner is a man called Sweeney Todd, and nobody is more skilful with a razor. Todd's closest friend is the baker, Mrs Lovett. Her bakery is famous for its tasty meat pies. When men in the neighbourhood begin to disappear, people suspect that Sweeney Todd is responsible. They see customers going into his shop, but nobody can remember seeing them come out. But if Sweeney Todd is a murderer, what has he done with the bodies?

4 Allan Quartermain is an English hunter living in Africa. One day, a man called Henry Curtis approaches him asking for help. Henry's brother has gone into the heart of Africa to look for King Solomon's mines and hasn't returned. Henry wants to rescue him – and perhaps find the mines, which contain a treasure of gold, diamonds, and ivory. He offers Allan a share of the treasure … if they can reach the mines. But first they must get past the fierce Kukuana warriors and their king.

How to describe the plot of a story

G *-ing* and *-ed* clauses   V stories, books, fiction   P *well* and *anyway*

A Read plot descriptions

1 Answer the questions in **The Bookshelf Detective** opposite about your book collection. You can use a dictionary. Ask the questions to your partner.

2 Say what you think your partner's book collection shows about him or her.
   Example You've got a lot of old textbooks – perhaps you used to be a student.

3 Look at the pictures in **Antique Book Covers** opposite, but don't read the texts. What can you guess about the stories? Answer the questions with a partner.
   1 Which genre does the story belong to? Choose one or more for each book.
   adventure   fantasy   horror   murder mystery
   romance   science fiction   western
   2 Which story do you think you will find these things in? Use your dictionary if necessary.
   barber   diamonds   dictatorship   hunter   Indian
   ivory   killer virus   love   murderer   razor   treasure
   wagon   war   warriors
   3 What can you guess about the setting, characters, and plot?

4 Read texts 1–4 and match them with covers a–d. Check your guesses in exercise 3.

5 Write *true*, *false*, or *doesn't say*.
   1 Mrs Lovett's bakery sells pies.   *True*
   2 Sweeney Todd is definitely a murderer.
   3 Phillip Raven often sees books in his dreams.
   4 *The Shape of Things to Come* was written over 70 years ago.
   5 Sam, Will, and Molly are travelling west.
   6 Molly prefers Will to Sam.
   7 Allan travels to the heart of Africa to rescue Henry.
   8 Henry's brother is inside the mines.

6 Which of these books would you most like to read? Why? Tell your partner.

B Grammar *-ing* and *-ed* clauses

7 Look at **Antique Book Covers** again. Underline sentences with the same meaning as the pairs of sentences below.
   1 The owner is a man. He is called Sweeney Todd.
   The owner is a man called Sweeney Todd.
   2 They see customers. They are going into his shop.
   3 This book is full of predictions. It was written in 1933.
   4 She is a pretty passenger. She is called Molly.
   5 Allan Quartermain is an English hunter. He's living in Africa.

8 Look at the grammar box. Make one sentence with an *-ing* or *-ed* clause from the pairs of sentences below.

	-ing clause	*-ed* clause
	He's a hunter.	The passenger was a woman.
+	He's living in Africa.	She was called Molly.
=	He's a hunter living in Africa.	The passenger was a woman called Molly.

   1 He found a painting. It was stolen from the Louvre.
   He found a painting stolen from the Louvre.
   2 They see a thief. He's stealing the diamonds.
   3 He finds a box. It was covered in gold.
   4 It's about a civilization. It was destroyed by war.
   5 It's about two men. They're fighting for survival.

   More practice? **Grammar Bank** >> p.147.

C Listen to a plot description

9 **12C.1▶** Listen to a description of a best-seller. Do you know the title? Have you read it? Tell a partner.

10 Write notes on these topics then listen again to check.
   genre   set in   characters   start of story

11 What can you remember about the story? Tell a partner.

D Pronunciation *well* and *anyway*

12 Read audio script **12C.1▶** on >> p.159. Underline the words *well* and *anyway*. Match them with these meanings.
   We use this word to show …
   a that we're moving on to the next part of the story.
   b that we're starting our description of the story.

13 **12C.2▶** Listen and repeat these sentences. *Well* and *anyway* are said in a high voice so that the listener notices.
   Well, it's a murder mystery.
   Anyway, it starts when they find a body.
   Well, it's a romance.
   Anyway, she meets an attractive stranger.
   Well, it's an adventure story.
   Anyway, they start their journey.

ABCD Put it all together

14 Think of a story you've read or seen. Make notes about the genre, setting, characters, and plot.

15 Work in pairs or small groups. Tell the others about your story. Listen to the other stories. Do you know them?
   Example Well, I read a story called …

I can describe the plot of a story. ▬▬▬▬▬▬
Tick ✓ the line.   with a lot of help   with some help   on my own   very easily   121

Extreme Decisions

1 Monica was putting up a shelf when she dropped a piece of wood from the window of her flat by mistake. It fell on a man's head. He fell into the road and a car hit him and killed him. The driver thought he was responsible. Nobody had seen the piece of wood fall, so Monica didn't tell the police.

2 Fernando was a prisoner of war. The enemy captain told him to shoot another prisoner. 'If you don't kill one, I will kill two,' he said. Fernando refused and the captain shot two prisoners.

3 Basia was travelling with her teenage daughter in a country where the penalties for smuggling are very severe. The customs officers found prohibited goods in her daughter's bag and asked, 'Whose bag is this?' Basia said it was hers so she was arrested.

4 A group of passengers were stuck on a high mountain after a plane crash. Many of the passengers had died in the crash and their bodies were lying around in the snow. It was impossible for the survivors to walk to safety, and there was no food. After a few days, they decided to eat the frozen bodies in the snow.

5 Jim and Neil's car broke down in the desert. They started to walk but Jim fell and broke his leg. He couldn't walk without help from Neil. The nearest water was two days' walk away but with Jim's broken leg it would take a week, and they couldn't survive that long without water. Jim told Neil to go alone. Neil did this and Jim died.

6 There was a cruel landlord who everybody feared and hated. One day, Ernesto was in a fight with the landlord and killed him, but nobody saw the crime. Ernesto told his best friend Toni about it and Toni promised to keep the secret. Some time later, an innocent man was wrongly accused of the crime and sentenced to death. Toni told the police what Ernesto had told him.

Karen's Life Map

leave school	study French at university	move to Los Angeles	get job as secretary in film company
travel to America	meet Martin	get married	be offered a part in a movie
return to Britain	become a French teacher	stay in New York	become an actor

How to talk about important decisions

G 3rd conditional   P *would have*

A   Read for detail

1 Put these decisions in order from easy to difficult.

☐ what to have for lunch   ☐ what career to choose
☐ whether to get married   ☐ whether to have children
☐ where to live   ☐ where to go on holiday

2 Read **Extreme Decisions** opposite. Say which story.

a ☐3☐ A parent saved her daughter from prison.
b ☐ A person refused to kill someone.
c ☐ A person broke a promise.
d ☐ People found an extreme method of survival.
e ☐ A person kept quiet about what happened.
f ☐ A person left a friend to die.

3 Match each story with the final sentences below.

a ☐2☐ If Fernando had shot a prisoner, the captain would probably have shot another one anyway.
b ☐ If he hadn't, the innocent man would have died.
c ☐ If Neil had stayed with Jim, he would have died too.
d ☐ If she'd told them, she'd have been in a lot of trouble.
e ☐ If they hadn't, they would have died.
f ☐ If they'd known it was her daughter's bag, her daughter would have been arrested.

4 Discuss with a partner. Which decision was the most difficult? Did any of the people make the wrong decision?

B   Grammar 3rd conditional

5 Read the sentence and answer the questions.

if clause	main clause
If Neil had stayed with Jim,	he would have died, too.

1 Did Neil stay with Jim?
2 Did Jim die?
3 Is the sentence about the past or present?
4 Is the sentence about a real or imagined result?
5 How do you form the verb ...
   a in the *if* clause?   b in the main clause?

6 Complete these sentences with a partner.

1 If Monica *had* told the police, they *would* have arrested her.
2 If Fernando _____ shot a prisoner, the result would probably have _____ the same.
3 If Basia hadn't _____ the bag was hers, her daughter would _____ been in trouble.
4 The survivors _____ have died if they _____ eaten the bodies in the snow.
5 Neil wouldn't _____ gone if Jim _____ asked him to stay.
6 If the police _____ arrested an innocent man, Toni _____ have stayed silent.

7 Underline the correct words to make these sentences true about your school days.

1 I was/wasn't good at maths so I passed/didn't pass the exams.
2 I lived/didn't live near school so I walked/didn't walk there.
3 I liked/didn't like music so I wanted/didn't want to learn an instrument.

8 Write a conditional sentence about the *opposite* situation from your sentences in exercise 7.

Example   I was/wasn't good at maths so I passed/didn't pass the exams.
If I hadn't been good at maths, I wouldn't have passed the exams.

9 **12D.1▶ Pronunciation** Listen and repeat the sentences. Notice the pronunciation of *would have* and *wouldn't have*.

I would have /wʊ dəv/ (done the same/waited/ said something/kept quiet/tried to escape)
I wouldn't have /wʊdn təv/ (done that/said that/ made that choice)

10 What would or wouldn't you have done in the situations in **Extreme Decisions**? Tell your partner.
More practice? **Grammar Bank** >> p.147.

C   Listen for detail

11 Look at **Karen's Life Map** opposite. Guess some of the things she has done in her life. Tell a partner.

Example   I guess she's been to university.

12 **12D.2** Listen to Karen describing the important decisions she has made in her life. Draw her route through the life map from leaving school to becoming an actor.

13 What were Karen's important decisions and what would have happened if she'd decided differently?

Example   Her decision to travel to America was important. If she hadn't gone, she wouldn't have met Martin.

ABC   Put it all together

14 Make a list of three or four important decisions or moments in your or your family's life.

Example   When I was young, my family moved to ...

15 Work in pairs or small groups. Tell the others about your decisions. Say what would have happened if you'd made the opposite decision.

I can talk about important decisions.

Tick ✓ the line.   with a lot of help   with some help   on my own   very easily

Writing A story with a moral

A Read a story with a moral

1 Work with a partner. Complete the sayings with these nouns.

baby ~~bird~~ book eggs hand houses

1 A _bird_ in the hand is worth two in the bush.
2 Don't bite the _____ that feeds you.
3 Don't put all of your _____ in one basket.
4 People who live in glass _____ shouldn't throw stones.
5 Don't throw the _____ out with the bathwater.
6 Never judge a _____ by its cover.

2 Work with a partner and answer the questions about the sayings in exercise 1.

1 What do you think the sayings mean? Match them with these meanings.
   a ☐ Don't choose things just because they look nice.
   b ☐ Don't keep all of your valuables in one place.
   c ☐ Don't say bad things about a person who's helping you.
   d ☑ It's better to have one thing for certain, than just a possibility of having two.
   e ☐ People who have done bad things shouldn't talk about other people doing bad things.
   f ☐ When you are changing old things for new, be careful not to lose good things too.

2 Are there similar sayings in your country?

3 Read this story and add a saying from exercise 1.

A Heart of Gold

Mrs Goodwill lived alone in a big old house. She wasn't strong enough to do a lot of cleaning so the place was filthy. The paint was falling off the window frames because she couldn't afford to keep the house in good condition. She wanted to sell the place and move somewhere smaller, but nobody would buy it.

Mrs Goodwill never used the upstairs, so she decided to rent it out in order to earn some extra cash. She advertised in the paper and rented the rooms to the first person who called. He was a young man called Mick, with a shaved head, a torn leather jacket, and a broken nose. One day, Mrs Goodwill's daughter Hillary came to visit, and when she saw Mick, she was horrified. 'Mother, he looks like a criminal,' she said, 'If I'd been here, I wouldn't have let him through the door!'

Hillary didn't visit again until three months later, and when she arrived, she couldn't believe her eyes. The house was beautifully clean, all the window frames were newly painted, and Mick was in the garden cutting the grass. 'Mick's been helping me a lot,' Mrs Goodwill explained, 'That boy's got a heart of gold!'

Moral: _____

4 Complete these sentences.

1 Mrs Goodwill's house was filthy because … *she wasn't strong enough to clean it.*
2 She couldn't afford to keep the house in good condition so …
3 She put an advert in the paper in order to …
4 Hillary was horrified because …
5 Hillary couldn't believe her eyes because …

B Think about paragraph structure

5 Cover the story in exercise 3. What extra information can you remember from paragraphs 1–3? Note key words and phrases with a partner.

Paragraph structure

para 1 – **situation** old woman lived in house in bad condition *filthy, paint falling …*

para 2 – **action** rented rooms to man called Mick; daughter didn't like him

para 3 – **result** Mick helped old woman a lot; daughter surprised

para 4 – **moral** Never judge a book by its cover.

6 Work with a partner. Decide how to finish these story outlines. Write notes for the missing parts.

1 **situation** woman won lottery
   action she invested all her money in an Internet company
   result _____
   moral Don't put all of your eggs in one basket.

2 **situation** politician said another politician was corrupt
   action the police investigated
   result _____
   moral People who live in glass houses shouldn't throw stones.

3 **situation** a man looking for work got a good job offer
   action he refused because he thought he could get a better offer
   result _____
   moral A bird in the hand is worth two in the bush.

AB Put it all together

7 Work with a partner. Choose one of the story outlines in exercise 6, or think of another. Add more notes to the situation, action, and result paragraphs.

8 Write your story. Don't include the moral at the end.

9 Work in groups. Read out your story to the others. Listen to the other stories. What is the moral? Does the story fit the moral well?

I can write a story with a moral. ████████

Tick ✓ the line.   with a lot of help   with some help   on my own   very easily

Unit 12 Review

A Grammar

1 *so, because, (in order) to* Complete the sentences with *so, because,* or *(in order) to.*

1 The grass is wet _because_ it's been raining.
2 It's been raining _____ the grass is wet.
3 She went to bed _____ she was tired.
4 She went home _____ rest.
5 I went to the market _____ buy some food.
6 I needed some food _____ I went to the market.

2 *wish* Complete the text with the correct form of the verbs in brackets.

Three wishes
OK, first – I wish I [1] _lived_ (live) somewhere nice. I wish I [2]_____ (not live) in a noisy city with terrible weather. Second – I wish I [3]_____ (be) rich. I wish I [4]_____ (not have) to work every day. And my third wish – I wish I [5]_____ (can speak) lots of languages. I wish people around the world [6]_____ (will communicate) with each other instead of fighting.

3 *-ing* and *-ed* clauses Complete the sentences with the verbs in the correct form to make *-ing* and *-ed* clauses.

1 The baby was in a bag _left_ on the step. Nobody saw the mother _leaving_ it. leave
2 Harry was in a pub _____ the Red Lion. He was on the phone _____ the police. call
3 There was a message on the wall _____ in red paint. No one was seen _____ it. write
4 There was a hole and there were dry leaves _____ it. Jim fell into it and came out _____ in mud. cover

4 3rd conditional Write sentences in the third conditional to give the opposite situation.

1 I ate the fish and I felt sick.
   If I hadn't eaten the fish, _I wouldn't have felt sick._
2 The CD was good so I bought it.
   If the CD hadn't been good, _____
3 It wasn't raining so we went out.
   If it had been _____
4 I heard a noise so I phoned the police.
   _____
5 They didn't study so they failed the test.
   _____

B Vocabulary

5 *wish, hope, be glad* Complete the sentences with these phrases.

I wish   I hope   I'm glad

1 Here's a little present for you. _I hope_ you like it.
2 **A** Thanks for the present. I love it.
   B You're welcome. _____ you like it!
3 _____ it would stop raining! I've got to go out to the shops.
4 _____ my flat wasn't so small. I haven't got enough space for my books.
5 _____ I'll have a job by this time next year.
6 _____ I've got a book to read, otherwise I'd be bored to death.

6 Stories, books, fiction Do the crossword.

Across
2 A genre: murder _____.
4 What happens in a story.
6 A genre with a lot of action.
8 The story happened in London. It is _____ in London.
9 A person in a story.
10 Something which happened, real or fiction.
11 A love story.
12 A book that thousands of people buy.

Down
1 A group of objects of the same sort, e.g. a book _____.
2 The person who kills in 2 across.
3 A genre: _____ fiction.
5 A story about cowboys and Indians.
7 A collection of gold, diamonds, jewellery, and other valuables.

Pairwork

1B Put it all together
Student A Two countries

Make notes to answer these questions.
1. How do people greet each other?
2. How do they address each other?
3. What do people say when they meet?

1 China
The Chinese bow slightly when they greet each other, and they often shake hands when they meet people for the first time. The handshake is not very strong, and it lasts quite a long time. People address each other by their surname and a title such as Mr or Mrs, Doctor or Teacher. They never use the surname without a title. The most common greeting in formal situations is 'How are you?' while in informal situations they often ask, 'Have you eaten?' People often reply, 'Yes, I have' to this question to be polite, so the other person doesn't have to offer food.

2 Jamaica
When Jamaicans meet for the first time, it is normal to shake hands, smile, and look each other in the eye. When people know each other better, women usually hug each other and kiss each other on both cheeks, starting with the right. Men often touch each other on the arm while greeting. To begin with, people address each other by their surname and a title such as Mr, Mrs, or Miss. Common greetings include 'Good morning', 'Good afternoon', and 'Good evening'. When people know each other, they use first names or nicknames.

1D Put it all together
Misunderstandings

In a shop …
A Can I have some pears, please?
B Some pairs of what?

At home …
A Where's the flour?
B The flower? It's in the vase on the table.

On holiday …
A How did you get here?
B Road.
A Rode what? A bike?

A stressed parent …
A I just want a little peace.
B A little piece of what?

Planning a meeting …
A Does anybody know when the meeting is?
B Mr Long knows.
A Who's Mr Long Nose?

2C Exercise 14
Object A

This is a kind of bag from Scotland, and it's called a *sporran*. Men wear it with the traditional Scottish Highland clothing. This sporran is made of fur and it has a metal part to close the top of the bag. It's used for carrying money or other things, which is useful because traditional Highland clothes don't have any pockets.

1C Put it all together
Student A Family photo

Ask and say who the people are.

Example A Who's the woman in the green T-shirt? She's sitting and talking to two other women.
B That's Clara. She's Billy's aunt. She's a graphic designer.

1. Billy. Aged 13. Loves sports. Wants to be a footballer.
3. Grace. Aged 14. Wants to be a singer.
5. Laura. Aged 15. Likes clothes. Wants to be a model.
7. Jean. Billy's mum. Works in a bank.
9. Raymond. Billy's grandfather. Retired.
11. Nina. Friend of the family. Lives in California.
13. Uncle Joe. Jean's brother. Taxi driver.
15. Belinda. Joe's girlfriend. Hairdresser.

2C Put it all together
Guess the objects

corkscrew	saw	ice cube tray	razor
nail clippers	paint brush	paper clip	drill
orange juicer	scissors	plaster	hairdryer
hole punch	tape measure	teaspoon	can-opener

3C Put it all together
Hospitality role play

Role play 1

A host	B visitor
– your visitor's coat is wet	– you've been out in the rain
– your visitor looks hungry	– you had dinner half an hour ago
– the radio is very loud	– you've got a headache
– your visitor looks bored	– you'd like to watch the news on TV
– your visitor looks thirsty	– you'd like a cup of tea

Role play 2

B host	A visitor
– your visitor looks very hot	– you've been playing tennis
– your dog is jumping on your visitor	– you love dogs
– your visitor must catch an early train tomorrow morning	– you left your alarm clock at home
– your visitor looks hungry	– you are very hungry
– your visitor goes to wash the dishes	– you want to help by washing up

4A Put it all together
Student A Feelings

Write one or two words in each shape.

1 Something you do when you're bored.
2 An amazing place you've visited.
3 An amusing film you've seen.
4 Something you're interested in.
5 Music you find exciting.
6 Something that makes you feel worried.
7 The most terrifying moment in your life.

Now look at the words in your partner's shapes and ask about them.

Example **A** Draw – what's that?
 B It's something I do when I'm bored. I draw little pictures on my notebook.
 A So when do you feel bored?
 B In meetings ...

4B Exercise 3
Are you into music? Answer Key

Calculate your partner's score.

1 Score 1 point for each tick and 1 point for the correct order: radio–records–tapes–CDs–MP3 player
2 Score 1 point for matching all three:
  a 3 **c** 2 **d** 1
3 Score 1 point for each tick.
4 Score 1 point each for **a**, **b**, **c**, and **d**. Score 3 points for **e**!
5 Score 1 point for each correct answer.
  a a grand piano is bigger than a keyboard
  b an electric guitar is louder than a Spanish guitar
  c a saxophone is heavier than a recorder
  d the violin is the smallest, the double bass is the biggest
6 Score 1 point each if you ticked **a** and **b**. Score 2 points if you ticked **c**. Score 3 points if you ticked **d**.
7 Score 1 point for getting all the correct answers and 1 point for the question.
  1 rap **2** rock **3** opera **4** country **5** jazz **6** reggae
  Opera is the oldest.
8 Score 1 point for each tick.
9 Score 1 point if you ticked **c**, and 2 points if you ticked **d**.

----

35 or more points You are a real music fan, maybe even obsessed! I don't think I'd like to share a flat with you.

Between 25 and 34 points You seem to be into music. We know what to get you for your birthday!

Between 15 and 24 points You're not especially into music. You don't mind what you listen to. Let somebody else make the party mix!

Fewer than 15 points I guess you're not too keen on music, then?

Pairwork

4B Put it all together
Music

Make notes in the table about the music, venues, and entertainment you prefer and why. Then discuss your ideas.

	I prefer ...	because ...
music	classical ...	most relaxing ...
venues	stadium ...	
entertainment	theatre ...	

4D Exercise 4
Types of film Research results

Order of preference		
	male	female
1	drama	drama
2	action	romance
3	science fiction	action
4	comedy	comedy
5	fantasy	fantasy
6	romance	musical
7	musical	science fiction

5A Put it all together
Politics

1 Who is the head of state and what is his/her title (president/prime minister/king ...)?
2 How often are there elections? Who can and can't vote?
3 What are the main parties? Which are more left wing and which are more right wing?
4 Where are the government buildings and what are they called?
5 What international organizations does the country belong to?
6 What does the flag look like? What does it represent?
7 Are there any animals, trees, or flowers which are used as symbols of the country?

5C Put it all together
Headlines

WOMAN ARRESTED IN HOUSES OF PARLIAMENT **MAN ATTACKED BY CROCODILE**

PRESIDENT'S SON KIDNAPPED **FIVE HURT IN TRAIN CRASH**

Write notes to answer these questions.
1 When and where did it happen?
2 Who were the people involved?
3 How/Why did it happen?
4 What are the details?

5E Exercise 10
Narrating a story

I was walking back to the hotel when I noticed that someone was following me. It was late at night and I was alone. This was in Barcelona. I'd been to a concert and I'd taken a taxi back to the hotel. The taxi couldn't take me to the door of the hotel because it was in a pedestrian area, so I had to walk the last 500 metres.

When I heard the footsteps behind me, I was scared and I walked faster. The person behind me walked faster too, so I started to run. The person behind me shouted, 'Stop!' but I didn't stop until I reached the hotel. At the hotel it was light and there was a night porter, so I felt safe. I had escaped from my attacker!

However, to my surprise, my attacker followed me into the hotel. But he wasn't a robber and he hadn't been trying to attack me. He was the taxi driver and he was returning my bag. I'd left it in the taxi!

6A Put it all together
Tell a story

Think of the best or worst ...
film you've seen or book you've read.
hotel or holiday place you've stayed at.
experience you've had while travelling.
experience you've had at school or work.

What happened? Why was it good or bad?

What extreme adjectives could you use to describe ...
the experience?
your feelings about it?

6B Put it all together
Student A Picture story

You are the person in the story. For each of the four pictures in the story, imagine some extra details – for example, when and where was it? How did you feel? Write notes.

6C Put it all together
Are you a good neighbour?

Interview your partner and tick ✓ the answers which are true for him/her.

1 Who do you know in your neighbourhood?
   I know the next-door neighbours.
   I know the upstairs/downstairs neighbours.
   I know some people in the building/street.
   I know some shopkeepers.
   Other ...

2 How well do you know your neighbours?
   We say hello.
   I know their names.
   We often stop for a chat.
   I often socialize with them.
   I never see them, and I'm happier that way.
   Other ...

3 What kinds of problems have you had with people in your neighbourhood?
   They're nosy.
   They're noisy.
   Their children are naughty.
   Their dog barks all day.
   They park their car in my space.
   They always complain.
   Other ...

4 How much do you help each other?
   We look after each other's pets or water each other's plants while we're away.
   We keep a key for each other in case of emergency.
   We help each other with shopping or housework.
   I go to community meetings.
   Other ...

6D Put it all together
Student A The Violin Story Part A

Sebastian, dressed in cheap clothes and carrying a violin, went into the Ritz Restaurant and had a meal. At the end, he said to the owner, 'I'm sorry. I've left my wallet at home. I'll go home and collect it. I'll leave my violin with you as security.'

Sebastian returned to the restaurant with his wallet and paid for his meal. The restaurant owner said, 'I like your violin. I'll give you $5,000 for it.' Sebastian agreed, took the money, and left.

Tell your part of the story to your partner, using reported speech. Then answer these questions with your partner.

1 How are the two parts of the story connected?
2 How much is the violin really worth?
3 Did John know Sebastian?
4 Who is telling a lie?
5 Who is the victim?

Now read the solution on >> p.133.

7A Put it all together
Portraits of men

Student A Choose a photo, but keep it secret.

The others Ask closed questions to guess which photo it is. Don't say the number until you are sure.

Example B Has he got long dark hair?
            A No, **short** dark hair.
            C Does he look happy?
            A No, he looks **worried**.

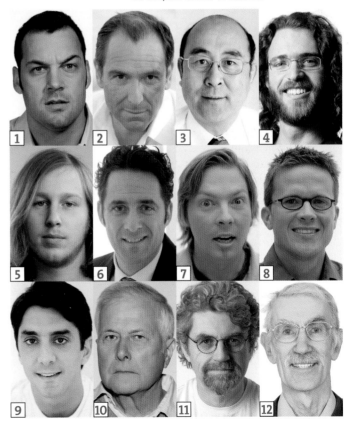

Pairwork

7D Exercise 4
The Bedroom in Arles

The picture is called 'The Bedroom' and it was painted by Vincent van Gogh (born 1853, died 1890). The room is in Arles, in the south of France. One of the portraits we see on the wall is this self-portrait by the artist.

Vincent moved to Arles from Paris in 1888 and rented this room and a couple of others. He had very little money and survived with help from his brother, Theo.

Vincent suffered from mental health problems and killed himself in 1890. The house in Arles was destroyed in the Second World War.

7D Put it all together
Two rooms – the photos

Tell your partner your guesses about the photos. Do you agree?

> *Example* **A** I think this must be a man's room.
> **B** Are you sure? It might be a woman's room.
> **A** I think it's a man's room because …

Then read about the people who live in these rooms on >> p.134. Were any of your guesses correct?

Room 1

Room 2

8A Put it all together
Phoning Frank

Choose roles, plan what you are going to say, and then do the role play.

> *Example* **A** This is the ABC Tyre Company. Can I help you?
> **B** Yes, I'd like to speak to Frank Jones on extension 123, please.

Caller

You are Mary Smith and you urgently need to speak to Frank Jones at the ABC Tyre Company. You phone the company and speak to his secretary. Ask for Mr Jones on extension 123. If he's busy, say you'll wait or call back again. You want to speak to him personally and you don't want to leave a message. You could ask for his mobile number. If you get cut off, call again. If you think the secretary is trying to stop you getting through to Mr Jones, say that you're calling about a *very* important business deal which could earn Mr Jones many thousands of euros, but you must speak to him today.

Answerer

You are Frank Jones's secretary at the ABC Tyre Company. Mr Jones has taken the afternoon off to go and play golf, but he doesn't want anybody to know. He has asked you to make excuses for him, saying he's busy in a meeting or speaking on the phone or his car's broken down or something. You could take a message or offer to put callers through to his colleague, Mrs Sandra Summers. You *mustn't* give his mobile phone number to anybody! If callers insist on speaking to Mr Jones, you could hang up and pretend that you got cut off.

8B Put it all together
Ideas

Look at these ideas. Write notes about your story in the box.

1 The first time you did something (went abroad; rode a bike; spoke in public …)
2 A time when you lost something (a key; a passport; money …)
3 A time when you wanted to do something but couldn't (start a car; find the way; remember a name …)
4 *Your ideas* …

When and where did it happen?	
Who is it about?	
What was the problem?	
What did the people do to solve the problem?	
What was the result?	

8D Put it all together
Questions

Look at these questions and write notes.

1 Where and when was it?
2 Why did you speak to him/her?
3 Was it a nice encounter or an unfortunate one?
4 Who spoke first – you or the other person?
5 Which of these things did you or the other person do?

    advise   agree   ask   invite   offer
    promise   refuse   tell   warn

6 What did you or the other person actually say? Write it down. If it was in another language, translate it into English.

9C Exercise 13
Student A Safety Leaflet A

Write notes to answer these questions.

1 Where could you face this danger?
2 What shouldn't you do, and why?
3 What *should* you do, and in what situation?
4 What can you do to protect yourself?

NATIONAL PARK GUIDELINES
BEAR SAFETY

What should I do if I meet a grizzly bear?

If a grizzly bear sees or hears you, it will probably run away. Most bears don't like contact with humans. For this reason, it is a good idea to make some noise while you're walking. You could carry a bell, or clap your hands and shout every few minutes.

However, if you get too close and surprise a bear, it might get aggressive. If the bear is angry, it will hit the ground with its paws, show its teeth and rush towards you. If this happens, stay calm. Do not turn and run. If you run, the bear will run after you – and bears can run up to 50 km per hour! Make yourself look big by putting your arms up. If you are in a group, stay close together. Don't take off your backpack – if the bear attacks, it will give you protection. Talk to the bear, and walk slowly backwards. You could climb a tree if you have time, but remember that bears can climb the lower part of a tree, so you will need to go up high.

If the bear attacks, you can use a bear spray. Wait until the bear is very near and direct the spray at its face. This will often stop an attacking bear. However, if it continues attacking, fall to the ground, protect your head and play dead. When the bear moves away, don't move immediately or it will come back again.

Please report all encounters with aggressive bears to the park ranger.

10D Exercise 3 and Put it all together
Personality Quiz!

Calculate your score to find your shopping personality. Circle your answers for each question and then count how many W, X, Y, and Z you've got.

	a	b	c	d
1	Z	X	W	Y
2	X	W	Z	Y
3	Z	Y	X	W
4	W	Y	X	Z
5	X	Z	W	Y

Are you mostly W, X, Y, or Z? Most people will have a little of all four, but you're probably more of one than the rest. Read your shopping personality below.

W You're an **organized shopper**. You plan what you're going to buy and shop around for the best deal. You like bargain hunting in discount shops. You do a lot of research about products and make notes. You always ask the shop assistant about what's included in the price. You read the small print of the guarantee. If the product is not perfect, you'll ask for a discount. It's a competitive world out there, and everybody's trying to get your money off you – but you won't let them!

X You're a **good-taste shopper**. You look for quality products and well-known makes. You often read about products in magazines or on the Internet so you know which is best and most up-to-date. You don't mind paying more for something good. There are lots of people out there trying to sell you cheap rubbish, but you know better!

Y You're a **pleasure shopper**. Shopping is one of the things you like doing in your free time. You like browsing in the shops to see what there is, and you quite often buy things you never planned to buy. How can you know what you want until you've seen what's available? You'll wander around the shops even if you haven't got any money – dreaming is free!

Z You're an **anti-shopper**. You buy what you need, when you need it. You go for the easiest option – you don't waste time shopping around. You sometimes surprise shop assistants by saying, 'I'll take it' immediately, with no questions asked. Maybe you could get a better deal if you spent more time looking, but life's too short and you've got better things to do!

Pairwork

11A Put it all together
Student A Map

You want to find:

Luigi's Restaurant   Stanton's Chemist   Public Library
Chaucer Monument   Post Office   Clancy's Coffee Shop

Example   **A**   (I'm at number 1) Excuse me, can you tell me
the way to Luigi's Restaurant?
B   Yes. Go straight along …

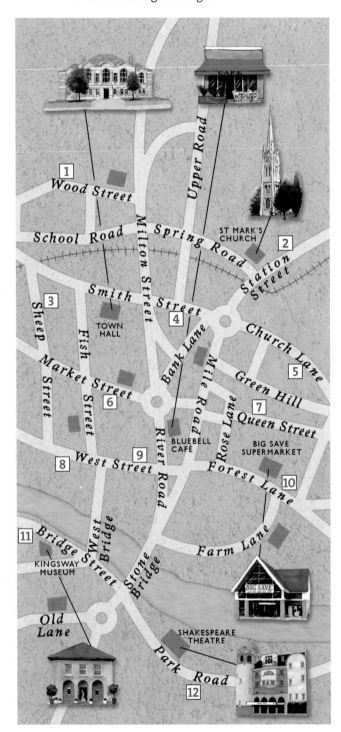

11C Put it all together
Travel advice

1   Tick ✓ the statements you agree with.
1   You don't need to prepare for holidays in advance.
2   You need to get travel insurance.
3   You ought to take all possible health precautions.
4   You should just get up and go.
5   Travel is more fun when you're not too well prepared.

2   Work in pairs or small groups. Choose two of these
holidays and tell the others where you're going and what
you plan to do. Listen and give the others travel advice.
– Backpacking in Asia
– Camping in Central Europe
– Carnival in Brazil
– Safari in East Africa
– Working holiday in the USA

Example   **A**   I'm going backpacking in Asia. What should
I do before I go?
B   You should have some injections.
C   You ought to …

12A Put it all together
Is it stealing?

Look at these situations. Do you think the person has done
anything wrong? Is it stealing?
1   Adam takes an apple from a tree. The tree is in a
private garden but the apple was hanging over the
pavement.
2   Barbara sits in the park working on her laptop. She
notices that somebody's wireless Internet connection
is available, so she checks her email.
3   Colin finds a valuable antique in a rubbish bin, so he
takes it.
4   Diana takes a video camera into the cinema and
records the whole film to watch again later.
5   Eddy downloads a film from the Internet. He records it
onto DVDs to sell around the college.
6   Fiona makes a copy of her new CD to give to a friend.
7   Gemma finds somebody's cat in her house. It doesn't
have an identification collar, so she decides to keep it.
8   Harry finds a €20 note in the street. Nobody has seen
him pick it up, so he keeps it.
9   Ian finds a €20 note on the floor of the bank and
keeps it.
10   Jenny drinks the mineral water from the hotel mini-
bar. Then she discovers that it's much more expensive
than normal, so she fills the bottle with tap water and
puts it back.

12B Put it all together
Wish box

Complete these sentences with a word or phrase. Write your word or phrase in one of the squares in the wish box below. For example, if your first sentence is *I wish I was rich*, write the word *rich* in one of the squares in the wish box.

I wish I was …		I wish I could …
I hope I'll be able to …		I hope I'll get …
I'm glad I've got a …		I wish I could travel to …
I'm glad I'm not …		I wish I had a …
I hope I won't meet …		I wish I didn't have to …
I'm glad I can …		I hope I'll never have to …

6D Put it all together
The Violin Story solution

Sebastian and John were working together to trick the restaurant owner. Sebastian ate at the restaurant, went home to collect his wallet, and left the violin as security. John went into the restaurant after Sebastian had left to collect his wallet. He convinced the owner that the violin was valuable, but in fact it was a very cheap violin. He offered to buy it and left his phone number. When Sebastian returned, the restaurant owner decided to buy the violin from him so that he could sell it to John. Sebastian and John earned $5,000 in the deal, minus the cost of the cheap violin and two meals.

1B Put it all together
Student B Two countries

Make notes to answer these questions.
1. How do people greet each other?
2. How do they address each other?
3. What do people say when they meet?

1 France
The French shake hands in formal situations, but with friends and family, they kiss on the cheeks. This can happen between two women or between a man and a woman. Two men sometimes hug or touch each other on the shoulder. The number of kisses in a greeting is different in different parts of the country – in some places it's two kisses, in other places three, and in Paris it's four. In formal situations, people address each other by a title – Mr, Mrs, or Miss and a surname. They use first names when they know each other well. Common greetings include 'Good day' and 'How are you?'

2 Indonesia
Indonesians usually shake hands with each other and say the word 'Selamat' when they meet. After shaking hands, they often bow slightly or put their hand over their heart. When they meet a few people at the same time, they greet the oldest first. People greet each other using a title such as Mr or Doctor and the person's name. Many Indonesians have only one name, and often it is very long, so when they know each other better, they use a nickname.

2C Exercise 14
Object B

This is a kind of water heater from Russia, and it's called a *samovar*. The hot water is used for making tea, and there is a teapot on the top of the samovar. The samovar is made of metal and looks like a vase. It stands on one leg, and it has handles on the sides for carrying it. It has a tap in the front for pouring the hot water out.

1C Put it all together
Student B Family photo

Ask and say who the people are.

Example **B** Who's the boy in the yellow T-shirt? He's catching a ball …
   A Well, that's Billy. He's 13, and he loves sports. He wants to be a footballer.

2 Clara. Aunt of the boy with the ball. Graphic designer.
4 Ellen. Aged 12. Interested in animals. Has a pet spider.
6 Kylie. Aged 9. Top in her class at school.
8 Frank. Jean's husband. Doctor. Owner of the house.
10 Jeff. Clara's husband. Comes from Puerto Rico.
12 Martin. Friend of the family. Actor.
14 Maya. Clara's sister. Works in a supermarket.
16 Lisa. Aged 18. Plays the guitar. Studying at university.

Pairwork

4A Put it all together
Student B Feelings

Write one or two words in each shape.

1 An exciting film you've seen.
2 A game you find entertaining.
3 Something that would make you feel embarrassed.
4 Something that fascinated you as a child.
5 Something that makes you worried.
6 Something that makes you feel annoyed.
7 The most amazing thing you've done.

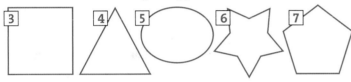

Now look at the words in your partner's shapes and ask about them.

Example **A** Draw – what's that?
B It's something I do when I'm bored. I draw little pictures on my notebook.
A So when do you feel bored?
B In meetings ...

6B Put it all together
Student B Picture story

You are the person in the story. For each of the four pictures in the story, imagine some extra details – for example, when and where was it? How did you feel? Write notes.

The next day ...

6D Put it all together
Student B The Violin Story Part B

John, dressed in expensive clothes, went into the Ritz Restaurant for a meal. He noticed a violin lying on the bar and said to the restaurant owner, 'I like the violin. I'm a collector. It's a very fine instrument. I'll give you $50,000 for it.'

The restaurant owner said, 'I don't know. I'll think about it.' John gave the restaurant owner his phone number and left.

Tell your part of the story to your partner, using reported speech. Then answer these questions with your partner.

1 How are the two parts of the story connected?
2 How much is the violin really worth?
3 Did John know Sebastian?
4 Who is telling a lie?
5 Who is the victim?

Now read the solution on ›› p.133.

7D Exercise 7
Mystery person

The mystery person is Nicole Kidman.

7D Put it all together
Two rooms – the people

Room 1
This room belongs to Jimmy Eberhard, from Bremen. He's in his late twenties and he's single. He lives in a rented flat with two friends. He's a sound engineer, and he sometimes works from home. He doesn't earn a lot of money and he doesn't save much from month to month. He plays the electric guitar in a heavy rock group.

Room 2
This room belongs to Aurora Gonzalez, from Valencia. She's in her sixties and she's a retired government worker. She never married. Her main interest is history – she has a lot of books and magazines about it, and she has studied the history of her own family tree. She has quite a lot of money saved in the bank as well as her pension, but she doesn't spend a lot.

9C Exercise 13
Student B Safety Leaflet B

Write notes to answer these questions.

1. Where could you face this danger?
2. What shouldn't you do, and why?
3. What *should* you do, and in what situation?
4. What can you do to protect yourself?

Citizens Advice
What to do in a tornado

A tornado can lift a person off the ground and carry them up to a mile away. However, this is very rare. The biggest danger is being hit by flying rubbish.

If you see a tornado, you shouldn't try to escape in your car. A tornado can move faster than a car, and cars are often lifted by tornados. In any case, the road may be blocked.

If you're in a house, you should go into the basement. If you haven't got a basement, find a place away from the windows – an inner room or cupboard perhaps. Bathrooms are often the best place. If you lie in the bath with something over you, you will be well protected. The bath is fixed to the ground by the water pipes, and sometimes it's the only thing left after a tornado has passed!

If you're in a mobile home, you should get out fast and find a safer place. Most tornado deaths happen in mobile homes.

If you are out in the open, the best thing to do is lie in a ditch. Try to find something to cover you to protect you from flying rubbish.

If you're in a school or workplace, go to an interior room or corridor on the lowest floor. Don't go into very large open rooms – corridors are better. Don't use the lift. Stay away from windows and doors. Sit on the floor, cover your head, and try to make yourself as small as possible!

11A Put it all together
Student B Map

You want to find:

St Mark's Church   Town Hall   Big Save Supermarket
Shakespeare Theatre   Bluebell Café   Kingsway Museum

Example   **B** (I'm at number 2) Excuse me, can you tell me the way to St Mark's Church?
   A Yes. Go straight along ...

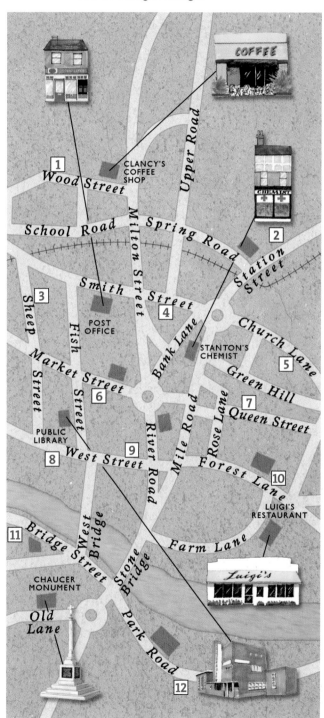

Grammar Bank

1A subject and object questions

Use a subject question to ask about the subject, who or what does an action.

Use an object question to ask about the object, who or what receives an action.

subject questions	object questions
Who lives here? Julie.	Who did you call? My sister.
Who lives with Wanda? Fatima.	Who was Jim talking to? His brother-in-law.

- Change the word order in an object question, e.g. *He works in an office. Where does he work?*
- Don't change the word order in a subject question, e.g. *Julie lives here. Who lives here?*
- Don't use the auxiliary verb *do* in subject questions. ~~*What did happen?*~~

>> Now go to **exercise 1.1** to practise.

1A wh- / how questions

Use *wh-* and *how* questions to ask for information.

Who's your boss?   What's your name?
Which is their flat? Number 6 or number 7?   Where does he live?
When did she call?   Why are we waiting?

>> Now go to **exercise 1.2** to practise.

1B reflexive pronouns

Use reflexive pronouns when the subject and object are the same.

Use *by* + a reflexive pronoun to mean *alone*, e.g. *I did my homework by myself.* (without any help)

subject pronouns	possessive adjectives	object pronouns	reflexive pronouns	
I	my	me	myself	I introduced myself to the rest of the group.
you	your	you	yourself	Why don't you get yourself a drink?
he	his	him	himself	He lives by himself.
she	her	her	herself	Ellen taught herself to paint.
we	our	us	ourselves	We enjoyed ourselves at the party.
they	their	them	themselves	Julie and Dave did everything by themselves.

>> Now go to **exercise 1.3** to practise.

1C present simple and continuous

Use the present simple for verbs which describe states, an action which happens often, and permanent or long-term facts.

Use the present continuous for actions happening at this moment and actions happening these days, but perhaps not at this moment.

present simple	present continuous
I sometimes visit art galleries.	I'm wearing my new shoes.
You're often late for lessons.	You're looking at a painting by Goya.
He doesn't live in Paris.	My computer isn't working.
Does she like modern art?	Is Simon enjoying his course?
How do we get to the museum?	Where are they sitting?

- Use the present simple with state verbs, e.g. *believe, know, see, understand, want,* etc.

>> Now go to **exercise 1.4** to practise.

1.1 Are the questions subject questions or object questions?
Example Who works in a bank?   *subject*

1 Who did you see at the party?
2 Who married Tom Cruise?
3 Who is learning to play a musical instrument?
4 Who divorced Brad Pitt in 2005?
5 Who does he work with?
6 Who did they meet in London?
7 Who left this message for me?
8 Who lives in this house?

1.2 Underline the correct question word.
Example Who/What is Tina's flatmate?

1 Where/When do your parents live?
2 Who/Why does your neighbour complain?
3 What/When do you do?
4 When/Which building does he work in?
5 What/When did they get married?
6 Who/What lives in that house?

1.3 Right or wrong? Tick ✓ or correct the underlined words.
Example I taught himself to play the guitar. ✗ *myself*

1 They cooked the meal themselves.
2 I cleaned the house herself.
3 He introduced herself to the class.
4 We did the homework by each other.
5 Have you known each other for a long time?
6 Julie, I want you to do this by myself.
7 She doesn't live by yourself.
8 We said 'Hello' to ourselves.

1.4 Underline the correct tense – present continuous or present simple.

A My mum sent me some old family photos. Do you want/Are you wanting to see them?
B Yes, please. I ¹ love/'m loving old photos.
A This is my friend Josie. She ² studies/'s studying maths at Oxford University now so we ³ don't see/aren't seeing each other very often.
B Oh, right!
A Her brother ⁴ has/'s having a house in Spain and we ⁵ sometimes spend/'re sometimes spending our holidays there.
B This is my family – we ⁶ have/'re having a picnic at my cousins' house. I ⁷ sit/'m sitting on the ground and my cousins ⁸ stand/are standing behind me.
A Where ⁹ do your cousins live/are your cousins living?
B In London. Oh, here's another picture of me.
A The sun ¹⁰ shines/is shining! Why ¹¹ are you wearing/do you wear a winter coat?
B I ¹² don't know/'m not knowing. I was only three years old!

2A *the* before geographical names

names with *the*	mountain ranges, rivers, oceans and seas, island groups, deserts, some countries, some regions	We visited the Andes. The River Seine flows through Paris. I worked in the Middle East.
names without *the*	most regions, single mountains, most countries, continents, single islands, cities, lakes	She lives in Western Australia. They climbed Mount Everest. France is in Europe.

>> Now go to **exercise 2.1** to practise.

2B adverbs of frequency

Use adverbs of frequency to say how often something happens.

100%   0%

always   often   sometimes   never
      usually   quite often   hardly ever / rarely

use an adverb of frequency before the main verb	Janet usually goes abroad on her holidays.
use an adverb of frequency after the verb *be*	She's rarely late.

- Put an adverb of frequency between an auxiliary verb and a main verb, e.g. *I've never been on a plane.*

>> Now go to **exercise 2.2** to practise.

2C phrases + prepositions / adverbs

use *made of* + a material or substance	The desk is made of wood.
use *use for / use as* + a purpose	This machine is used for making coffee. Vegetable oil can be used as fuel for cars.
use *covered with* + a material or substance	Baseballs are covered with leather.
use *a kind of* + a classifying noun	A sporran is a kind of bag.
use *look like* + a noun to compare two things	The fishing floats look like balls.

>> Now go to **exercise 2.3** to practise.

2D past simple and past continuous

Use the past continuous for longer actions / to describe the context of a story.
Use the past simple for shorter actions / to describe the events of a story.

past continuous	past simple
While I was sitting on the train,	my mobile phone rang.
They were having dinner	when we arrived.

>> Now go to **exercise 2.4** to practise.

2E time expressions

period of time	relate two times	put events in order
in / during / for a moment / for a while	before / after / (a couple of years) ago / later / when	first / second / then / next / in the end / finally
We met in the evening. I lost my watch during the first week of term.	Put your coat on before you go out. I saw him a few days ago.	It was our first time in Japan. I got up, then I had a shower.

>> Now go to **exercise 2.5** to practise.

2.1 Right or wrong? Tick ✓ or correct the sentences.
Example Washington is in ⟨*the* USA.

1 The highest mountain in Africa is the Mount Kilimanjaro.
2 United Arab Emirates and India are countries in Asia.
3 They crossed Sahara on foot.
4 We went sailing on Lake Windermere last year.
5 There are some beautiful beaches in California.
6 The Paris is on the River Seine.
7 My sister is working in Far East.
8 Cuba and the Bay Islands are in Caribbean.

2.2 Rewrite the sentences using the adverbs of frequency.
Example I buy souvenirs when I go to a new place.   always
         I always buy souvenirs when I go to a new place.

1 They go to Spain on their holidays.   often
2 I've been to South America.   never
3 He enjoys sightseeing.   rarely
4 We visit museums when we go abroad.   hardly ever
5 Tourists say that Britain is expensive.   sometimes
6 The trains to London are late.   quite often
7 The weather is good in July and August.   usually

2.3 Complete the sentences with these phrases.
made of   used for   ~~used for~~   used as
covered with   a kind of   look like

Example Chopsticks are _used for_ eating Chinese and Japanese food.

1 A kilt is _____ skirt that is sometimes worn by Scottish men.
2 The floors in the house are _____ carpet to keep the rooms warm.
3 DVDs _____ CDs, but you can store more information on a DVD.
4 These books are _____ teaching English.
5 I only wear shoes that are _____ leather.
6 Nowadays, the Internet is often _____ a way of sending messages to people.

2.4 Underline the correct verb form.
I was having/had lots of interesting experiences while I was [1] living/lived in Hong Kong. One evening my boss, Lin, [2] was inviting/invited me to a dinner party in a very expensive Chinese restaurant. When I [3] was arriving/arrived at the restaurant, Lin and her family [4] were waiting/waited at the table. Everyone [5] was wearing/wore traditional Chinese clothes. We [6] were starting/started to eat our meal. It [7] was being/was a bit difficult because I [8] wasn't knowing/didn't know how to use chopsticks. I [9] was sitting/sat opposite Lin's parents and halfway through the meal I [10] was noticing/noticed that they [11] were looking/looked at me. They [12] were trying/tried not to laugh. Lin [13] was explaining/explained that I [14] was holding/held my chopsticks upside down!

2.5 Complete the text using the time expressions.
after   ~~ago~~   before   during   first   for a while
in the end   in the morning   then   when

Four years _ago_ I went to Syria. I had a few problems [1]_____ the first few days because I didn't speak Arabic. I decided to buy a phrase book and every morning, [2]_____ I left the hotel, I practised a few new phrases. At [3]_____ I found the language difficult, but gradually I learnt enough words to say 'Hello' and ask for things in the shops.

I spent a few days in Damascus, [4]_____ I travelled to Palmyra to see the old Roman city. [5]_____ Palmyra, I took a bus to Aleppo. It was so nice that I decided to stay [6]_____ and enrol on an Arabic course. I had lessons [7]_____ and [8]_____ they were over, I explored the city and applied for teaching jobs. [9]_____, I got a job in a language school and stayed for a year.

3A used to

Use *used to* to talk about repeated actions in the past or states in the past that aren't true now.

+	I/You/He/She/It/We/They	used to	get good grades.
			be shy.
–	I/You/He/She/It/We/They	didn't use to	get good grades.
			be shy.
?	Did I/you/he/she/it/we/they	use to	get good grades?
			be shy?

short answers	
Yes, I/you/he/she/it/we/they did.	No, I/you/he/she/it/we/they didn't.

>> Now go to **exercises 3.1 and 3.2** to practise.

3B present perfect and past simple

Use the past simple to talk about past actions which happened in a finished time.

Use the present perfect to talk about past actions which happened in an unfinished time.

past simple	present perfect
I took an exam a few days ago.	She's taken several exams in the last few days.
We didn't have a maths test last term.	They haven't had a maths test this term.
Did you learn any new words last week?	Have you learnt any new words this week?
What did he do yesterday?	What have you done today?

>> Now go to **exercise 3.3** to practise.

3B time expressions

Use expressions of finished time with the past simple.
Use expressions of unfinished time with the present perfect.

expressions of finished time	expressions of unfinished time
yesterday/last week/last year/ in 2002/(a few minutes) ago/ when (you started)	today/this week/this year/ in the last few (minutes)/ since (you started)/in (my) life

>> Now go to **exercise 3.4** to practise.

3C phrasal verbs (1)

A phrasal verb is a verb used with an adverb. Together, they have a particular meaning, e.g. *make up = invent*.

Phrasal verbs can have more than one meaning, e.g. *Take your coat off. The plane took off on time.*

non-separable phrasal verbs without an object (intransitive)	Come on, Jim! I grew up in Italy.
non-separable phrasal verbs with an object (transitive)	Who's looking after the children?
separable phrasal verbs with an object (transitive)	Turn the TV on. He turned it on.

- Phrasal verbs have two parts: a verb + an adverb particle.
- Intransitive phrasal verbs do not have an object. The verb and adverb cannot be separated.
- Transitive phrasal verbs have an object that can be a noun or a pronoun. Sometimes it is possible to put the object between the verb and adverb.
- If the object of a separable transitive verb is a pronoun (*me, you, him, it*, etc.), it must come before the particle. Nouns can go before or after the particle.

>> Now go to **exercise 3.5** to practise.

3.1 Complete the sentences using the correct form of *used to*.
Example **A** Do you ever think about Park School?
B No, I <u>used to hate</u> going to school. hate

A We ¹_____ those blue uniforms. wear
B And the boys from Don School ²_____ at us! laugh
A Our teachers were OK though.
B They ³_____ all the time. shout
A Mr Hinchley was nice.
B Did ⁴_____ history? he/teach
A That's right. Did ⁵_____ to his lessons? you/go
B Yes, but I ⁶_____ good grades. not/get

3.2 Tick ✓ the correct sentence in each pair. In some cases both sentences are correct.
Example a We did sport on Wednesdays. ✓
b We used to do sport on Wednesdays. ✓

1 a They had lunch in the school dining room.
  b They used to have lunch in the school dining room.
2 a We had our school disco in the hall yesterday.
  b We used to have our school disco in the hall yesterday.
3 a One year there was a fire in the science classroom.
  b One year there used to be a fire in the science classroom.
4 a Did you have a lot of homework?
  b Did you use to have a lot of homework?
5 a My son went to Park School for four years.
  b My son used to go to Park School for four years.

3.3 Complete the text using the present perfect or the past simple.
8.15 a.m.
Today is Maria's first day at school. Last week we <u>visited</u> (visit) the school together and ¹_____ (meet) her new teacher. Maria ²_____ (not/talk) about anything but school since then. A few minutes ago she ³_____ (put on) her new uniform and Jim ⁴_____ (take) a photo of her. I can't believe how much she ⁵_____ (grow) this year.

11.30 a.m.
Jim and I ⁶_____ (be) really busy since we ⁷_____ (leave) Maria at school and we ⁸_____ (not/have) any time to miss her. I ⁹_____ (clean) the house, and Jim ¹⁰_____ (do) the washing and it's only half past eleven! I think we ¹¹_____ (achieve) quite a lot. I wonder if Maria ¹²_____ (enjoy) herself this morning.

3.4 Order the words to make sentences.
Example didn't Spanish when was school I at I study .
I didn't study Spanish when I was at school.

1 week We test didn't this a have .
2 exams passed of He's year all his this .
3 few finished lesson a ago The minutes .
4 you Have started learnt course lot the a since ?
5 school week The closed last was .
6 Have a had they today lesson maths ?

3.5 Underline the correct phrase.
Example The story wasn't true. The journalist <u>made it up</u>/ made up it.

1 Hurry up!/Hurry you up! We're late.
2 Will you turn up the radio/turn up? I want to listen to the news.
3 Why did you wake up me/wake me up? It's only 5 a.m.
4 Shall I put on/on put the new DVD?
5 I'm going to take off/take them off these shoes when I get home.
6 If you've got a mobile phone, please turn off it/turn it off.

4A -ed and -ing adjectives

Use -ed adjectives to talk about how someone feels.
Use -ing adjectives to talk about the cause of a feeling.

-ed adjectives	I'm bored, there's nothing to do here. Mike is interested in art.
-ing adjectives	I think football is boring. Have you got an interesting hobby?

>> Now go to **exercise 4.1** to practise.

4B comparatives and superlatives

Use a comparative adjective or adverb + *than* to compare two things.

We use *slightly/a bit* before comparative adjectives and adverbs to show that two things are not very different, e.g. *The Spanish guitars are a bit cheaper than the electric guitars.*

We use *much, far, a lot* before comparative adjectives and adverbs to show that two things are very different, e.g. *Madonna is much more famous than Rhianna.*

to make comparative adjectives and adverbs		
one-syllable adjectives and adverbs	+ *er*	Keyboards are cheaper than pianos. Henry sings louder than anyone else.
adjectives and adverbs with more than one syllable	*more* + adjective or adverb	Are the *Spice Girls* more famous than *Madonna*? You can hear the notes on a piano more clearly than the notes on a guitar.
irregular adjectives and adverbs	change their form	Rap is good but I think reggae is better. Sheila sang badly but Maria sang worse.

Use a superlative adjective or adverb to compare more than two things.

to make superlative adjectives and adverbs		
one-syllable adjectives and adverbs	+ *est*	He bought the cheapest guitar in the shop. This MP3 player sounds the clearest.
adjectives and adverbs with more than one syllable	*the most* + adjective or adverb	They're the most popular band in the UK. Mandy practised the most frequently.
irregular adjectives and adverbs	change their form	My brother is the worst singer in the world. Of all the CD players, this one is the best.

>> Now go to **exercises 4.2 and 4.3** to practise.

4C comparing with *as*

Use *as ... as* to say that two things are equal or unequal.

as + adjective or adverb + as	I've never had a meal as nice as this. She can cook as well as a professional chef.
not as + adjective or adverb + as	My cooking isn't as good as my mother's cooking. We don't eat out as often as we used to.

>> Now go to **exercise 4.4** to practise.

4D defining relative clauses

Use defining relative clauses to identify the person, thing, or place you are talking about.

people	who/that	Bridget Jones is a woman who is looking for love. Renée Zellweger is the actress that played the part of Bridget.
things	which/that	A comedy is a film or a play which is funny. *Nemesis* is one of the stories that Agatha Christie wrote.
places	where	This is the town where *Mr Bean* was filmed.

- We don't need to use a subject or object pronoun (*he/they/it*, etc.) when we use a relative pronoun.
- We can leave out *who*, *which*, or *that* when they are the object of a relative clause, e.g. *He's an actor (that) I like.*

>> Now go to **exercise 4.5** to practise.

4.1 Underline the correct word.
Example She doesn't enjoy watersports because she's <u>terrified</u>/terrifying of water.
1 I'm a bit worried/worrying about my exam tomorrow.
2 Mark's stamp collection is fascinated/fascinating.
3 The view as we climbed to the top of the mountain was amazed/amazing.
4 They were annoyed/annoying because their football team didn't win the match.
5 Body building? That's disgusted/disgusting!
6 They're excited/exciting because it's the first time they've been skiing.

4.2 Complete the sentences with the comparative or superlative form of the adjective. Add any extra words you need.
Example Is flamenco music _more popular_ than opera in Spain? popular
1 This band is _____ the other one. noisy
2 Wembley Arena is one of _____ concert venues in Britain. big
3 Can you be a bit _____? I'm trying to practise for my music exam. quiet
4 I think this is _____ song Elton John has recorded. bad
5 What's _____ concert venue you've been to? unusual
6 Which is _____ club in town? good

4.3 Complete the sentences with these adjectives and adverbs.
earlier   harder   worst   loudest   carefully   ~~better~~

Example Do you think that Coldplay's music sounds _better_ than the Beatles'?
1 All of my family dance badly, but my dad dances the _____.
2 You will need to practise _____ than the others to succeed.
3 Look after that violin more _____ or you'll break it.
4 I arrived late – the concert started _____ than I thought.
5 You can always hear Sam – he plays the _____.

4.4 Rewrite the sentences using (not) as ... as and the words in red.
Example The Crown and the Red Lion have both been open for three years.
The Crown has been open *for as long as* the Red Lion. long
1 Tom ate a lot of food and Mike ate a lot of food.
Tom ate _____ Mike. much
2 A meal in the cafeteria is €8. A meal in the restaurant is €15.
The cafeteria _____ the restaurant. expensive
3 The Italian restaurant and the Chinese restaurant both have 20 customers.
The Italian restaurant _____ the Chinese restaurant. busy
4 I bought the melons today and the strawberries last week.
The strawberries _____ the melons. fresh
5 Thai curries are hot. Indian curries are hotter.
Thai curries _____ Indian curries. hot

4.5 Underline the correct relative pronoun.
When I was a Singer is a love story <u>which</u>/where takes place in France. Alain is a middle-aged man [1] which/who sings in a local nightclub. He meets Marion in the club [2] that/where he sings and falls in love with her. The next day he visits the office [3] where/who she works but she isn't interested in him. Marion is trying to get over a marriage [4] which/who failed. She wants to find a place [5] which/where she can build a new life with her young son. There are some scenes in the film [6] where/which are very sad, but it's a story [7] that/who I enjoyed very much.

5A the or no article in names of institutions

institutions with *the*	positions	the president of France the managing director
	organizations	the World Health Organization
institutions with no article	the names of individual people	King Juan Carlos President Sarkozy

- Don't use an article with *Mr, Mrs, Miss,* or *Ms*, e.g. *Has Mrs Smith arrived?*

>> Now go to **exercise 5.1** to practise.

5B modals of obligation

Use *can* to say what is allowed.
Use *can't* and *mustn't* to say that something is forbidden.
Use *must* and *have to* to say that it's important to do something.
Use *don't have to* to say that it's not necessary to do something.

can + verb	You can take photos in the museum.
can't + verb	You can't take dogs into restaurants in Britain.
must + verb	You must have a licence to drive a car.
mustn't + verb	You mustn't smoke in the classroom.
don't/doesn't have to + verb	You don't have to pass a test to ride a bicycle.

>> Now go to **exercise 5.2** to practise.

5C active or passive?

Use the passive when you don't know who does an action, or when the action is more important than the person who does it.

Use the active when you know who does an action, or when the person is more important than the action.

We can use the passive with *by* to show who did the action. *A man was bitten by a crocodile.*

active	passive
The police arrest criminals.	Criminals are arrested.
The police are arresting the murderer.	The murderer is being arrested.
The police arrested the criminals.	The criminals were arrested.
The police have arrested the burglars.	The burglars have been arrested.

>> Now go to **exercises 5.3** and **5.4** to practise.

5D past perfect

Use the past perfect when you are talking about the past and want to say that an action happened at an earlier time in the past.

+	I/You/He/She/It/We/They	'd been to a concert.
–		hadn't been to a party.
?	Had	I/you/he/she/it/we/they	been to a party?

>> Now go to **exercise 5.5** to practise.

5E linkers

Use *and then/after/while* to say when something happened.
Use *and then* to show the sequence that things happen in.
Use *after* to show that one thing was completed before another started.
Use *while* to say that one thing was happening when another happened.

and then	I wrote the email and then I left the office.
after	After I'd written the email, I left the office. I left the office after I'd written the email.
while	Liz arrived while I was writing the email. While I was writing the email, Liz arrived.

>> Now go to **exercise 5.6** to practise.

5.1 Right or wrong? Tick ✓ or correct the sentences.
Example Do you think ⌄*the* Socialist Party will win the next election?
1 Head of state is Queen.
2 Do you know where headquarters of UN are?
3 Government is worried about the rate of inflation.
4 George Washington was first president of USA.
5 Britain, Republic of Ireland, and Denmark joined European Union in 1973.
6 Grace Kelly was married to Prince Rainier III of Monaco.

5.2 Underline the best modal verb.
Example All passengers must/don't have to wear a seatbelt.
1 You can't/don't have to pass a test to ride a bike.
2 Cyclists under 14 years old must/mustn't wear a helmet.
3 You can/have to pay to drive in London.
4 You mustn't/don't have to switch your bicycle lights on to see during the day.
5 You can't/must ride a horse on a motorway.
6 Drivers can/mustn't use mobile phones while driving. It's forbidden.

5.3 Put the words in order to make sentences.
Example was bank A yesterday robbed .
A bank was robbed yesterday.
1 robbers Guns the used were by .
2 tied customers up were The .
3 One hurt was woman .
4 filled with The bags cashiers money .
5 bags money robbers with The of escaped the .
6 The arrested been have robbers .

5.4 Underline the correct verb form.
A young student attacked/was attacked in the park this morning. Lee Yin was on his way to his language school when two men ¹stopped/were stopped him. One of the men ²hit/was hit Lee Yin and the other ³stole/was stolen his bag. A passer-by ⁴called/was called an ambulance and Lee Yin ⁵took/was taken to hospital, where a doctor ⁶examined/was examined him. Luckily Lee Yin ⁷didn't badly injure/wasn't badly injured. The police ⁸have sent/have been sent a description of the attackers to all the local language schools.

5.5 Complete the sentences using the past simple and the past perfect.
Example Before he _died_, King Edward _had asked_ his brother Richard to look after his two sons. die/ask
1 No one _____ the princes – Richard _____ them into the Tower of London. see/put
2 Richard finally _____ the king of England – he _____ to be king for a long time. become/want
3 Henry Tudor, Richard's enemy, _____ to England in 1485 – he _____ the previous two years in France. return/spent
4 Henry _____ the title of King of England after he _____ Richard in battle. took/kill
5 People _____ to talk about the princes. They said Richard _____ them. continue/murder
6 In 1502, James Tyrell _____ to the murder of the two princes. Richard _____ him to kill them. confess/order

5.6 Complete the sentences with *and then, after,* or *while.*
Example The phone usually rings _while_ I'm having a shower.
1 I didn't see Mike. He arrived _____ I'd left.
2 Our house was burgled _____ we were on holiday.
3 We watched a film _____ we'd finished dinner.
4 Sally bought a dress _____ she went home.
5 I read a book _____ I was waiting for you.
6 They had a party _____ they'd decorated the house.

6A so and such

Use *so* to make an adjective or adverb more extreme.
Use *such* to make a noun more extreme.

so + adjective	The children were so tired that they fell asleep immediately. Why are you so happy?
such + article + noun	It was such a bad experience that I just want to forget it. Why is he such a fool?

>> Now go to **exercise 6.1** to practise.

6B infinitives and gerunds

to + an infinitive	I decided to visit my sister.
verb + gerund	Do you fancy going for a walk?
preposition + gerund	They arrived after travelling for two hours.

- Use *to* + an infinitive after verbs such as *decide, expect, forget, hope, phone, want, refuse*, etc.
- Use a gerund after verbs such as *enjoy, fancy, finish, mind*, etc.
- Use a gerund after a preposition (e.g. *after, before, for*, etc.).

>> Now go to **exercise 6.2** to practise.

6C pronouns in reported speech

direct speech	reported speech
She says, 'I'm tired.'	She says she's tired.
He says, 'You can't play in the hall.'	He says I/we can't play in the hall.
She says, 'He/She/It's noisy.'	She says he/she/it's noisy.
He says, 'We don't play loud music.'	He says they don't play loud music.
She says, 'They shout a lot.'	She says they shout a lot.

- Pronouns sometimes change in reported speech, depending on the situation.
- We don't need to change the tense of the reporting verb, i.e. *say*, when it is in the present tense.

>> Now go to **exercise 6.3** to practise.

6D tenses in reported speech

	direct speech	reported speech
present simple	I play the violin. I don't like the music.	He said (that) he played the violin. She said (that) she didn't like the music.
past simple	We played tennis. They didn't win the game.	They said (that) they had played tennis. They said (that) they hadn't won the game.
future simple	He'll get better soon. She won't need a doctor.	She said he would get better soon. He said that she wouldn't need a doctor.

- We can shorten *had* and *would* to *'d*.

>> Now go to **exercise 6.4** to practise.

6E connectors

Use connectors to join ideas.
Use *anyway* to mean *also* or *and*.
Use *by the way* to introduce an unconnected topic.
Use *however* and *although* to mean *but*.

anyway	I don't really want to go out. Anyway, I've got too much homework to do.
by the way	Well, I think I've told you all my news. By the way, did you know that Sam and Alice have split up?
however / although	We haven't finished painting the house. However, we've done the most important rooms. He likes his job, although he has to travel a lot.

- Use a comma after *by the way, however*, and *anyway*.

>> Now go to **exercise 6.5** to practise.

6.1 Complete the sentences with *so* or *such*.
Example Joanne is _such_ a horrible woman!
1. Why are you _____ angry?
2. Her son behaves _____ badly!
3. This is _____ a brilliant CD!
4. We had _____ an amazing time in Japan!
5. It's _____ a lovely surprise to see you again!
6. He speaks _____ quickly that I can't understand him!

6.2 Complete the text with the gerund or infinitive form of the verbs.
My friend Annie phoned to _ask_ (ask) me if I fancied [1]_____ (spend) a weekend in Paris. She wanted me [2]_____ (feed) her cat while she was in New York. Of course I said yes. I always enjoy [3]_____ (visit) Paris and, after [4]_____ (finish) my exams, I was ready for a break. And I didn't mind [5]_____ (look after) her cat either. Before [6]_____ (set off) on my journey, I checked that I had everything I needed.
After [7]_____ (drive) for three hours and [8]_____ (get) lost twice, I finally arrived. I was hoping [9]_____ (see) Annie but she'd already left. There was a note on the door thanking me for [10]_____ (look after) the cat, but Annie had forgotten [11]_____ (leave) her key. Luckily, I found the cat in the garden so we spent the weekend in a hotel!

6.3 Rewrite the sentences as reported speech. Use the pronouns.
Example Mrs Smith says, 'My neighbours are horrible.' her
         She says her neighbours are horrible.
1. He says, 'Your children are badly behaved.' our
   He says _____
2. She says, 'I don't like them.' she
   She says _____
3. He says, 'You should move.' we
   He says _____
4. She says, 'Your music is too loud.' my
   She says _____
5. He says, 'I can hear them arguing.' he
   He says _____
6. She says, 'We can't sleep at night.' they
   She says _____

6.4 Underline the correct form of the verb.
Example 'My birthday is in July.'
         Sally said her birthday will be/<u>was</u> in July.
1. 'We'll give you some money.'
   They said they would give/had given me some money.
2. 'I bought a new dress.'
   Jill tells/told me she'd bought a new dress.
3. 'She lost her purse.'
   He said that she lost/she'd lost her purse.
4. 'I don't know him.'
   She said that she didn't know/hadn't known him.
5. 'They won't invite you to the party.'
   He says/said that they wouldn't invite me to the party.
6. 'We live in Prague now.'
   Linda told me that they would live/lived in Prague now.

6.5 Put the connecting word in the correct place. Add any necessary punctuation.
Example I don't like my new job it's very well paid. although
         I don't like my new job, although it's very well paid.
1. My new neighbours are friendly. They've got a big dog. however
2. We've just moved house. Did I tell you I met Susan last week? by the way
3. I've joined a gym. I've only been twice. however
4. He plays his music very loudly. I can't really say anything because I practise my trumpet every day. anyway
5. We bought a new car. We couldn't really afford it. although

7B wh- clauses

Use wh- clauses like nouns to refer to things, people, etc.

	clause begins:	
things	which / what	She can't decide which outfit looks best. They don't know what they want.
people	who	Do you know who designed this skirt?
places	where	This is where we buy most of our clothes.
times	when	I can't remember when I bought this suit.
reasons	why	He doesn't understand why his wife buys so many shoes.
methods/ conditions/ quantities	how	Does she know how to sew? I know how you feel about dressing up. I don't mind how much you spend.

- We often use a wh- clause after know.

>> Now go to **exercises 7.1 and 7.2** to practise.

7C future intentions

Use the present continuous to talk about arrangements and appointments.
Use going to to talk about plans you've had for a while.
Use will to talk about plans you've just decided.

present continuous	going to	will
I'm having a haircut on Friday. They aren't doing anything tomorrow. Are you meeting Jim later? What are we having for dinner tonight?	He's going to do more exercise. I'm not going to go abroad this year. Are you going to learn Thai? Where are you going to stay?	Maybe we'll have a big party after the exams. I won't study tonight. Will you give me a lift to work today? What shall we do at the weekend?

- Use shall instead of will in questions with I and we.

>> Now go to **exercises 7.3 and 7.4** to practise.

7D modals of deduction must, might, can't

Use must to say what you are sure is true.
Use might to say what you think is possibly true.
Use can't to say what you are sure is not true.

must + verb	He must be very rich if he's got a Rolls-Royce.
might + verb	The shutters are closed. She might be asleep.
can't + verb	They can't be poor if they live in the most expensive part of town.

- Use an infinitive without to after a modal verb.

>> Now go to **exercise 7.5** to practise.

7.1 Order the words to make sentences and questions.
Example what likes She she knows .
She knows what she likes.

1 when Does know she the close shops ?
2 clothes cheap where They to know buy .
3 know how you this is much dress Do ?
4 why suit I know this don't bought I .
5 fashionable are which know Do colours you ?
6 well dress know to how We .

7.2 Complete the sentences with the wh- words.

how how ~~what~~ when where which

Example I like _what_ you're wearing today.

1 When he saw _____ cheap the shirts were, he bought six.
2 I can't remember _____ I bought this tie – maybe in Japan.
3 I'm not sure _____ the sales start – probably in June or July.
4 I can't believe _____ many clothes you've got.
5 She liked all the shoes and didn't know _____ ones to buy.

7.3 Complete each sentence by adding one word.
Example I'm tired, I think I'll _go_ to bed.

1 Paul and Terry _____ visiting their parents tomorrow.
2 I think I _____ stay in and watch this film.
3 _____ Tom coming to the party?
4 What _____ you going to do during the holidays?
5 Who _____ Italy playing tonight?
6 We _____ going out. We're too tired.

7.4 Underline the correct verb form.
Example **A** Do you fancy a game of tennis?
      B Sorry, I 'm meeting/'ll meet Javi.

1 **A** Have you made any plans for the weekend?
  B Yes, I 'll/'m going to relax.
2 **A** Did you phone the doctor?
  B Yes, I 'm seeing/'ll see him on Thursday.
3 **A** Are you doing/Will you do anything interesting tonight?
  B No. I'm studying/going to study for the test.
4 **A** Have you booked your holiday?
  B No, we aren't going to go/won't go away this year.
5 **A** What time are you meeting/will you meet Mandy?
  B We won't meet/aren't meeting her. She's cancelled her trip.
6 **A** Oh no! I've left my wallet at home.
  B Don't worry. I 'll pay/'m paying with my credit card.

7.5 Choose the best sentence.
Example There's a lot of cat food in the cupboard.
    a ☐ They can't have a cat.
    b ☑ They must have a cat.

1 I don't know what time the bank closes.
  a ☐ It can't be open now.
  b ☐ It might be open now.
2 They argue all the time.
  a ☐ They can't be happy.
  b ☐ They must be happy.
3 He speaks English.
  a ☐ He might be from Canada.
  b ☐ He can't be from England.
4 The lights are out and the doors are locked.
  a ☐ The party must be over.
  b ☐ The party might be over.
5 They've been walking for six hours.
  a ☐ They can't be tired.
  b ☐ They must be tired.

8A phrasal verbs (2)

phrasal verbs which can't be separated	The car broke down. We called by the garage on the way home.
phrasal verbs which can be separated	You can pick up your messages later. You can pick your messages up later. I'll put you though.

- If the object of a separable verb is a pronoun (*me, you, him, it,* etc.), it must come before the particle, e.g. *Pick it up.*
- Nouns can go before or after the particle, e.g. *Pick up a message. Pick a message up.*

>> Now go to **exercise 8.1** to practise.

8B ability *can, could, be able to, manage to*

general ability in the present	I can speak French. Many dogs are able to swim.
general ability in the past	She could swim when she was a child. He had a car so he was able to travel a lot.
general ability on one occasion in the past	They were able to book the flights on the Internet. We all managed to pass the English test.
other tenses or modals	We've been able to save enough money for a holiday.

- Put the infinitive form of the verb after *can, could, be able to, managed to.*

>> Now go to **exercises 8.2 and 8.3** to practise.

8C reported questions

Use *ask* when you want to report a question.

	direct questions	reported questions
present simple	Where is he from? Where does he work?	They asked him where he was from. She asked him where he worked.
past simple	How was your interview? When did your course start?	She asked me how my interview had been. He asked us when our course had started.
future tenses	Where will you be? What will you do?	She asked me where I would be. We asked him what he would do.

>> Now go to **exercise 8.4** to practise.

8C reported questions: open and closed questions

	direct questions	reported questions
open questions (*Who, Where,* etc.)	Why are you looking for a new job?	She asked him why he was looking for a new job.
closed questions (*Are, Do, Can,* etc.)	Can you speak any foreign languages?	They asked her if she could speak any foreign languages.

- Open questions are questions with many possible answers.
- Closed questions have only two possible answers.
- We use *if* when we report a closed question.

>> Now go to **exercise 8.5** to practise.

8D reported imperatives and requests

Use *told* + person + infinitive with *to* to report imperatives.
Use *asked* + person + infinitive with *to* to report requests.

	direct speech	reported speech
imperatives	Be careful! Don't move!	She told the children to be careful. I told him not to move.
requests	Can you tell me the time?	She asked me to tell her the time.

>> Now go to **exercise 8.6** to practise.

8.1 Underline the correct words.
Example He can't <u>get through</u>/get him through to the manager's office.
1 Pete said he'd call back/call back you later.
2 Why did you hang me up/hang up on me?
3 I'll have to hand you over/you hand over to my manager.
4 She was cut off/cut her off in the middle of her call.
5 Could you put through/put me through to the office, please?
6 Can you hang on/hang on you while I go and find Terry?

8.2 Order the words to make sentences.
Example able are birds Most fly to .
       Most birds are able to fly.
1 was was when able walk he old ten to Toby months .
2 can My walk his dog legs back on .
3 to able We the be competition win might .
4 next go year to be I'll to university able .
5 meeting the managed She for time to arrive on .
6 were We our able to night homework last finish .

8.3 Complete each sentence by adding one word.
Example Luckily, I _was_ able to find a parking space near the office.
1 She _____ to complete the marathon in four hours.
2 We might _____ able to come to the party.
3 My mum _____ dance very well when she was young.
4 He _____ been able to learn Greek, even though he's tried.
5 Holland managed _____ score three goals against Italy.
6 She _____ cook very well – this food is delicious.

8.4 Report the direct questions.
Example What is your name?
       The officer asked _me what my name was_____.
1 What's your address?
   He wanted _____.
2 Where do you come from?
   He asked _____.
3 What is your profession?
   His colleague wanted to know _____.
4 When did you leave the USA?
   He asked me _____.
5 Why did you move to Australia?
   They wanted to know _____.

8.5 Complete the reported questions. Use *me* where it is appropriate.
Example How old are you?
       She asked _me how old I was_____.
1 Where do you go to school?
   She wanted to know _____.
2 Are you a good student?
   She asked _____.
3 What's your favourite subject?
   She asked _____.
4 Do you speak any foreign languages?
   She wanted to know _____.

8.6 Complete the sentences with the correct form of the verbs.
give   help   not leave   show   not smoke   ~~tell~~   turn off
Example He asked me to _tell_ him where the ticket office was.
1 She asked me _____ her a single ticket to Brighton.
2 The guard told us _____ him our tickets.
3 He advised us _____ our bags in the aisle.
4 The passenger refused _____ her mobile phone.
5 The guard told me _____ on the train.
6 A man offered _____ the old lady put her bags on the train.

9A tag questions

Use tag questions to check something that you think is true.
Use sentences with tag questions to start a conversation.

positive questions	negative questions
It's cold, isn't it?	It isn't a very nice day, is it?
The flowers are **pretty**, aren't they?	The days aren't very long, are they?
There's **a lot of snow**, isn't there?	There isn't a cloud in the sky, is there?
They live in **Mexico**, don't they?	They don't have a big garden, do they?
She enjoys **the snow**, doesn't she?	He doesn't like the rain, does he?

>> Now go to **exercise 9.1** to practise.

9B future perfect

Use the future perfect to talk about something that will be finished by a certain time in the future.

+	I /You/He/She/It/We/They	'll have finished work by six o'clock.
−		won't have finished work by six o'clock.
?	Will I /you/he/she/it/we/they have finished work by six o'clock?

>> Now go to **exercise 9.2** to practise.

9C 1st conditional

Use the first conditional to talk about possible future actions and predict their results (e.g. to give advice or warn about danger).

if clause	main clause
If we make a noise,	the bear will run away.
If you stay in your car during a tornado,	you won't be safe.
If there's a tornado,	where will you go?

- Use the present simple in the *if* clause and *will* + verb in the main clause.
- The *if* clause can go before or after the main clause.
- When a conditional sentence begins with the *if* clause, use a comma to separate the two clauses.

>> Now go to **exercise 9.3** to practise.

9C other *if* clauses

Use an *if* clause followed by a main clause with an imperative or *should* + a verb to give advice.

if clause	main clause
If there's an accident,	call the police.
If the road is flooded,	don't try to drive.
If you cycle on a busy road,	you should wear a helmet.
If you see a bear,	you shouldn't run after it.
If there's a fire,	what should we do?

>> Now go to **exercise 9.4** to practise.

9D 2nd conditional

Use the second conditional to talk about situations which are not true now and probably won't be true in the future.

if clause	main clause
If I had a dream programmer,	I'd choose dreams about travelling.
If someone gave us a personal helicopter,	we would fly to Barbados.
If I didn't have a car,	I would walk to work.
If you could buy anything in the magazine,	what would you buy?

- Use the past simple in the *if* clause and *would* + verb in the main clause.
- The contraction of *would* is *'d*.
- The *if* clause can go before or after the main clause.

>> Now go to **exercise 9.5** to practise.

9.1 Complete the sentences with a tag question.

aren't they   do we   doesn't it
don't they   ~~don't we~~   is it   isn't it

Example We spend a lot of time talking about the weather, _don't we_?

1 The days are getting longer, _____?
2 It isn't snowing there, _____?
3 We don't need an umbrella, _____?
4 Sailors listen to the weather forecast every day, _____?
5 It rains a lot in Ireland, _____?
6 It's quite mild today, _____?

9.2 Complete the sentences with the future perfect form of the verbs.

Example I _won't have finished_ cleaning the house by lunchtime.   not finish

1 I hope I _____ weight by the end of this diet.   lose
2 He _____ 42 kilometres when he finishes the marathon.   run
3 Sally's worried that she _____ her exams.   not pass
4 I _____ this essay by Friday.   not do
5 Next year we _____ married for 25 years.   be
6 By the end of their trip, they _____ almost 6,000 miles.   drive

9.3 Make 1st conditional sentences.

Example If/you/not/hurry up/we/leave/you/behind.
If you don't hurry up, we'll leave you behind.

1 If/you/not/give/us/a safety leaflet/we/not/know/what/to/do.
2 What/he/do/if/there/be/an emergency?
3 How/they/find/their way/to/the campsite/if/it/be/dark?
4 You/get/lost/if/you/not/take/a map.
5 She/make/a camp fire/if/it/be/very cold.
6 If/you/leave/food/near/the tent/it/attract/the bears.

9.4 Match 1–6 with a–f.

1 [a] You shouldn't play dead
2 [ ] You shouldn't stand under a single tree
3 [ ] Swim parallel to the beach
4 [ ] Don't move a lot
5 [ ] You shouldn't run
6 [ ] You should go into a basement and sit under a table

a if you're attacked by a shark.
b if you see a tornado coming towards you.
c if there's a lightning storm.
d if a bear comes towards you.
e if you are stuck in quicksand.
f if a current pulls you out to sea.

9.5 Complete the sentences with the correct form of the verb. Add a pronoun where necessary.

Example Where _would you go_ if you _could go_ anywhere you wanted?   go/can go

1 I _____ a house if I _____ more money.   buy/have
2 If we _____ so much homework, we _____.
   not have/can go out
3 My parents _____ happy if I _____ all my exams.
   be/passed
4 If he _____ his own computer, he _____ to use mine.
   had/not need
5 What _____ if you _____ a teacher?   do/not be
6 If you _____ a bit harder, you _____ better grades.
   work/get

144

10A articles *the*, *a*, *an*

Use *a/an* with singular countable nouns, e.g. *a shop, an engineer*.
Use *the* with singular or plural nouns, e.g. *the shop, the shops*.

a / an	the first time you mention someone / something	There's a lorry outside my house.
	to say what someone's job is	He's an engineer.
	to say what something is	It's a new shopping mall.
the	when there is only one of something	I saw him in the high street.
	when it's clear who / what you are talking about	Mr Jones is talking to the butcher.
	with places in a town	Have you been to the bank?

>> Now go to **exercise 10.1** to practise.

10B quantifiers

Use quantifiers to say and ask about how much or how many of something there is / are.

	plural countable nouns	uncountable nouns
+	There are a lot of shops. There are a few shops.	I've got a lot of money. I've got a little money.
–	There aren't many shops. There aren't any shops.	I haven't got much money. I haven't got any money.
?	Are there many shops? Are there any shops?	Have you got much money? Have you got any money?

- Use *a lot of* with plural countable and uncountable nouns. Only use *of* before a noun.
- Use *too* + an adjective, *too much* + an uncountable noun, and *too many* + a countable noun to say there is more than we want, e.g. *There is too much sugar in this coffee.*
- Use *not* + an adjective + *enough*, and *not enough* + a noun to say that there is less than we want, e.g. *There isn't enough sugar in this coffee.*

>> Now go to **exercises 10.2 and 10.3** to practise.

10C present perfect continuous

Use the present perfect continuous to talk about an activity which started in the past and has continued until now.

+	–	?
I/You/We/They've been learning English for a long time.	I/You/We/They haven't been learning English for a long time.	Have I/you/we/they been learning English for a long time?
He/She/It's been learning English for a long time.	He/She/It hasn't been learning English for a long time.	Has he/she/it been learning English for a long time?

- Don't use the present perfect continuous with state verbs (*be, believe*, etc.)

>> Now go to **exercises 10.4 and 10.5** to practise.

10D time and conditional clauses

if / as long as	I'll buy the camera if / as long as it's cheap.
unless	I won't buy the camera unless it's cheap.
when / as soon as	We'll buy a car when / as soon as we've saved enough money.
until	We won't buy a car until we've saved enough money.

- Time clauses and conditional clauses can go before or after the main clause.

>> Now go to **exercise 10.6** to practise.

10.1 Complete the text with *the, a,* or *an*.
Looking for *a* nice place to spend ¹_____ afternoon? Come to Old Basing, ²_____ old-fashioned English village in Hampshire. During ³_____ summer you can visit ⁴_____ ruins of Basing House. ⁵_____ original house was destroyed in 1645 during ⁶_____ English Civil War. Today, you can walk around ⁷_____ gardens and enjoy ⁸_____ ice-cream or ⁹_____ cup of coffee in ¹⁰_____ café. If you're hungry after your walk, why not have dinner in ¹¹_____ pub next door? They have ¹²_____ award-winning chef and you are always sure of ¹³_____ warm welcome from ¹⁴_____ pub owner and his family.

10.2 Complete the sentences with *a little, a few, a lot of, much,* or *many*.
Example I've got *a little* money so I can lend you some.
1 We haven't got _____ potatoes.
2 Hurry up! There's only _____ time before the shop closes.
3 There isn't _____ food in the house.
4 Don't buy any more eggs – there are _____ in the fridge.
5 There are _____ strawberries here. Too many for me to eat.
6 Are there _____ good restaurants in the town centre?

10.3 Underline the correct words.
Example How much/<u>many</u> plastic bags do you use when you go shopping?
1 We don't recycle enough/too many rubbish.
2 A few/lot countries have banned plastic bags.
3 Are there a few/little recycling centres near your house?
4 A lot of/lot this packaging is unnecessary.
5 Why do people buy so many/much bottled water?
6 We are producing too much/enough waste.

10.4 Complete the sentences using the present perfect continuous form of the verbs.
go out   play   not rain   read   ~~use~~   not work
Example Who *'s been using* my mobile phone?
1 I _____ a book about sailing.
2 There's a problem with the computers. They _____ today.
3 How long _____ Tom _____ with Sue?
4 They _____ computer games all day.
5 It _____ for long. Maybe it will stop soon.

10.5 Underline the correct form of the verbs.
Example I 've tried/<u>'ve been trying</u> to finish this report all day.
1 We haven't waited/haven't been waiting for long.
2 I 've written/'ve been writing four emails today.
3 Has he passed/Has he been passing his English exam?
4 How long have you studied/have you been studying Russian?
5 I haven't seen/haven't been seeing Debbie for 20 years.

10.6 Write sentences with the same meaning using the word or phrase in red.
Example I won't buy it unless they reduce the price.
  as long as
  I'll *buy it as long as they reduce the price* .
1 I won't leave until I find what I'm looking for.   as soon as
  I'll _____
2 Buy it if you're sure it's what you want.   unless
  Don't _____
3 You have to pay when you leave.   until
  You don't _____
4 They won't replace the camera unless you show the receipt.   as long as
  They'll _____
5 She won't order those shoes until she gets paid.   when
  She'll _____

11A indirect questions

Use an indirect question when you want to be more polite.

	direct question	indirect question
closed questions with *be*	Is there a newsagent's near here?	Can / Could you tell me if there's a newsagent's near here?
closed questions with an auxiliary verb and a main verb	Can I buy a map here?	Do you know if I can buy a map here?
open questions with *be*	Where is the town hall?	Do you know where the town hall is?
open questions with an auxiliary verb	When does the shop open?	Can / Could you tell me when the shop opens?

>> Now go to **exercise 11.1** to practise.

11B *to have something done*

> I have my hair styled every week.
> My sister's having her house painted.
> They've had a new garage built.

• Make the causative (*to have something done*) with subject + *have* + object + past participle.

>> Now go to **exercise 11.2** to practise.

11C *have to, need to, should, ought to*

Use *have to / need to* to say that it is necessary to do something.
Use *don't have to / needn't* + verb to say that it isn't necessary to do something.
Use *should / ought to / shouldn't* + verb to give advice.

have to / need to + verb	You have to take the pills three times a day. You'll need to show your passport at the hotel.
should / ought to / shouldn't + verb	You should make an appointment to see the doctor if you're ill. You ought to keep a first aid kit in your car. You shouldn't leave medicine where children can reach it.

>> Now go to **exercise 11.3** to practise.

11D non-defining relative clauses

Use defining relative clauses to identify the person, thing, or place you are talking about. See **4D**.

Use non-defining relative clauses to add extra information to a sentence.

people	My sister, who is from Barcelona, speaks Castellano and Catalan.
possessive	Sam, whose father is a doctor, is studying French.
things, places (subject)	Edinburgh, which is in the east of Scotland, is a beautiful city.
places (object)	Edinburgh, where we spent our holiday, is a beautiful city.
times	The accident happened on Tuesday, when I was driving home.

• We don't need to use a subject or object pronoun (*he / they / it*, etc.) when we use a relative pronoun.
• We can't leave the relative pronoun out of a non-defining relative clause.
• Use commas to separate a non-defining relative clause from the rest of a sentence.

>> Now go to **exercise 11.4** to practise.

11.1 Rewrite the questions as indirect questions. Add *me* where necessary.
Example Is the museum open today?   Do you know …
Do you know if the museum is open today?
1 Where is the tourist information office?   Could you tell …
2 Can we take photos inside the theatre?   Do you know …
3 Is this Bridge Street?   Could you tell …
4 How old is that building?   Do you know …
5 When does the library close?   Can you tell …

11.2 Rewrite the sentences using the correct form of *to have something done*.
Example They replaced the broken windows.
They had the broken windows replaced.
1 They redecorated the house.
2 They repaired the heating.
3 They've put an alarm system in the house.
4 They've built a new garage.
5 They're fitting the new carpets today.
6 They're making new curtains for all the rooms.

11.3 Put the words in order to complete the dialogues.
Example **A** I money change the Should my at airport ?
Should I change my money at the airport?
B No, you can change it at any bank.
1 **A** I don't know what to take.
  B need pack to clothes warm some You'll .
2 **A** Is anything shouldn't my suitcase there in which I put ?
  B Yes, here's the list.
3 **A** Where's my hairdryer?
  B You hairdryer take needn't your .
4 **A** Perhaps taxi order I a should .
  B It's OK, I've already ordered one.
5 **A** have When we to do check in ?
  B At 1.30.
6 **A** I've never flown before.
  B You relax to need .

11.4 Complete each sentence with the correct non-defining relative clause. Add commas where necessary.
~~which is a small village in Spain~~
whose apartment I share
when she was working in Paris
who is teaching me Arabic
where I used to live
which meant I was late for work
Example Luis and Eva come from Belchite, *which is a small village in Spain* .
1 There was a long traffic jam _____.
2 She met her husband 17 years ago _____
3 Anna _____ is coming to visit me.
4 I was on my way to Rome _____.
5 Alain _____ loves animals.

12A so, because, (in order) to

Use *so* to talk about the result of a situation.
Use *because* to talk about the cause of a situation.
Use *(in order) to* to talk about a purpose.

so	I got up late so I missed the bus.
because	I missed the bus because I got up late.
(in order) to	I got up early (in order) to catch the bus.

>> Now go to **exercise 12.1** to practise.

12B wish

Use *wish* to talk about unreal situations in the present.
Use *hope* to talk about things that we want to happen in the future.
Use *be glad* to say that you are happy about a situation.

real situation	wish / hope / be glad
I'm so tired.	I wish I wasn't / weren't so tired.
I'm not rich.	I hope I'll be rich soon.
I live in the city centre.	I wish I didn't live in the city centre.
I haven't got any problems.	I'm glad I haven't got any problems.
I can't drive.	I wish I could drive.
They won't speak to me today.	I hope they'll speak to me tomorrow.

- Change the tense in sentences with *wish* to show that the situation is unreal.

>> Now go to **exercise 12.2** to practise.

12C -ing and -ed clauses

Use *-ing* and *-ed* clauses to add extra information about the subject of a sentence.

-ing clauses	The story is about a man. + He's working in London.	The story is about a man working in London.
-ed clauses	The author was a man. + His name was Emerson Hough.	The author was a man called Emerson Hough.

- Form *-ed* clauses with any past participle, including irregular past participles, e.g. *written, seen, said,* etc.
- Use *-ed* and *-ing* clauses when both clauses in a sentence have the same subject.
- Use *-ed* for past tenses and *-ing* for continuous tenses.

>> Now go to **exercise 12.3** to practise.

12D 3rd conditional

Use the third conditional to talk about an imagined situation in the past (something that didn't happen) and its imagined result.

If we'd worked harder at school,	we'd have passed our exams.
If they'd invited me to the party,	I wouldn't have gone.
If he hadn't gone to Mexico,	he wouldn't have met his future wife.
If you'd won the lottery last week,	what would you have done with the money?

- Use the past perfect in the *if* clause and *would have* + past participle in the main clause.
- *'d* in the *if* clause is a contraction of *had*, but *'d* in the main clause is a contraction of *would*.
- The *if* clause can go before or after the main clause.
- When a conditional sentence begins with the *if* clause, use a comma to separate the two clauses.

>> Now go to **exercises 12.4 and 12.5** to practise.

12.1 Complete the sentences with *because, (in order) to,* or *so*.
Example He couldn't get a job _because_ he didn't have any qualifications.
1 I spent a year in Cuba _____ improve my Spanish.
2 He read the book _____ he wanted to learn more about the Internet.
3 I didn't want to pay for the DVD _____ I copied my friend's.
4 We grow our own vegetables _____ save money.
5 We bought a guide book _____ we could plan our trip.
6 She downloaded some music _____ she could listen to it.
7 I stayed up all night _____ finish the homework exercises.
8 My dad was angry _____ I crashed his car.

12.2 Rewrite the sentences. Use the words in blue.
Example My brother won't tidy up.   I wish
    I wish my brother would tidy up.
1 I don't share a room with my sister.   I'm glad
2 The football isn't over.   I wish
3 Her friends won't stop talking.   I wish
4 We didn't go out.   I'm glad
5 They might buy me a present.   I hope
6 It isn't raining.   I'm glad
7 I can't find a nice boyfriend.   I wish
8 Our kids might stop arguing soon.   I hope

12.3 Complete the sentences with the *-ing* or *-ed* form of the verbs.
    talk call direct injure read take ~~wearing~~
Example Who is the woman _wearing_ the red coat?
1 It's an adventure film _____ by Steven Spielberg.
2 A man _____ Pete left these flowers for you.
3 The coach _____ us to the airport broke down.
4 This is a picture of Tom Cruise _____ to fans at the opening of his new film.
5 Everyone _____ in the train crash was taken to hospital.
6 The only person in the library was a man _____ a newspaper.

12.4 Match 1–6 with a–f to make 3rd conditional sentences.
1 [b] He wouldn't have broken his leg
2 ☐ If I'd driven any faster,
3 ☐ You would have hurt yourself
4 ☐ If he hadn't gone to the party,
5 ☐ What would we have done
6 ☐ Which language would you have learned

a if you'd had a choice?
b if he'd been more careful.
c he wouldn't have met his old school friend again.
d if we'd had an accident?
e I would have crashed.
f if you'd fallen down those stairs.

12.5 Rewrite the sentences using the 3rd conditional.
Example I didn't fail my exams so I was able to go to university.   *If I'd failed my exams, I wouldn't have been able to go to university.*
1 I studied and did well in my course.
2 I saved some money and spent a year travelling around Africa.
3 I stopped in Egypt and saw the pyramids.
4 I didn't go to Kenya so I didn't climb Mount Kilimanjaro.
5 I got a job in Botswana and I met my husband.
6 I wrote a book and I became famous.
7 I earned a lot of money and I bought a big house.
8 My wife wasn't happy so she left me.

Irregular verbs

verb	past simple	past participle
be	was	been
	were	
become	became	become
begin	began	begun
bite	bit	bitten /ˈbɪtn/
blow	blew	blown
break	broke	broken
bring	brought /brɔːt/	brought /brɔːt/
build /bɪld/	built /bɪlt/	built /bɪlt/
burn	burnt	burnt
	burned	burned
buy	bought /bɔːt/	bought /bɔːt/
catch	caught /kɔːt/	caught /kɔːt/
choose	chose /tʃəʊz/	chosen /ˈtʃəʊzn/
come	came	come
cost	cost	cost
cut	cut	cut
do	did	done
draw	drew	drawn
dream	dreamt /dremt/	dreamt /dremt/
	dreamed	dreamed
drink	drank	drunk
drive	drove	driven /ˈdrɪvn/
eat	ate	eaten
fall	fell	fallen
feel	felt	felt
find	found	found
fly	flew	flown
forget	forgot	forgotten
forgive	forgave	forgiven /fəˈgɪvn/
freeze	froze	frozen
get	got	got
give	gave	given
go	went	gone
		been
grow	grew	grown
hang	hung	hung
have	had	had
hear	heard /hɜːd/	heard /hɜːd/
hide	hid	hidden /ˈhɪdn/
hit	hit	hit
hold	held	held

verb	past simple	past participle
hurt	hurt	hurt
keep	kept	kept
know	knew /njuː/	known /nəʊn/
learn	learnt	learnt
	learned	learned
leave	left	left
lend	lent	lent
let	let	let
lie	lay	lain
lose	lost	lost
make	made	made
mean	meant /ment/	meant /ment/
meet	met	met
mistake	mistook /mɪˈstʊk/	mistaken
pay	paid	paid
put	put	put
read	read /red/	read /red/
ride	rode	ridden /ˈrɪdn/
ring	rang	rung
rise	rose	risen /ˈrɪzn/
run	ran	run
say	said /sed/	said /sed/
see	saw /sɔː/	seen
sell	sold	sold
send	sent	sent
set	set	set
shake	shook /ʃʊk/	shaken
shine	shone /ʃɒn/	shone /ʃɒn/
show	showed	shown
shut	shut	shut
sing	sang	sung
sink	sank	sunk
sit	sat	sat
sleep	slept	slept
smell	smelt	smelt
	smelled	smelled
speak	spoke	spoken
spell	spelt	spelt
	spelled	spelled
spend	spent	spent
split	split	split

verb	past simple	past participle
spoil	spoilt	spoilt
stand	stood /stʊd/	stood /stʊd/
steal	stole	stolen
stick	stuck	stuck
swear	swore	sworn
swim	swam	swum
take	took /tʊk/	taken
teach	taught /tɔːt/	taught /tɔːt/
tear	tore	torn
tell	told	told
think	thought /θɔːt/	thought /θɔːt/
throw	threw	throne
understand	understood	understood
wake up	woke up	woken up
wear	wore	worn
win	won /wʌn/	won /wʌn/
write	wrote	written /ˈrɪtn/

≪ Look at the verb column. Cover the past simple and past participle columns and test yourself.

Pronunciation

Vowel sounds

/æ/	/e/	/ɪ/	/ɒ/	/ʌ/	/ʊ/
apple /æpl/	egg /eg/	fish /fɪʃ/	office /ˈɒfɪs/	uncle /ˈʌnkl/	book /bʊk/
/ɑː/	/ɜː/	/iː/	/ɔː/	/uː/	
car /kɑː(r)/	girl /ɡɜː(r)l/	eat /iːt/	four /fɔː(r)/	two /tuː/	
/eə/	/ɪə/	/ʊə/	/əʊ/	/aʊ/	
hair /heə(r)/	ear /ɪə(r)/	newer /njʊə(r)/	phone /fəʊn/	mouth /maʊθ/	
/aɪ/	/eɪ/	/ɔɪ/	/ə/		
ice /aɪs/	eight /eɪt/	boy /bɔɪ/	cinema /ˈsɪnəmə/		

Consonant sounds

/p/	/b/	/t/	/d/	/tʃ/	/dʒ/
pen /pen/	bed /bed/	table /teɪbl/	door /dɔː(r)/	chair /tʃeə(r)/	jeans /dʒiːnz/
/f/	/v/	/θ/	/ð/	/k/	/g/
food /fuːd/	visit /ˈvɪzɪt/	thing /θɪŋ/	father /ˈfɑːðə(r)/	cup /kʌp/	garden /ˈɡɑːdən/
/s/	/z/	/ʃ/	/ʒ/	/h/	/l/
sister /ˈsɪstə(r)/	zoo /zuː/	shoe /ʃuː/	television /ˈtelɪvɪʒn/	house /haʊs/	lunch /lʌntʃ/
/m/	/n/	/ŋ/	/r/	/w/	/j/
man /mæn/	nine /naɪn/	sing /sɪŋ/	red /red/	water /ˈwɔːtə(r)/	young /jʌŋ/

The alphabet

A	B	C	D	E	F	G	H	I	J	K	L	M	N
/eɪ/	/biː/	/siː/	/diː/	/iː/	/ef/	/dʒiː/	/eɪtʃ/	/aɪ/	/dʒeɪ/	/keɪ/	/el/	/em/	/en/

O	P	Q	R	S	T	U	V	W	X	Y	Z
/əʊ/	/piː/	/kjuː/	/ɑː(r)/	/es/	/tiː/	/juː/	/viː/	/ˈdʌbljuː/	/eks/	/waɪ/	/zed/, American /ziː/

Stressed and unstressed words

Stress 'vocabulary' words ...	
nouns	book, girl, time ...
main verbs	walk, speak, play ...
adjectives	big, green, old ...
adverbs	easily, fast, slow ...
question words	Who, What, How, ...
negatives	not, aren't, can't ...

Don't stress 'grammar' words ...	
articles	a, an, the ...
prepositions	in, on, of ...
conjunctions	and, but ...
auxiliary verbs	is, was, do ...
pronouns	you, we, them ...
possessives	me, your, their ...
demonstratives	this, that ...

Example stress patterns

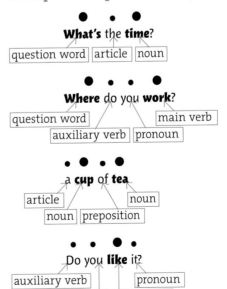

Audio scripts

1

1A.1

1 Oh, eh … hello, this is Margaret speaking. A young man visited today. He had a horrible red jumper and he frightened my cat! He knocked on your door for half an hour. Knock knock knock! What a noise! I couldn't sleep! Please could you tell your friends to be quieter. Thank you!

2 Hi, this is a message for Wanda. This is Mr Robbins from the office. Listen, we have a big job tomorrow and, ehm, well, I thought ehm … could you work a bit later tomorrow evening? Just an extra hour or something … and then, ehm … I'll buy you dinner, if you want … OK, well, we can talk about it in the morning. Ciao.

3 Hi Wanda, it's me. I called at your flat today but you were out. That horrible woman in the next flat came out and shouted at me. I was only knocking on the door! Anyway, let's meet up for a coffee some time. Or maybe we could go to the cinema … How about tomorrow? I'll call round at seven o'clock then, OK? Alright, see you tomorrow. Bye.

4 Wanda, it's me. Listen, can you come to our house and look after Grace tomorrow night? Me and Ray want to go to a concert. Could you come at seven o'clock? It's easy, just give Grace a bath, put her in bed, and watch TV. I'll leave some soup for you. Right, see you tomorrow then. Bye-bye.

5 Hi Fatima, it's your mother. Are you there? … Go on, pick up the phone … OK, you're not there … I'll call back later, OK? Bye.

6 Hello, Wanda, it's me. Listen, Roxette's coming to London tomorrow, and she's got quite a lot of baggage, so maybe you could help her? Could you meet her at the airport? It's flight 6254 from Malaga, and it arrives at seven o'clock. Thanks a lot darling. Love you. Bye for now. Bye.

7 Hi Wanda, are you there? … It's me, calling from Nottingham. Having a great time. Listen, I'm coming home tomorrow evening, but ehm … I forgot my keys when I left the flat yesterday, so, ehm could you let me in? I'm arriving back at about seven o'clock, so could you stay home and open the door for me? Cheers! See you tomorrow.

8 Hello Wanda, it's me. Why don't you come round for dinner one night this week? Me and Costas would love to see you. And could you bring my pink umbrella back? I left it at your flat last time I was there. So how about tomorrow evening? Seven o'clock? Give me a ring. Bye love.

1B.1

OK, number one, ehm … well in Britain, shaking hands is quite common, yeah, and sometimes you put your hand on the other person's shoulder, yeah, but ehm … we never bow – well, people bow when they meet the Queen I guess, but we don't normally bow.

Hugging is quite common in the family and with good friends. Some people kiss their friends on the cheeks. Kissing on the lips – well, I guess girlfriends and boyfriends do this – couples, or whatever, OK, and waving, well yeah, that's very common.

Number two … when I meet a good friend, well, with women we kiss each other on the cheeks and with men, we usually shake hands. An acquaintance, well, I guess I just say 'Hello' or something, and the same for an older neighbour – or maybe I'd say 'Good morning' or whatever. The same for my boss. If I meet one of my parents after a long time, we hug each other, and I kiss my mum on the cheeks. OK, and my nephew or niece – well, I hug them or just touch them on the head.

Question three … well, actually I address all of these people with their first name, but some people would use 'Mr' or 'Ms' and the surname when they talk to their boss, I think.

OK, number four … in this situation, in the café, my friend would introduce me to the other people I think, but they wouldn't all stand up or anything.

Number five … well, I never say 'Enchanted', I mean that's really old fashioned, nobody says that nowadays. I often say 'Pleased to meet you'. I would never ask 'How old are you?' – well, maybe to a child, but not to an adult. I never introduce myself with Mr and my surname, I just say 'Hi, I'm Greg'. Ehm … I would never say 'Peace be with you', very strange, that, and 'Greetings', I would never say that either.

OK, six … meeting my teacher in the street, I'd say 'Hello' and the first name, ehm … I guess children would say 'Mr' or 'Miss' and the surname.

And finally seven … to attract attention, I'd say 'Excuse me'. The other ones are rude, I think.

1B.2

This is Mrs Mirren.
Good afternoon, Mr Brown.
Please come in, Miss Jones.
He introduced me to Ms White.
I saw Mr Costas.
Are you Ms Phillips?
Pleased to meet you. I'm Mrs Smith.
Where are you from, Miss Wilson?

1C.1

Barbara Who are those two people?
Guide Which two?
B At the back of the room – I think they're in a mirror?
G Ah, well, that's the king and queen. King Phillip the fourth and Queen Mariana.
B So *is* it a mirror?
G Yes, it is.
B So that means the king and queen are in the room as well?
G That's right. They're probably standing where we are.
B So we're looking through their eyes?
G Yes. And in fact the princess and the other people are looking at the king and queen, not at us.
B Oh, OK.
G There's something else interesting in the picture, too. You see the painter Velázquez there on the left?
B Uh huh?
G Well, he's wearing a black jacket and there's a red cross on the front of it.
B Yes.
G Well, that's the symbol of the Order of Saint James. The king made him a member of that order.
B Oh, yeah?
G But that was three years *after* Velázquez painted the picture.
B Oh – so how is it in the picture?
G Well, some people say that the king painted it there himself.
B Oh, right.

1D.1

Nose, N-O-S-E, is pronounced the same as … knows, K-N-O-W-S.
Piece, P-I-E-C-E, is pronounced the same as …
Guest, G-U-E-S-T, is pronounced the same as …
Threw, T-H-R-E-W, is pronounced the same as …
Road, R-O-A-D, is pronounced the same as …
Meet, M-double E-T, is pronounced the same as …
Knew, K-N-E-W, is pronounced the same as …
Board, B-O-A-R-D, is pronounced the same as …

1D.2

A Can I have some bananas, please?
B Yes, of course. Which ones do you want?
A Oh, ehm … I'll take that pair.
B Pardon? Don't you want any bananas then?
A I'm sorry, I don't understand …
B You want a pear?
A Oh, I see! No, no, no. I meant pair, P-A-I-R! I'd like those two bananas, please.
B Oh, ha ha. OK. Sorry, I misunderstood. I thought you said pear, P-E-A-R!

1D.3

I don't understand.
No, I meant pair.
I thought you said pear.
Oh, I see!
Pardon?
Sorry, I misunderstood.

2

2A.1

This picture shows a woman standing beside Lake Titicaca in Bolivia. She's wearing a traditional black hat and carrying a brightly coloured cloth bag. The Aymara people have their own language, called Aymara.

2A.2

a This picture shows a young man from the Atlas Mountains in Morocco. His people are mostly Muslims. He's got a cloth tied around his head to protect him from the sun. The bright blue colour of his clothing is typical of the region.

b This is a photo of a young man with a black head cloth. He has white lines and spots painted on his face, and his lips are painted black. His people live in the Sahara Desert, in Niger. He's at a marriage festival and he wants to find a wife.

c This young man holding two birds is from Jordan. He's wearing the typical red headscarf of the region. The Bedouin people live all over the Middle East and they are Muslims. Behind him you can see a wall made of mud and stones.

d This is a picture of a woman in the north of Tanzania. She's wearing the traditional red costume of her tribe and a wide necklace of coloured beads. She's got short hair and she's wearing earrings. She's standing in front of a wooden door.

e This is a man from the island of Raiatea in French Polynesia. His skin is decorated with traditional tattoos. He's got a marker pen through a hole in his ear, and his long hair is tied up. You can see the sea behind him.

f Here we see a young girl from Guatemala in Central America. She's wearing a blue shirt or dress and she's smiling at the camera. Behind her you can see some traditional blue handmade local cloth.

g This girl with pieces of wood through her nose and lower lip is an Indian from Brazil. She's also wearing a necklace made of beads. Her hair is straight and black. Her people live in the Amazon rainforest in the north of the country.

h This man with white paint in his beard is a tribesman from Papua New Guinea. Papua New Guinea is part of an island to the north of Australia. The man has lots of necklaces made from coloured beads, and he's carrying some spears. He has red spots painted on his face.

i This picture shows a man from Baffin Island in the far north of Canada. He's wearing a thick fur coat to protect him from the cold arctic weather. He's got straight black hair. Behind him, you can see clouds and sky.

2A.3
My name's Gerry. I'm 19 and I work in a garage. I'm from a village near Galway in the west of Ireland. I speak English and Gaelic. I'm not religious but my parents are Catholic. I come from a working class family. I've got cousins in America because my aunt Celia married an American man and moved to the USA. They live in Georgia. I enjoy motor racing and I write articles for a car magazine.

2B.1
They always like the city lights
They usually go to see the sights
They often go to see Big Ben
They quite often visit 'Number Ten'
They sometimes take a photo there

They rarely miss Trafalgar Square
The action hardly ever stops
They never want to miss the shops

2B.2
Country one
First clue – When people think of this country, they usually think of mountains. There are a lot of mountains here and some of them are very famous, such as the Eiger and the Matterhorn.

The next clue is food. The country is quite famous for cheese and chocolate, and they often eat them in a fondue. People who visit this country often buy chocolate to take home.

OK, the last clue is about typical goods. People often buy watches from this country, for example Rolex watches, or Swatch. Other souvenirs include army penknives and coloured pencils.

Country two
First clue – When people think of this country, they often think of flowers. It's very flat, there aren't any mountains, and they grow a lot of flowers. It's also well-known for cheese.

Clue number two – People usually visit the most famous city, and there are a lot of canals; you can take a boat on the canals, and you see a lot of people on bicycles here.

Next clue – There are a lot of famous painters from this country, for example Rembrandt and Vincent Van Gogh.

Country three
First clue – People always think this country is very big and very cold, and there are a lot of forests. In fact, it's the biggest country in the world.

OK, next clue – There are a lot of very well-known writers from this country, for example, there's Tolstoy, who wrote War and Peace, and there's Dostoyevsky.

Last clue – When people visit the capital, they usually go to see Red Square and the Kremlin.

Country four
First clue – When people think of this country, they often think of Carnival and dancing in the street and samba, and tropical fruit and sunshine.

OK, next clue – People usually visit the beaches in the most famous city, and they go to the top of some of the mountains in the city such as Sugar Loaf.

Last clue – There are a lot of famous footballers from this country, including Pelé and Ronaldo.

2C.1
What's it used for?
It's used for cutting fruit.
It's used for opening tins.

What's it made of?
It's made of metal.
Where's it from?
It's from Africa.
What's it used as?
It's used as a stool.

2C.2
Elaine What's this?
Nilson It's a kind of cup.
E Uh huh.
N Ehm, it's used in the south of Brazil for drinking maté – that's a kind of tea. The cup's called a chimarrão in Portuguese.
E Oh yeah? What's it made of? It looks like wood …
N It's made of dried gourd – you know gourd? It's a kind of fruit.
E Oh yeah, I know. And what's this metal thing for? Is it for mixing the sugar or something?
N No, that's used as a straw for drinking the tea. It's called a bomba.
E Why don't people just drink out of the cup?
N Ah, I guess you've never seen maté! There are lots of leaves on the top, so if you drink it from the cup, you get leaves in your mouth.
E Oh, OK. And how do you put the cup down? I mean, the bottom's round. Doesn't it just fall over when you put it on the table?
N You don't put it down. Where I come from, people hold these things all day, and when they've finished, they just put more hot water in.
E Wow, that's so strange. I've never heard of that.
N Uh huh.

2D.1
Linda I lived in Spain a couple of years ago, and …
F Oh yeah? What were you doing there?
L I was studying Spanish.
F Uh huh.
L So anyway, in the first week I didn't go out because I had a cold, but in the second week I was feeling better …
F Mmm.
L And, ehm, some friends from the university invited me out to eat in the evening.
F Uh huh.
L So we met at ten and we went to a bar for a drink before dinner, you know.
F Uh huh.
L Anyway, my friends ate the 'tapas', you know, the bar snacks, while we had a drink, but I didn't have any tapas because I wanted to be hungry for dinner.
F Oh yeah?
L Anyway, after a while, we went to another bar and the same thing happened again.

More drinks and tapas. And again. And again.
F So didn't you have any dinner?
L Well, no. Finally, I asked, 'When are we going to have dinner?', and my friends laughed and said the tapas WERE the dinner!
F Oh no!
L Yeah, so in the end I went to bed hungry.

3

3A.1
The **first time** I **fell** in **love**
How could **I forget**?
She **used** to **sit** at the **front** of the **class**
And her **name** was **Berna**dette
She **nev**er **used** to **get** it **wrong**
A **real teach**er's **pet**
'A' in **Sci**ence, 'A' in **Maths**
I used to **love** her, **my** sweet **Berna**dette

She **used** to **sing** in as**sem**bly
And **play** the **clar**inet
She **did**n't **use** to **make** mi**stakes**
And her **name** was **Berna**dette
She **ran** a**round** the **play**ing **field**
And **did**n't **use** to **sweat**
The **cap**tain of the **hock**ey **team**
I used to **love** her, **my** sweet **Berna**dette

She **did**n't **use** to **look** at **me**
Our **eyes nev**er **met**
She **used** to **be** too **good** for me
And her **name** was **Berna**dette
Last week I **met** her
I **found** her on the **Internet**
She's **married** with two **kids** now
I used to **love** her, **my** sweet **Berna**dette

3A.2
first time
last week

used to **sit**
get it **wrong**
teacher's **pet**
make mi**stakes**

sit at the **front**
front of the **class**

3A.3
Antonia
Ehm, I remember I used to sit by the window, and there was a heater there so it was really warm, and I used to sit and look out of the window, and ehm, sometimes the teacher got really angry and she used to say 'Pay attention, Antonia!' … ehm …
I remember one teacher especially – his name was Mr Collins but we called him Collie, and he used to teach Maths, and he always used to wear really big ties, very wide ties, with pictures on them. Maths was my worst subject, I always used to get a D or E in Maths exams and Collie was angry and he gave me extra homework. I hated that.

Jeremy

OK, well, my first school ... ehm ... I think the place I remember most was the big room where we used to have assembly – a big dark hall and it had these pictures of old head teachers and things on the wall, and a piano, oh and I remember the playground – we used to go out there in the breaks and it was always raining ... Erm, another thing I remember is we used to have a uniform – it was a green jacket and grey shorts, and we had to wear these grey shorts, even in the freezing cold in winter. Then, there were the school trips – that was the best thing, because we didn't have to wear the uniform, and we used to sit on the bus and sing songs, and the teachers were always more friendly on school trips, so it was quite good fun.

3C.1

Mum Daniel Peter Marston! Just look at the time! Where have you been? This isn't a hotel, you know!

Daniel I wish my mum understood me!

M You look tired, Danny. Don't get up. Shall I wake you up when the football starts?

D What? Eh ... yeah, thanks Mum.

Emma Mum – Danny's left the bathroom floor wet!

M I'm sure that's not true, Emma. Don't make stories up about your brother. Hurry up Danny, the football's about to start. Don't tidy up. I'll put your clothes away if you like.

M I'll turn the telly on for you. Just sit down, take off your trainers, and put your feet up. Help yourself to crisps.

M Lunch is on the table, Danny!

D Oh Mum! I'm watching The Simpsons!

M Oh sorry! Would you like me to bring your lunch on a tray?

D Yes, please.

M Don't worry about the dishes, Danny. I'll wash up today. Why don't you turn your music up – it's very nice! Is everything alright?

D No, I'm fed up!

M Why don't you try something new? Take up the electric guitar. Get a tattoo.

D Alright! I'll invite 30 friends for a party next Friday. We'll put heavy metal music on, turn it up really loud, and dance on the furniture. Is that OK?

M Oh, that sounds great! I'm looking forward to it already!

D Aargh! I can't stand it! You're too NICE! You're my mum – you're supposed to shout at me and tell me off! If you carry on like this, I'll grow up SPOILT!

M Daniel, it's nine o'clock! Get up at once!

D Oh! Good morning, Mum! I love you!

3C.2

Mrs Marston Hello, Jessica! Come in!

Jessica Hello, Mrs Marston. Thanks.

M I'll take your coat if you like.

J Thank you.

M Just leave your bag on the sofa.

J OK.

M Would you like me to make you a cup of tea?

J No, thanks. I'm fine.

M Danny isn't home yet. Why don't you watch TV for a bit?

J OK, thanks.

M Shall I change the channel for you? I'm not watching this programme.

J No, it's fine, thanks.

M Help yourself to some of these biscuits.

J Thanks, Mrs Marston.

M Don't worry about the dog. He won't bite.

J OK.

M Do you need anything, or is everything alright?

J I'm fine, thanks.

M OK, well, I'll leave you in peace then.

J OK, thanks.

3C.3

I'll take your coat if you like.
Just leave your bag on the sofa.
Would you like me to make you a cup of tea?
Why don't you watch TV for a bit?
Shall I change the channel for you?
Help yourself to some of these biscuits.
Don't worry about the dog.
Do you need anything, or is everything alright?

3D.1

educate	educ**a**tion
qualify	qualific**a**tion
graduate	gradu**a**tion
apply	applic**a**tion
technical	tech**no**logy
photograph	pho**to**graphy
public	pub**li**city

3D.2

Well, I left school after my GCSE exams when I was 16. I wanted to get a job and earn some money, you know, so I signed on at the job centre and, anyway, they offered me a job as an assistant in an old people's home, so I took the job, and ehm ... well, I quite liked the work, and I stayed there for a couple of years, but it was going nowhere, I couldn't move up in the job – I couldn't get promotion without qualifications, so in the end I decided to leave and go to night school. I studied marketing and publicity, I don't know why, but anyway, I did well, and I went on to do a master's. After that, I got a job in an international advertising agency. I worked hard and got promoted up and up, and

now I'm the head of the design team. So that's where I am now. It's OK. The money's good, but it's not a secure job. You never know where you'll be tomorrow.

4

4A.1

/d/
amazed
bored
/t/
embarrassed
/ɪd/
excited
fascinated
disgusted
interested

4B.1

a nice venue
a nicer venue
an old song
an older song
a deeper sound
a deep sound
a bigger stage
a big stage
a small studio
a smaller studio

4B.2

Jan I don't buy CDs any more. I just download MP3s off the Internet.

Andrea Oh, I still buy CDs. I think the quality's better, you know, the sound's much clearer.

J Yeah, people say that, but I can't tell the difference myself. And you can find the songs you want much more easily on the Internet, especially if you're looking for a more unusual track, you know, there's a lot of stuff you can't find in the normal shops.

A Maybe I'm old-fashioned, but I like having the CD. I don't know ... I like looking at the picture on the box. If I can't find the CD in the shop, I'll order it, no problem.

J That's much slower.

A So what's the hurry?

J Well ... Anyway, MP3 music's much more convenient, too. You can put it on your iPod. They're much smaller than a CD walkman. And CDs jump if you're moving around. No, iPods are much better.

A Why do you want to move around? The best place to listen to music is on the stereo system at home. It's much more comfortable. And anyway, I hate listening to music through headphones. It gives me a headache, and I think two good quality speakers give a much better sound.

J Alright, but what about the family? They always ask you to play it more quietly, and you

can't hear it properly.

A I live on my own, so I don't have that problem. You can have your MP3s, but I'm happier with my CDs.

4C.1

Sarah Shall we go out for a meal on Friday evening?

Tom Friday? Ehm ... **yes, OK, good idea**. Where shall we go?

S Let's look at the restaurant reviews and choose somewhere different. Let's see ... ehm ... OK, here we are ... well, there's the Café Paradiso, but we've been there before ...

T Yeah. I can't stand that place. It's always full of children. What about this one ... Old Peking ... 'The Old Peking is under new ownership, but it's just as good as ever'. That sounds good.

S **Well, I'm not too keen on Chinese food**. I prefer Indian food. How about the Bombay Palace?

T **Ehm, well, I don't know** ... How about this French place, for example? ... Chez Dominique ... I absolutely adore French cooking.

S It looks a bit expensive ...

T Alright. Why don't we try this place ... The Chestnut. It looks really good, and it isn't as expensive as the French place.

S It's vegetarian.

T Yeah. Why not? Do you want a place that serves meat?

S No, it's alright. I don't mind vegetarian food. **OK then, let's try it**. We'd better book – it says book as early as you can.

T OK. I'll do that now.

4C.2

Yes, OK, good idea.
Well, I'm not too keen on Chinese food.
OK then, let's try it.
Ehm, well, I don't know.

4C.3

Sarah Shall we go for a pizza?

Tom Mmm mmm mmm.

S Let's go for an Indian meal.

T Mmm mmm mmm.

S Why don't we go to a French restaurant?

T Mmm mmm mmm.

S How about going out for a Chinese meal?

T Mmm mmm mmm.

4D.1

Interviewer On today's programme, we're going to talk about women's films, and here to talk to us is Janet Shaw, professor of Media Studies at Midland University.

Professor Hello.

I First of all, Professor Shaw, what ARE women's films? Are they all about romance and relationships?

P Well, they aren't just one

kind of film, in fact, there are lots of different kinds of women's films. Yes, a lot of them are about romance and relationships. Women's films focus more on the people and dialogue, and men's films often focus more on the action.

I So action films are men's films.

P Well, not necessarily. Some women's films are action films too – but they take a woman's point of view, and the main characters are often women – characters that a female audience can identify with. For example, there was the film *Thelma and Louise*, about two female criminals, or the science fiction film *Alien*, with Sigourney Weaver.

I Ah. Are the main characters always female?

P No – a lot of women's films have lead actors like Nicolas Cage or Hugh Grant or Mel Gibson – male actors who a lot of women find attractive.

I Uh huh. Are women's films actually made for women? I mean, do the film makers sit down and say 'We're going to make a women's film here'?

P Yes, they often make a story which they think women will like. But often it's the other way round. For example, films from classic literature, such as *Pride and Prejudice* – these could be called women's films.

I Because they focus on characters ...

P Yes, characters and relationships – more dialogue, less action.

I OK, and finally – do women watch only women's films?

P No – that would be impossible! There are far fewer women's films than men's films, so women have to watch men's films, too. And of course, people aren't just stereotypes. There are a lot of men who like women's films, and a lot of women who actually prefer men's films.

I OK ... and what about you?

P Ooh, now that's a difficult question! Actually, I prefer reading books!

I Ah ha, yes, I see. OK, well, thank you very much for joining us today.

P You're welcome.

I Goodbye.

5

5A.1
Question 1. An election is a system in which the people choose their political leaders. In the past, only men were allowed to vote. Which country, in 1893, became the first nation to allow women to vote in elections?

a The United Kingdom
b Indonesia
c New Zealand

5A.2
Question 2. We often think of kings and queens as historical figures, but many countries today still have them – for example the United Kingdom and Spain. Which of the following countries does NOT have a king or queen?

a Norway
b The Czech Republic
c Saudi Arabia

Question 3. Many countries have a president as the head of state. Which of these countries does NOT have a president?

a The United Kingdom
b Brazil
c France

Question 4. In most countries, the main centre of government is in the capital city. For example, the United States congress is in the capital, Washington DC. Which of these capital cities is NOT the centre of government of the country?

a Amsterdam
b Buenos Aires
c Tokyo

Question 5. The world is divided into nations, and nearly all of them are members of an international organisation called the United Nations, or UN. The UN was formed in 1945 and has over 190 member states. Where is the headquarters of the UN?

a Geneva
b Beijing
c New York

Question 6. In Europe, many countries have joined together to form the European Union. Which of the following countries is NOT in the European Union?

a Switzerland
b Bulgaria
c Finland

Question 7. We sometimes use the name of a famous government building to refer to the government of that country. For example, people often say 'The White House' to refer to the United States government. What famous building is used to refer to the government of Russia?

a The Bundestag
b The Kremlin
c The Winter Palace

Question 8. Many of the world's flags have three stripes of different colours. For example, the French flag has one stripe of red, one of white, and one of blue. Which of these countries does NOT have a flag with stripes of three different colours?

a Germany
b Italy
c Australia

5A.3
Question 1 – the answer is c, New Zealand.

Question 2 – the answer is b, the Czech Republic doesn't have a king or queen.

Question 3 – the answer is a, the United Kingdom doesn't have a president.

Question 4 – the answer is a, Amsterdam is the capital, but the centre of government isn't Amsterdam – it's The Hague.

Question 5 – the answer is c, the headquarters of the UN is in New York.

Question 6 – the answer is a, Switzerland is not in the European Union.

Question 7 – the answer is b, the Kremlin.

Question 8 – the answer is c, the Australian flag doesn't have stripes of three different colours.

5A.4
the emperor of Japan
the US president
the Australian prime minister
the head of state
the European Union
the United Nations
the Irish government
the Liberal party

5B.1
Jeff What are you going to do with your old one?

Sally Oh, I don't know. I hadn't thought about that. I'll put it out with the rubbish bins, I guess.

J But you can't do that, I mean, it isn't allowed, is it?

S Oh?

J Yeah, it's got some dangerous chemical in it, apparently, so ...

S So what do I have to do with it?

J I'm not sure. I suppose you have to phone somebody to come and take it away.

S What, for free?

J No, you have to pay, I think. I don't really know. When I got my new one, the people from the shop took the old one away.

S Oh, that was good.

J Yeah.

5C.1
baseball bat
birthday party
cash machine
earrings
headline
sports car
steering wheel
taxi driver

5C.2
A Renoir painting worth three million euros has been stolen from the National Gallery. Police believe it was done with the help of someone who works in the gallery. Apparently, a door of the gallery was left open and the alarms were switched off. The security guards were drugged and all the film from the security cameras was deleted. The thieves knew exactly what they were looking for, and less valuable paintings were not taken.

Hold on, some news is just coming in. We've just been informed that the painting has been found in Hong Kong and three men have been arrested. We'll get back to you as soon as we have any more news on that story.

5D.1
Part 1
Interviewer Welcome to Mysteries from History, and on today's programme, Dr Andrew Griffiths is going to talk to us about one of the most famous murder mysteries in British history – the murder of the princes in the Tower of London in 1483. Good morning Andrew!

Dr Griffiths Morning.

I So ... did Richard the Third kill the princes in the Tower?

D Well, it's a good question. Most people think they were murdered by Richard the Third, but I'm not so sure. I think somebody *wanted* people to think he was the murderer. You have to remember that the people who first wrote about the princes in the tower wrote about it when Henry the Seventh was in power.

I And Henry was Richard's enemy.

D Exactly. So these writers wanted to please Henry. Very dangerous to make the king angry in those days!

I So they had to write the story Henry wanted to hear.

D That's right. And Henry wanted people to think Richard had murdered the princes.

Part 2
D Now, remember that in 1502, Richard's friend Sir James Tyrell confessed to the murder. Well, we know that he confessed under torture. He was *forced* to confess. But he didn't say where the bodies were. I don't think he knew. I don't think he *had* killed the boys at all.

I Oh, right. And what about the bones – the children's bones they found in 1674?

D Well, it's not clear that they were the princes' bones. They were examined in 1933, and guess what? Some of them were animal bones! I don't think it's clear at all. And then there's the painting of Richard the Third.

I Uh huh.

D Well, the painting has been examined with X-rays, and we know that it was changed later. Somebody had made one shoulder bigger than the other – someone tried to make Richard look ugly afterwards. Remember, in those days, a deformed body was a sign of an evil mind.

I Interesting.

Part 3

I So who do *you* think did it?

D Well, I don't know of course, but I think possibly Henry the Seventh. I think the princes had still been alive when Henry won the Battle of Bosworth Field. Now, remember that Prince Edward's father had been king; Prince Edward was next in line.

I So Henry wanted him out of the way?

D Exactly. I think Henry murdered the princes and told everybody that Richard had murdered them. Maybe Richard was framed after he had been killed – in other words, Henry made it look like Richard was guilty.

I Oh, I see. Hmm, interesting. Well, thanks for coming to talk to us today.

D Thank you.

6

6A.1

Paul Look what you've done to my car! Women! They're absolutely awful drivers! Suzi! Is that you Suzi? I can't believe it! It's me, Paul!

Suzi Paul. What a surprise.

P This is absolutely amazing! It's such a strange coincidence! Are you hurt?

S No, I'll be fine.

P This is unbelievable. It's so wonderful to see you again!

S So ... How's your super-model girlfriend, Mercedes?

P We've split up. Look, I'm so sorry about what happened. You and I were so good together. I was such a fool to leave you for Mercedes.

P And don't worry about the car. We'll have to tell the police it was your fault, of course – you were driving so badly. You always were such a terrible driver! But I don't mind about the car – I'm just so happy I've found you again!

S Oh, Paul, you're so kind! Listen, I've got a bottle of champagne in the car – let's have a drink to celebrate.

P Whew, I needed that. More?

S No, I'm fine for now, thanks. Help yourself.

P You haven't touched your cup. Aren't you going to have any?

S No, thanks. You go ahead and drink. I'll just wait for the police.

6A.2

I'm **so** ex**haust**ed!
It's **such** a **bril**liant **film**!
It's **such** an e**norm**ous **car**!
It's **absolutely aw**ful!
She's **so fur**ious!
It's **absolutely** a**maz**ing!
It's **absolutely ter**rible!
I was **absolutely ter**rified!
It's **absolutely won**derful!

6A.3

1
A I thought it was quite good.
B Yeah! I thought it was **absolutely bril**liant!
A Yeah – it had a good ending.
B Yeah I know. It was **such** an a**maz**ing story.
A Great music, too.
B Yeah. It was **so good**. I could see it again tomorrow.
A Really?
B Yeah, absolutely!

2
A How was it?
B It was **absolutely won**derful!
A Oh, really? Great!
B Yeah, we had **such** a **bril**liant time!
A So you liked the place, then?
B Yeah, it's **so** a**maz**ing we've decided to go again next year!
A Wow! Sounds good. Maybe I'll go there, too!
B Yeah, you should! You'll love it!

3
A Have you got them yet?
B Yeah.
A So how are they?
B **Absolutely aw**ful!
A Oh no!
B My parents are **so fur**ious that they won't let me go to the camp.
A What – were they so terrible then?
B Yeah. I'll have to do them again. I'll have to spend all summer preparing!
A Oh no! Poor you!

6B.1

Ben Did you read the story about that man who lost his wallet?

Julia Yeah, yeah, and he got it back after 39 years. Amazing, eh?

B Yeah, I bet he didn't expect to see that again!

J I know. I hate losing things. I lost my handbag last year, it was awful, because I had all my documents in there, you know – bank cards, ID card and all of that ...

B What a pain!

J Yeah. I forgot to pick it up when I was getting off a train.

B Uh huh.

J And my mobile phone was in there too, so I lost everybody's phone number ...

B Oh no! And was there much money in there?

J There was a bit of money, yeah, but the worst thing was the ID card ... and the phone.

B Mmm ... yeah ... And did you get it back?

J No, no, no. So I cancelled all the bank cards and everything.

B Mmm.

J And it took months to get a new ID card ...

B Yeah, all the paperwork and everything ...

J Ha ha – maybe I'll get it back in 39 years, like that man in the story, no ...

B It'll be a bit late by then!

J Yeah, right.

6C.1

OK, well top of the list is noise. Noise is the biggest problem for neighbours in the UK, according to our survey. The second in the list is rough behaviour, and after that, in third place – naughty children. The fourth place is problems with walls and fences. After that in fifth place are problems to do with car parking. In sixth place are animal problems, for example dogs barking. And finally, in seventh position are problems to do with rubbish.

6C.2

Love Your Neighbours

Mrs Dickson thinks the Lanes
Are noisy and rough
She says the kids are naughty
She says she's had enough
Mr Dickson says they leave
Their rubbish by the door
'You can't complain', says Mrs Lane
'It's not against the law'
Love Your Neighbours ...

Mrs Dickson says their children
Play their music loud
She says she hears them swearing
It shouldn't be allowed
Mr Dickson says he hears them
Fighting all night long
'You can't complain', says Mrs Lane
'We're doing nothing wrong'
Love Your Neighbours ...

Mrs Dickson says they kick
Their ball along the hall
She says she saw their daughter
Writing on the wall
Mr Dickson says he hears them
Talking on the phone
'Don't complain', says Mrs Lane
'Leave us all alone'
Love Your Neighbours ...

6D.1

he tried to
he'd tried to

she needed
she'd needed

6D.2

He said he'd tried to help.
He said he tried to help.
He said he'd try to help.

She said she'd need money.
She said she needed money.
She said she'd needed money.

7

7A.1

This man's in his early twenties, and he's got straight dark hair ... ehm ... it's quite long. He's got quite a long face, and his nose is long and thin too. His eyes are wide open – he looks a bit surprised. He looks a bit shy, nervous perhaps, I don't know.

7A.2

a This woman's in her early fifties, and she's got wavy light brown hair ... ehm ... it's quite short and parted on the side. She's got quite a long nose, and she looks like an ambitious character. She looks very confident, serious maybe, like a school headmistress or something.

b This girl's in her late teens or early twenties, and she's got very long ginger hair, and it's straight. It's parted in the middle and she hasn't got a fringe. She looks like an outgoing character, she's got a friendly smile. She looks imaginative and artistic.

c I guess this man's in his mid thirties. He's got short dark hair and he's clean-shaven. He's got a round face with a high forehead and a short nose. He looks unfriendly – he looks aggressive, in fact.

d This woman's in her late sixties and she's got short, curly grey hair. She looks like a happy grandmother. Ehm ... she looks kind – she's probably quite a generous woman, and she looks lively and active.

e This man's in his seventies, and he's got shoulder-length white hair and a beard and moustache. He's got bushy eyebrows as well. He looks quite lively and intelligent – he looks like he wants to ask you a question.

7A.3

A Is it a man or a woman?
B A man.
A A man, OK. Has he got long dark hair?
B No, he's got long **white** hair.
A Long **white** hair. OK, I know who it is ...

7A.4

No, long **fair** hair.
No, **long** fair hair.

No, curly **ging**er hair.
No, **curly** ginger hair.

No, **late** twenties.
No, late **twen**ties.

No, **big** brown eyes.
No, big **brown** eyes.

7B.1

Wang Li
I'm not fashion-conscious. I wear what I'm expected to wear for work. After that, I don't mind what I wear as long as it's comfortable. I don't understand what's so special about designer clothes – I never look at labels. I don't like clothes shopping – I don't know what to look for.

Heather
I dress how I want, and I don't care what people think! I know what I like and I don't just follow everybody else. I don't spend a lot on clothes – I wear what I can afford. I don't think it's important how much your clothes are worth. The cheapest things can look cool.

Marcela
How I look is very important to me. My outfit changes how I feel, so I spend a lot on clothes. I think people notice what you're wearing, and if you're well dressed, they treat you differently. I love how it feels when I go out in a new outfit and I know everybody's looking at me.

7B.2

1 I don't mind what I wear.
2 I don't care what people think!
3 I never look at labels.
4 If you're well-dressed, they treat you differently.
5 I wear what I'm expected to wear.
6 My outfit changes how I feel.

7C.1

A Are you doing anything interesting this week?
B No, not much. I'm doing my French exam on Monday, so I'm going to stay home and study.
A So you're not going out at the weekend?
B No. Maybe I'll go out to celebrate after the exam! What about you? Are you doing anything special?
A Well, I'm starting dance classes on Thursday.
B Really? What sort of dancing?
A We're going to study salsa, tango, rumba ... that sort of thing.
B Wow, sounds great.

7D.1

This is a young woman's bedroom. There's a big birthday card on the wall saying 'Happy Birthday Liz', so her name must be Liz and it must be her birthday. There are two party dresses hanging up, so she must be having a party and she's deciding which one to wear. It must be an important birthday because the dresses are expensive. Perhaps it's her 18th or 21st birthday. She might be American or British, because of her name, and the birthday card's in English.

There's a photo of a young woman on the wall, which might be her. It looks like a graduation photo. She's a white girl with long dark hair. She might be a student. There are lots of books in her room. It might be a student flat or maybe it's a room in her parents' house.

She probably isn't married. She must like babies because there are photos of babies and children on the wall. She probably plans to get married and have children in the future.

There's also a painting on the wall. Perhaps the girl likes painting. This might be a portrait of her sister or a friend.

7D.2

perhaps it's her 18th or 21st birthday
maybe it's a room in her parents' house
she probably isn't married
she probably plans to get married and have children
perhaps the girl likes painting

8

8A.1

1 Look, I'm with a client and I can't get away right now. Can I ring you back tomorrow?
2 Have you got her mobile number please? ... Great. Hang on, I'll just get a pen to write it down ... OK, go ahead.
3 Look, I've tried that number already, but I can't get through. I either get cut off or I just get the engaged signal. Is there another number I can call? Please don't hang up!! Hello?
4 Hi, Lucy. It's me. I'm calling from the hospital. Gloria has had the baby. It's a beautiful boy! Hang on, I'll hand you over to Gloria ...
5 Extension 483? Who's calling please? ... Hold on. I'll put you through ... I'm sorry, the line's busy right now. Would you like to leave a message or call back in five minutes?
6 Hello, can you put me through to the emergency rescue service, please. My car's broken down ... Thanks.
7 Hello, it's Mike calling from Bike World. I'm calling to let you know the spray paint you ordered has arrived, so you can call by and pick it up some time ...

8A.2

a I **called** by **public phone**.
b I **called by** this **morn**ing.

8A.3

Stephanie Hello?
Voicemail Hello, this is Max Motors. I'm sorry, all our lines are busy. Please call back in five minutes.
Secretary Max Motors. Can I help you?

S Oh, ehm, hello, can you put me through to the emergency rescue service, please. My car's broken down. I'm on a main road near Stratford upon Avon.
Sec Hang on, I'll put you through.

Sec Max Motors. Can I help you?
S Hello, I called a minute ago but I got cut off.
Sec Oh yes, sorry about that. What was the problem again?
S My car's broken down. The engine won't start. I'm on the side of a road near Stratford upon Avon.
Sec OK, so you want to speak to a mechanic. If you hold the line, I'll put you through.
Mechanic 1 Hello?
S Hello. My car's broken down near Stratford upon Avon ...
M1 I'm sorry, I'm in the middle of something right now. I'll hand you over to my colleague.
Mechanic 2 Hello. Can I help you?
S Hello. There's a problem with my car – something's wrong with the engine, and I need someone to look at it.
M2 I see. Well, if you call by the garage, I'll check your car and we'll see what the problem is.
S I'm sorry, you don't understand. I can't call by. The car's broken down on the side of the road and the engine won't start.
M2 Ah well, I'm sorry, I can't help you then. We don't have a call out service. Goodbye.
S Wait – don't hang up! ... Oh no!

8B.1

able	**a**bility
popular	popu**lar**ity
active	ac**tiv**ity
curious	curi**os**ity
real	re**al**ity
possible	possi**bil**ity

8C.1

Ricardo Oh, hi Cath. How was the interview? Was it alright?
Cath Hmm, well. I don't think it went very well, actually.
R Oh, really? What happened?
C I don't think I gave very good answers to their questions.
R Oh. What did they ask?
C Well, they asked why I wanted to work for them, and I couldn't think of an answer.
R So what did you say?
C I said I needed the money. I couldn't think of anything else to say.
R Hmm. What else did they ask?
C They wanted to know what foreign languages I spoke.
R Uh huh.
C And in particular, they asked if I spoke German.
R So what did you say?
C What could I say? I told them I didn't speak any foreign languages.
R Oh. Is that a problem?
C Well, it's a German company. They need their staff to travel to Germany sometimes.
R Oh I see. So how did it end?
C Well, they asked me what salary I wanted. I said £30,000 a year.
R And what did they say about that?
C Nothing. They just thanked me for coming to the interview, and that was it. They said, 'Don't call us, we'll call you'.
R Hmm. It doesn't sound very good. Have you got any other interviews lined up?
C No.

8D.1

I asked her to wait.
She told me not to wait.
I told him not to go.
He asked me to go.

8D.2

Anita Hi, Vikram. When did you get back from Paris?
Vikram Last night.
A So how was the journey?
V Great, except I was tricked out of some money by a man at the station.
A Why? What happened?
V Well, when I arrived at the Gare du Nord, an English man approached me and asked me if I spoke English. So I said yes, and then he asked me to give him ten euros for his train ticket.
A So did you give it to him?
V Yes, and he promised to send it back to me when he got home, but I just told him to keep it.
A That was very nice of you.
V Well, it wasn't very much. I felt sorry for him – in fact, I invited him for a coffee.
A Uh huh.
V And he told me to be careful because there were thieves in the station.
A Mmm.
V So anyway, we said goodbye, and then the next day I was in the station again, and guess what: he was there again.
A So that story about the train ticket was a lie ...
V Exactly, **and** he was asking a woman to give him money. Another victim!
A Did you say anything?
V Yeah, I did. I went over and I warned the woman not to give him anything.
A Quite right too!

8E.1

Sandra Hi. I'm doing a survey about communication habits. Can I ask you a question?
B Uh huh, sure.
S Do you send a lot of text messages?
B Quite a lot, yeah.
S Uh huh. Why do you send them? I mean, why don't you just phone?
B Well, it's a quick way to send information, because you don't have to have a conversation.

And it's convenient. If the other person is busy and isn't able to answer right at that moment, they can read it later.

S   Yes, right. OK, thank you very much.

9

9A.1
heavy showers
blowing a gale
boiling hot
freezing cold
pouring rain
soaking wet

9A.2
1   Winter

Susan   Ooh, there's a cold wind out there!

Tom   Yeah, I know. It's freezing, isn't it? It goes right through your coat.

S   And they say it's going to rain later.

T   Oh, yeah?

S   Yeah. Still, it could be worse I suppose. They're having snowstorms in the north, aren't they?

T   Yes, I saw that on the news. The heaviest snow in 50 years, they say.

S   Yeah, it's amazing, isn't it? Some villages are completely cut off.

2   Spring

S   It's a lovely day, isn't it?

T   Yes. It's so mild for the time of year.

S   Yeah, I know. Normally this time of year we have the heating on!

T   Yeah, it's great, isn't it? Do you think it will last until the weekend?

S   Probably not. I'm going away. It'll probably rain.

T   Oh well, I guess we need it, don't we? You know what they say: April showers bring May flowers.

S   Yeah, but the showers are always at the weekends, aren't they?

3   Summer

S   It's hot, isn't it?

T   Yeah, I know. It's terrible, isn't it? I prefer cold. At least you can put more clothes on. When it's hot, there's nothing you can do about it.

S   Mmm. They say it's the hottest August since 1920.

T   Really? And there's no wind at all, is there?

S   No. I wonder how long it will go on for.

T   I don't know. They say there's a heat wave all over Europe. In some parts of the Mediterranean it's over 45 degrees.

S   Wow. I guess we shouldn't complain, then.

4   Autumn

S   The days are getting shorter again, aren't they?

T   Yeah. Dark at six thirty!

S   It's a clear night though, isn't it? Look at that moon!

T   Yeah, it's going to be a cold one. You know what they say: Clear moon, frost soon.

S   It's cold already, isn't it? My ears are freezing.

T   Yeah, but it'll be nice and sunny tomorrow.

S   Mmm.

9A.3
It's freezing, isn't it?
It's amazing, isn't it?
It's a lovely day, isn't it?
It's great, isn't it?
It's terrible, isn't it?
It's a clear night though, isn't it?
It's cold already, isn't it?

9B.1
My **hair** will have **grown**.
I'll have **cut** my **nails**.
Things won't have **changed much.**
I'll have **passed** the ex**am**.

9B.2
1
Five years from now I'll be 66. Hopefully, I'll be in good health, because I don't want to retire. I don't want to sit in front of the television all day. I want to be active and look after the business. My husband and I started this business from nothing and now it's listed in the best restaurant guides. Unfortunately, Luigi won't be here. That's Luigi behind me – he's the head chef. He's going to retire next year and go back to Italy. Hopefully, I'll have found a new chef by then, but it won't be easy to get someone as good as Luigi. Maybe one day my son will return and work with me. He's working in America at the moment, but I don't think he's happy. Hopefully, in five years' time he'll have moved back here and we'll be together again.

2
In five years' time, I'll be 24 and I'll have finished university. I'm going to study Art History. Hopefully, I'll get good final exam results. I'll probably have found a job. I'd like to be a fashion designer. I'll probably work for a company at first, and then maybe I'll start my own business. Hopefully, I'll have bought my own little flat, and maybe a cat called Toby. I probably won't be married – it's too soon, and I want to start my career first. Perhaps I'll never get married, I don't know. I don't think I want children, really. I won't have a car, because of pollution and all that – I think we'll have to take more care of the environment, so I'll still use my bicycle.

9C.1
1   The worst option is b. If you run, the bear will probably run after you. The other options are all recommended.

2   The worst option is b. If you disturb the quicksand a lot, it'll pull you downwards. The best option is to try to lie on your back on top of the quicksand and get your legs out little by little.

3   The worst option is a. If your mouth is open, it'll get filled with snow. Breathing is the biggest problem when you're trapped in the snow. The other options are all recommended.

4   The worst option is c. If you try to swim against the current, you'll probably just get exhausted. The best option is to swim parallel to the beach to get away from the current.

5   The worst option is b. A tornado can easily lift up a car. The other options are all recommended. Sometimes, the bath is the only part of the house which is left after a tornado has passed!

6   The worst option is c. The tree may attract the lightening. The other options are all recommended. If you are in a pool when lightening strikes, the electricity will pass through the water to you.

7   The worst option is a. Sharks won't get bored and go away like grizzly bears. The eyes and gills are the shark's weakest places.

8   The worst option is c. If any lava comes from the volcano, it will flow downwards in the valleys on the mountain side. Also, the worst of the gases are heavier than air and are close to the ground.

9D.1
Nicola   If you could have one of these devices, which one **would you** choose?

Kurt   Ehm … I don't know … ehm … I think I'd have the personal helicopter. Yeah, that looks great fun.

N   Uh huh, yeah. So what **would you** do with it? Where **would you** go?

K   Oh, I don't know – I guess I'd fly over the town, see what it looks like from up there. Maybe go across the channel to France.

N   Mmm. Very nice.

K   So what about you. Which device would you choose?

N   I'd quite like the brain keyboard.

K   So what **would you** do if you had that?

N   Well, I work at the computer all day long and I'm not very good at typing, so I waste a lot of time. If I had that, I could just think what I want to write

and that would be it.

K   So you'd use it for work?

N   Yeah, I'd use it for work.

9D.2
Which one would you **choose**?
What would you **do** with it?
Where would you **go**?
What would you **do** if you had **that**?

10

10A.1
Death of the High Street
The butcher on the high street
Listens with alarm
They say that Farmer Jones
Is going to sell the farm
The greengrocer was driving past
And saw the land for sale
The cashier in the bank thinks
They're going to build a jail

The chemist tells the optician
The optician tells the nurse
The people on the high street
Say there's nothing worse
The newsagent saw an engineer
Walking on the land
The grocer on the corner
Saw a lorry full of sand

The baker saw a bulldozer
Driving through the town
'Did you hear about the farm house?
They've knocked the old place down!
They're building roads and walls
A big new shopping mall
We're going to lose our customers
The mall will take them all!'

The mall kills the high street

10A.2
Jerry   Hi Amrita. How are you?

Amrita   Oh, hi Jerry. I'm fine, and you?

J   Not too bad thanks. Hey, have you seen they're building a new shopping centre out near the motorway?

A   Are they? That's great. We need a good shopping mall around here.

J   I don't think so. I mean, there are lots of good shops on the high street, aren't there?

A   Yes, maybe, but shopping centres are more convenient, don't you think?

J   Not really, no. They're always a long way out of town.

A   OK, that's true, but there's no traffic and it's always easy to park the car …

J   Alright, but that's no good if you haven't got a car – like me.

A   Well, OK, you're right, I suppose. But you could get the bus. And things are always cheaper in malls …

J   I'm not so sure about that. They're cheap at first, and then when all the small shops close, they put up the prices! Anyway, you get much better service in smaller shops.

A Yes, I agree, but I haven't got time to go round lots of little shops. I think it's better to get everything in one place.

J OK, well you go to the new mall, but all the small shops will close, you'll see!

A Oh Jerry, you can't stop time, you know. You can't keep living in the past!

J Hmm.

10A.3

I don't think so.
Yes, maybe, but shopping centres are more convenient.
Not really, no.
OK, that's true, but there's no traffic.
Alright, but that's no good if you haven't got a car.
Well, OK, you're right, I suppose.
I'm not so sure about that.
Yes, I agree, but I haven't got time.

10B.1

a jar of coffee
a packet of biscuits
a box of eggs
a carton of milk
a pot of yogurt
a tin of tomatoes
a bottle of ketchup
a bag of potatoes
a tube of toothpaste
a tub of margarine

10B.2
Linda

Interviewer Hi, I'm doing a survey of shopping habits. Do you mind if I ask you a few questions?

Linda No, go ahead.

I OK, well, first of all, can you tell us what you're buying today?

L Let's see … I've got a two-litre bottle of milk, ehm, eight cartons of yogurt, a box of cereal, ehm, some packets of kitchen paper, a bottle of olive oil, two big bottles of water, some boxes of tissues …

I That's a lot of stuff. How are you going to get it all home?

L I've got the car in the car park.

I OK, that's good. Why are you buying so much?

L Well, I've got two children, and I haven't got time to go shopping during the week, so I just do one big weekly shop.

I OK. You've got lots of packets and bottles here, but there isn't much fresh stuff. Is this what you normally buy?

L Yes, but I buy fresh stuff from other shops, too. I normally buy my fruit in the greengrocer's across the road. I think it's better.

I I see. And do you write a shopping list?

L Yes, I need a shopping list, because if I forget something, I won't have time to come back.

I OK, last question. Do you pay in cash or by card?

L I usually pay with my debit

card. I don't like carrying too much cash, or I'll just spend it!

Mark

Interviewer Hi, I'm doing a survey of shopping habits. Do you mind if I ask you a few questions?

Mark No, go ahead.

I OK, well, first of all, can you tell us what you've got in your basket today?

M Let's see, there's a packet of pasta, a loaf of bread, a couple of toilet rolls, a tin of tomatoes, a bag of carrots, a jar of honey, a bottle of wine, some fresh fruit and veg …

I And are these the kinds of things you normally buy?

M Yes, this is more or less normal. I like cooking so I buy quite a lot of fresh stuff.

I And how often do you shop for food?

M Oh, two or three times a week.

I Do you write a shopping list?

M Yeah, sometimes, especially if there's something I know I'll forget.

I OK, and last question – do you normally pay in cash or with a card?

M Cash. I usually get cash out of the cash machine. I don't like paying by card.

10C.1

Ms Sayles We haven't been selling many of these sunshades lately. I want you to try harder. The one who sells the most over the next month or so will get a bonus.

Ms S Right. What have you been doing to sell more sunshades, Winston?

Winston I've been offering two for the price of one, Ms Sayles.

Ms S And how many have you sold?

W I haven't sold many recently. People don't want sunshades with pink rabbits on.

Ms S How many, Winston?

W Well, none, in fact.

Ms S None. And how long have you been working here?

W Almost six months.

Ms S Nearly six months and you haven't learnt anything. It's not good enough!

Ms S What about you, Janet?

Janet I've been advertising in the daily paper, Ms Sayles. I've also been phoning people at home.

Ms S And how many have you sold?

J About five. It's been raining for weeks. Nobody wants a sunshade.

Ms S You're a saleswoman, Janet. It's your job to sell things that nobody wants.

Ms S And you, Charlie? How many have you sold?

Charlie Two thousand, more or less. People have been queuing

to buy them.

Ms S That's amazing! What have you been doing?

C I've been selling them outside the station as umbrellas.

10C.2

It's been **rain**ing.
I've been **sleep**ing.
You've been **wait**ing.
It **has**n't been **rain**ing.
I **have**n't been **sleep**ing.
You **have**n't been **wait**ing.
Has it been **rain**ing?
Have I been **sleep**ing?
Have you been **wait**ing?

10C.3

Teresa Hi Simon!

Simon Oh, hello Teresa.

T What have you been doing lately? I haven't seen you around for ages.

S Oh, I haven't been going out much. I'm trying to save some money for a trip to India.

T India? Oh, very nice. Are you still working at the sports shop?

S No, I've been working in a travel agent's for the last three months. What about you? Have you been doing anything interesting? Still playing the piano?

T Well, I've been learning to play the trumpet, actually.

S Oh really? That must be nice for your flatmate! What's her name? Sarah?

T Sarah. I don't live with Sarah any more. I've been living on my own for nearly a year.

S Oh yeah. Are you enjoying it?

T Yeah, it's great. I've been going away most weekends, to the coast.

S Oh yes, I remember – you go windsurfing, don't you?

T Yes, windsurfing. I'm still doing that.

S Listen, I've got to go, but I'll give you a ring. Have you still got the same phone number?

T Yeah, still the same.

S Yes, mine's the same too. I'll be in touch. Bye!

T See you!

10D.1

Dan Can I help you?

Tina Yes, I'm looking for a cheap digital camera.

D A digital camera? OK. How much do you want to spend?

T £100 or so.

D Well, this one is normally £120, but it's reduced at the moment to £99.99.

T Does that include the batteries, the memory card, and everything?

D Yes, all included. And there's a six-month guarantee. If you have any problems with it, we'll repair it free of charge. Here, try it …

T Mmm. Oops, I've taken a photo of my foot!

D It's all right. We can delete it

unless you want to keep it!

T No, thanks. I hate these shoes! OK, I think I'll take the camera. And I'll buy some spare batteries while I'm here.

D Sorry, we don't sell batteries, but you can buy them at any supermarket.

T How much do they cost?

D £2.50, more or less. Would you like to buy a leather case for your camera? Brown, to match your shoes!

T Ha ha. No, thanks. That's all, thanks.

D OK. How would you like to pay – by cash or card?

T I'll pay by credit card, please.

D Can you enter your PIN number, please … Thanks. And here's your receipt. Keep it in case you need to bring the camera back.

T OK. Thanks. Goodbye.

D Bye.

11

11A.1
Paola

Paola Excuse me, do you know the way to (beeeeep!)

M Yes, go out of the building and go straight across the road and up Chapel Lane, and you'll see a church on your left.

P OK, up Chapel Street and …

M No, Chapel LANE, and you'll see a church on the left and the Great Garden on your right, OK? And at the crossroads, turn right along Chapel Street and then turn left up Ely Street.

P Ely Street, uh huh …

M Yes, and at the top of Ely Street, you'll come to a T-junction, and you turn left on Rother Street. You'll find the place you're looking for on the right.

P On the right. OK, thanks.

Ignacio

Ignacio Excuse me, can you tell me how to get to (beeeeep!)

W OK, go out of the building and cross High Street, then go down Sheep Street.

I Ship Street, OK …

W SHEEP Street.

I Sheep Street, OK.

W Ha ha, yeah, like the animal, and at the end of Sheep Street you'll come to Bancroft Gardens, take the path across the gardens until you come to the canal.

I A path to the canal, OK.

W Walk across the lock to the other side of the canal and you'll see the Tramway Bridge. Go over the bridge to the other side of the river and you'll come to Swan's Nest Lane.

I Swan's Nest Lane.

W Yeah, you'll see a car park there, and the place you're looking for is just the other side of the car park.

I OK, thanks very much.
W Hope you enjoy it!

Laura

Laura Excuse me, can you tell me the way to (*beeeeep!*)
M OK, so go across the river on the foot ferry and turn right on Southern Lane.
L The foot ferry?
M Yes. A boat across the river.
L Oh, I see. OK.
M OK, and take the second left.
L Second left …
M And go straight up to the crossroads. Go straight across and along Ely Street.
L Along Ely Street, yes.
M Yes, go along Ely Street until you reach Rother Street, then turn right. Then take the second left, which is Mansell Street.
L Mansell Street.
M Yes, Go along Mansell Street and across Arden Street, and the entrance is right there.
L OK – sounds complicated!
M Yes, well maybe you can ask someone else when you're nearer.
L OK, well, thanks very much.

11B.1

Claire Oh, you're going to Honduras? We went there last year.
Ian Oh yeah? Where did you stay?
C We stayed in a place called Punta Paloma on the Caribbean coast. It's a great place, set in a national park with mountains and rainforests. The hotel rooms are all separate cabins in the forest and they're really quiet and secluded – the only noise is the birds.
I Oh, wow. Sounds lovely!
C Yeah, really nice. The food's delicious and you can eat in the restaurant or have it served in the garden. There's a nice bar. For breakfast, there's a buffet, or you can have it brought to your room.
I Great. And what's there to do, you know, during the day?
C Oh, there's nothing to do really, but it's such a beautiful place just to spend time. We just relaxed by the pool and read a few books.
I And what are the people like – the hotel staff and so on?
C They're really efficient and helpful, you know, and if you want to have your clothes washed for example, you just leave them in a basket by the bed and they're clean the next day. So yeah, it's really comfortable. I'd recommend it.
I Right, OK. The Playa Paloma, you say?
C Punta. Punta Paloma.
I OK. Is it expensive?
C Ah! That's the thing. It's not cheap!
I Hmm … that could be a problem.

11C.1

Are there any **injections** that you need to have?
Will you have to show any **vaccination certificates**?
Are there any **pills** that you need to take?
Do you need to take out **medical insurance**?
Should you drink the **tap water**?
Are there any **local foods** that you ought to avoid?
Do you need to take **sun block**?
Should you carry a **first aid kit**?
Will you need to take **insect repellent**?
Should you carry a **mosquito net**?
What should you do in an **emergency**?

11C.2

Do you need to carry your **passport**?
Are there any **documents** that you need?
Are there any **guide books** I should buy?
Should you take **travellers' cheques**?

11D.1

Fiona What about you, Feliks?
Feliks My worst journey was about four years ago, when I was live … eh living in Scotland.
Fi Oh, really? Did you live in Scotland?
Fel Yeah, it was in Edinburgh, where I was a student, and, ehm … anyway, I went away one weekend with a Scottish friend called Duncan, who was my flatmate at the time, and eh … we drove to the Highlands, which is a few hours away by car, and we stayed in a youth hostel, but the next day it rained a lot and in the end we decided to go home early.
Fi Uh huh.
Fel So anyway, we got in the car and set off, and then we … eh … how do you say … the petrol finished.
Fi You ran out of petrol?
Fel Yes, we ran out of petrol.
Fi What, in the middle of nowhere?
Fel No, luckily. This was in a town called Perth, which was about half way home. But anyway, we had to take the spare petrol can and walk to a petrol station. We had to leave the car on the side of the road. We got completely wet 'cause it was raining hard, and eh … and I got petrol on my coat, which was new. And then when we got back to the car, we had a parking ticket … eh … a parking fine.
Fi Oh no!
Fel Yeah, we had a parking fine 'cause it was a no-parking zone.
Fi How annoying! That's so unfair!

Fel Yeah, I know. But that's not the end of the story. Later on, we stopped at a service station in a town called Stirling, where we had something to eat, and then when we came out, the car was … how do you say … not there … ehm …
Fi Gone? Stolen?
Fel Yeah, stolen.
Fi Really? So what did you do? Did you call the police?
Fel Well, Duncan tried to phone them on his mobile, but his batteries were … had no power, ehm …
Fi Flat?
Fel Yeah, his batteries were flat and we had to walk to the nearest phone box, which was a kilometre away. Anyway, the police came and Duncan filled in a report, and then we had to catch a bus home.
Fi What a horrible trip!
Fel Yeah, but it was worse for Duncan. It was his car!

11D.2

I changed the tyre which was flat.
I changed the tyre, which was flat.

They stopped the driver, who was speeding.
They stopped the driver who was speeding.

The man, who was lost, asked for help.
The man who was lost asked for help.

12

12A.1

Serge S-o what do you think is the point of that story?
Lucia Well, I think it's that you can't e-h, you can't own the smell of your food, you know, e-h-m I mean, I think the richer woman's very selfish so she doesn't want to give anything away, not even the smell of her food, I mean, she thinks e-h … she thinks the smell belongs to her.
S Yeah, so she thinks the poor woman i-s is stealing from her, stealing the smell. That's really stupid, isn't it?
L Yeah. And so I think the chief's very clever, b-e-c-a-u-s-e e-h he shows her how stupid it is, e-h stealing a smell is l-i-k-e like hitting a shadow, you know, what's the point of that?
S Uh huh, yeah.

12A.2

Lucia Yeah. And so I think the chief's very clever, b-e-c-a-u-s-e e-h he shows her how stupid it is, e-h stealing a smell is l-i-k-e like hitting a shadow, you know, what's the point of that?
Serge Uh huh, yeah. It reminds

me of that stuff with Internet, you know, t-h-e the wireless Internet connection thing …
L Wireless?
S Yeah, you know – those people who use other people's wireless connections in order to get onto the Internet. I don't think that's stealing because e-h-m because if it's out in the street, it belongs to everybody. I think it's out in public space, so everybody can use it, you know s-o e-h-m so it's like the smell of soup …
L I don't think it's the same, because you have t-o to pay for the Internet connection, so it's different. You don't have to pay for the smell of your soup.
S Yeah, but what difference does it make if somebody else uses your Internet connection? I mean, it doesn't take anything from you, so what's the problem? It's like this … You're playing your car radio, and e-h-m the window is down so everybody can hear it – are they stealing your sound?
L No, of course they aren't. But they aren't out there in order to hear your radio, are they? So it's different. People use your Internet connection in order t-o to get free Internet. In my opinion, that's stealing.
S But you don't have to pay more if somebody uses your connection, I mean, e-h you probably won't even notice.
L E-h-m but it makes your Internet connection wor – e-h-m slower, doesn't it?
S No, I don't think so.
L And what if they use your Internet connection to do s-o-m-e-t-h-i-n-g e-h criminal?
S Ah yes, OK, but that's different. If you're worried about that, you should put a a password on your connection.

12A.3

… the chief's very clever, b-e-c-a-u-s-e e-h he shows her …
… stealing a smell is l-i-k-e like hitting a shadow …
… you know s-o e-h-m so it's like the smell of soup …
… People use your Internet connection in order t-o to get free Internet …

12B.1

There were two men – Lofty and Shorty, and they were stuck on a desert island.

'Oh, I wish I was somewhere far, far away from here', said Lofty, 'I can't stand this place!'

Shorty, on the other hand, said, 'Oh, it's not so bad!'

Lofty spent all his time trying to make a signal. 'I hope a passing ship rescues us soon', he said, 'And I hope I never see another coconut